COLERIDGE'S POLITICAL THOUGHT

Also by John Morrow

T. H. GREEN: Lectures on the Principles of Political Obligation and Other Writings (*co-editor with Paul Harris*)

COLERIDGE'S WRITINGS, volume 1: On Politics and Society (*editor*)

Coleridge's Political Thought

Property, Morality and the Limits of Traditional Discourse

JOHN MORROW
Department of Politics
Victoria University of Wellington

St. Martin's Press   New York

© John Morrow 1990

All rights reserved. For information, write:
Scholarly and Reference Division,
St. Martin's Press, Inc., 175 Fifth Avenue,
New York, N.Y. 10010

First published in the United States of America in 1990

Printed and bound in Great Britain

ISBN 0-312-03645-0

Library of Congress Cataloguing-in-Publication Data
Morrow, John, Ph. D.
Coleridge's political thought: property, morality, and
the limits of traditional discourse / John Morrow.
    p.   cm.
  Includes bibliographical references.
  ISBN 0-312-03645-0
  1. Coleridge, Samuel Taylor, 1772-1834 —
    Political and social views.
  I. Title.
PR4487.P6M67 1990
821'.7 — dc20
                               89-36457
                                   CIP

For Di, Daniel and Kate

Contents

Preface ix

Introduction 1

1 Coleridge and Contemporary Radicalism: The Bristol Lectures (1795) and *The Watchman* (1796) 11

   I   Moral enlightenment and political reform 11
   II   Radical religion: the critique of property and government 19
   III   Radical religion and 'civic humanism' 27
   IV   Corruption and parliamentary reform: Coleridge's critique of the two bills 32
   V   Political progression and the diffusion of property: Coleridge, Thelwall and *The Watchman* 35
   VI   Conclusion: radical Christianity and 'civic humanism' 38

2 Constitutions, Concordats and Country Party Ideology: The Realignment of Coleridge's Political Theory, 1799–1802 43

   I   The critique of the French Constitution of 1799: property and political personality 45
   II   Landed and commercial wealth 55
   III   Independent property and church establishments 61
   IV   Conclusion: the Church, Constitution and Country Party argument 67

3 Principled Morality and Prudential Politics: *The Friend* (1809–10) 73

   I   Morals and politics 74
   II   Political obligation 77

III	Prudence in politics	83
IV	Property and political participation	89
V	Land, commerce and social progress	93
VI	Conclusion: property and the ends of government	97

4 Politics, Property and Political Economy, 1810–19   100

I	The 'reputed masters of political economy'	102
II	Radical reform: new Jacobins and old demagogues	107
III	Jacobinism's 'quality cousin'	111
IV	Landed property and the 'commercial spirit'	115
V	The spiritualised intellect and the spirit of commerce: education and religion in the 'Lay Sermons'	121
VI	Conclusion: moralism and institutionalisation	125

5 Property, Politics and Cultivation: *On the Constitution of the Church and State* (1829)   126

I	The context of *Church and State*: Catholic Emancipation and the Church of England	127
II	The Constitution of the Church and state as 'ideas'	130
III	Property and government in the Constitution	133
IV	The National Church and the Constitution of the nation	142
V	The National Church and the Church of Christ	149
VI	Conclusion: Coleridge and state theory	154

Conclusion: Land, Commerce and the Limits of Tradition   156

List of Abbreviations	165
Notes	167
Bibliography	197
Index	207

Preface

This study presents an account of Samuel Taylor Coleridge's political writings in relation to the history of political theory. Coleridge's thought has been the subject of a vast amount of scholarly analysis, and, while much of this has focused on his poetry and criticism, the fact that he wrote political theory has not gone unnoticed. Over the years, a number of books and articles have contributed greatly to the understanding of Coleridge's political ideas. In the last two decades, however, the history of political thought has undergone a renaissance, one of the fruits of which has been the development of new perspectives on eighteenth- and early nineteenth-century political theory. As a result, it is now possible to re-examine Coleridge's writings and to relate his political philosophy to features of contemporary political thought which have been unearthed by recent scholarship. The chapters which follow discuss Coleridge's use of a definable body of political languages which were the stock-in-trade of writers located in the historical context of which he was a part. These discourses were largely concerned with the significance of property for political relationships and political structures, and are of great importance for understanding Coleridge's political philosophy.

The typescript of this study was sent to the publishers in September 1987 before I had the opportunity to see three of the latest books discussing aspects of Coleridge's politics: Deirdre Coleman's *Coleridge and 'The Friend' (1809–10)*, Nigel Leask's *The Politics of Imagination in Coleridge's Critical Thought*, and Nicholas Roe's *Wordsworth and Coleridge: The Radical Years*. However, in revising the typescript for publication I have been able to consult these works, and have referred to them in the notes. Unfortunately, Peter Allen's article, 'Morrow on Coleridge's *Church and State*', *Journal of the History of Ideas*, 49 (1989) pp. 485–9, and Christopher Turk's book *Coleridge and Mill* have come into my hands at too late a date to be noted in this study.

In writing this book, I have made extensive use of recently published definitive versions of Coleridge's opus, and I wish to record my appreciation to the editors of the various volumes of the *Collected Coleridge*, to Kathleen Coburn, the general editor of this series and editor of the *Notebooks*, and to Earl Leslie Griggs, the editor of Coleridge's correspondence. I would like to think that these people will find something of interest in this study, but, in any case, I am most grateful to have had the benefit of their meticulous scholarship. I must also thank the editor of the *Journal of the History of Ideas* for permission to use material in Chapter 2 which originally appeared in an article published in volume 47 of that journal.

Over the last few years I have received invaluable help from a number of institutions and individuals. I must acknowledge the direct and/or indirect financial support of the Internal Research and Leave Committees of Victoria University, of my own department, and of the Claude McCarthy Foundation administered by the New Zealand University Grants Committee. During the (northern) winter of 1984–5 I drew on the resources of the Cambridge University Library, particularly the Rare Books Room. I am grateful for the help of the staff of this library and to the Warden and Fellows of Robinson College, Cambridge, who provided a comfortable and congenial environment for my stay in Cambridge. My parents, Dorothy and Henry Morrow, Peter and Rachel Morrow, Andrew and Polly Morrow, Bob and Kelly Law, and Peter Mahoney also deserve thanks for their hospitality while I was engaged in research in England. Thanks are also due to the staffs of the Folger Shakespeare Library in Washington, DC, and of the Library of Congress, but I am particularly indebted to the members of the Acquisitions and References Departments at the Victoria University Library. Aidan Lanham, Head of Acquisitions, has been especially helpful.

My friend Mark Francis of the University of Canterbury has greatly encouraged my interest in Coleridge's political thought and has offered most valuable advice on draft chapters of this study, as have Geoffrey Debnam and Paul Harris of Victoria, and J. C. Davis of Massey University. I have also benefited from responses to papers I delivered before the New Zealand Early Modern Studies Association in Wellington in March 1984; at meetings of the New Zealand Political Studies Association held in Hamilton in May 1984 and in Christchurch in May 1986; and in seminars at Exeter

University in January 1985, at York University in Toronto in April 1987, and at the Folger Institute Centre for the Study of British Political Thought in the same month. I must particularly thank Iain Hampsher-Monk (at Exeter), John Pocock (at both Wellington and the Folger) and Neal Wood (at York). Lindsey Shaw kindly helped me find the illustration for the jacket. Marion Beardsmore, Jenny Berry and Coula Pastelides have typed and retyped the script with accuracy and good humour. While thanking these individuals for their help, I naturally take sole responsibility for any shortcomings of this study.

I started writing this book in the month that our first child was born and completed it shortly after the birth of our second. During this time, and in the years before when I was engaged on research, my wife has been a constant source of practical help, sympathetic criticism and encouragement. The dedication of this volume attempts to convey my thanks to Di for her support, and to Daniel and Kate for the delight they have brought us both.

J.M.

Wellington, New Zealand

Introduction

Throughout his literary career, Coleridge discussed politics in relation to moral autonomy, or the free action of self-willed human actors.[1] Coleridge's focus on moral personality, and his understanding of what this entailed, was derived from his view of the necessity for free action in fulfilling God's purposes for humankind. However, these purposes were to be realised in a world where human interaction and the possibilities of moral autonomy were influenced by the effects of property ownership on the structure of political and social power. The relationship between property and political personality was a central theme in the moral and political discourses of the late seventeenth and the eighteenth century, and it will be argued here that the ethical and constitutional implications of these discourses provide valuable clues to the historical location of Coleridge's political theory and are also of great importance in recovering its general significance.[2]

By the late eighteenth century, presuppositions and arguments about the moral and political significance of property hinged upon a quite explicit differentiation of 'landed' and 'commercial' wealth. The former was associated with traditional patterns of authority, particularly those based on responsibility and deference, and with such politically significant qualities as independence and participation. By contrast, the term 'commerce' denoted features of contemporary economic activity – particularly debt-funding of government and speculation in stocks – that distinguished eighteenth-century society from its predecessors and made it 'modern'. Commerce generated new forms of wealth, but its apologists claimed that its benefits were not merely material. Commercial society was defended on the grounds that economic expansion undercut the position of traditional elites and thereby extended opportunities for human freedom; it also produced a range of intellectual, moral and social advances – 'sentiment and sympathy, transaction and conversation, taste and science, the polite together with the commercial arts'[3] – that provided an elevated, non-traditional basis for human interaction.

As we shall see, Coleridge's response to these discourses played a central role in his political theory, but his engagement with the languages of the eighteenth century took place in an ideological context that was marked by the impact of the French Revolution and by English responses to it. His earliest essays (derived for the most part from a series of lectures given in Bristol in 1795), showed how some of the benefits of the assault on the *ancien régime* in France could be of relevance to English conditions and problems. In taking such a stance, Coleridge aligned himself with the forces of radical Dissent which confronted the aristocratic Anglican establishment, but he was careful to distance himself from the atheistic strands in English radicalism evident in the writings of men such as William Godwin, Thomas Holcroft and Tom Paine. Indeed, the Bristol lectures were based on the premise that some of the goals of the Revolution were closely related to the Christian stipulation that individuals were moral equals and the belief (common in Dissenting circles) that this requirement should have a direct effect on the organisation of political life. However, these lectures combined elements drawn from radicalised Christianity with categories ingeniously and unusually derived from traditional discourses on property. The result was the development of a position that not only was critical of English religious and political institutions, but also called into question the very ideas of property and government.

After this brief flirtation with radical reform and with anarcho-communism, Coleridge began to develop a more favourable perspective on both government and property. He regarded the former as a necessary feature of a world filled with potentially wayward individuals, and the latter as a significant factor in human interaction. It facilitated free, and hence moral, action and also provided the basis for political institutions that preserved both liberty and order. This theoretical reorientation, which began in the closing months of the eighteenth century, again reflected Coleridge's response to events in France. In leading articles contributed to the *Morning Post* between 1799–1802, and in a short-lived periodical publication, *The Friend* (1809–10), Coleridge considered Napoleon's rise to prominence in French politics and analysed his role in subverting what was left of the old European order. Initially Coleridge reassessed potentialities in the prevailing structure of social and political relationships, argued that moral equality was not of direct political importance and extolled the virtues of property and of political systems that reflected its distribution. In *The Friend*, however, he also developed a philosophical defence of property-based polities and considered why modern societies failed to combine an acceptance of the material benefits of 'commerce' with the pursuit of the humanitarian moral goals which provided the ultimate rationale of political institutions. The villain of the piece was philosophical materialism, a tradition he identified particularly with John Locke but which stretched from Thomas Hobbes to William Paley, and manifested itself in a popular form in the pages of journals such as the *Edinburgh Review*.

Coleridge continued this line of argument in the 'Lay Sermons' of 1816 and 1817. In these writings he claimed that the correct antidote to philosophical materialism could be found in the tradition of Christian Platonism that had seen its most recent flowering in the works of the seventeenth-century Cambridge Platonists. The immediate context of the 'Lay Sermons' was the difficult years that followed the conclusion of the war against Napoleonic France. In his consideration of the problems facing the country at this time, Coleridge adopted a particularly sharp tone in his critique of 'new Jacobin' agitators, and warned of the destructive tendencies of their economic, moral and political views. However, these writings are also significant because they contain an analysis of the effect of materialism on the landed classes' ability to play their traditional role in a society in which commerce was becoming increasingly important.

Although Coleridge specified the problematic nature of the interaction of commerce, philosophical materialism, morality and traditional elites in his 'Lay Sermons', the solution was only formulated fully in *On the Constitution of the Church and State* (1829), his last and most significant contribution to political thought. In this work, Coleridge confronted both the attackers and the would-be defenders of the political and ecclesiastical establishment and developed a complex defence of traditional institutions and of some aspects of modernity.

The general direction of Coleridge's development as a political thinker, and the role played in this process by responses to events in France, had much in common with the path taken by the original, self-styled 'Romantics' based in Jena in the last years of the eighteenth century, who developed a critique of the philosophy of the French Enlightenment.[4] However, while this parallel may be illuminating in some respects, Coleridge's case is rather more complex than it might suggest. In the first place, he was largely concerned with the *British* manifestations of the philosophical spirit of the eighteenth century. Secondly, Coleridge's response to contemporary problems involved an attempt to infuse forms of political and social understanding that were very much part of the eighteenth century with principles derived from seventeenth-century Platonism. In so doing, he developed an interesting and sophisticated state theory that can loosely be described as conservative, but was neither archaic nor reactionary.

The development of Coleridge's political theory will be traced in the main body of this study; this is organised into five chapters, each of which deals with one of Coleridge's major contributions to political theory. These chapters focus on Coleridge's successive, and in a significant sense, incremental attempts to deal with the crucial issues of property and its constitutional and ethical implications. However, the character and import of Coleridge's earliest political writings (the subject of Chapter 1) can only be appreciated fully in the light of aspects of his career as an undergraduate at Cambridge in the early 1790s, and his involvement in the promotion of an ideal society in the United States in the second half of 1794. Because these episodes are pre-theoretical (in the sense that they predated Coleridge's reasonably formal statements of a political philosophy), they will be discussed briefly in the remainder of this introduction.

Political affairs were not an absorbing concern of Coleridge's during most of his undergraduate days, but contemporary accounts suggest that he did have political interests. In particular, he identified with those who welcomed the Revolution in France and hoped that it was a precursor of political and religious change at home. Charles Le Grice, a Cambridge contemporary, portrayed Coleridge as an avid reader of radical pamphlet literature and a lively disputant on political matters. In addition, there are stories of his involvement in a plot to etch the words 'Liberty' and 'Equality' on the lawns of St John's and Trinity Colleges.[5] Of course, this prank does not indicate the precise nature of Coleridge's early political views, but it suggests that he was prepared to align himself *with* the forces of reform, and *against* students who, with the support of some of the senior members of the University, rioted in the cause of 'Church and King'.[6]

In 1793 Coleridge took part in a demonstration in the Vice-

Chancellor's Court in support of William Frend (1751–1841), a Fellow of Jesus College, who was charged with 'impugning religion, as by law established'.[7] Frend's trial arose because of his attack on the beliefs, institutions and rituals of the Church of England in *Peace and Union Recommended* (1793), but he was already notorious for having given up Holy Orders, rejecting Trinitarianism and becoming an avowed Unitarian. The Vice-Chancellor's Court was primarily interested in Frend's religious views, but the offending pamphlet also contained statements in apparent approval of the execution of the French King, commented on the condition of the poor and the effects of the war upon them, and advanced a radical programme of political reform calling for a greatly extended franchise and for triennial parliaments. It thus exhibited the conjuncture of religious and political heterodoxy that was a feature of contemporary Unitarianism. This combination was also found in Coleridge's early political writings.

While Coleridge was an undergraduate, or shortly thereafter, he abandoned orthodox Anglicanism and became a Unitarian. In a letter to the radical lecturer John Thelwall, Coleridge provided an account of his early religious faith in clearly Unitarian terms. He suggested that Christianity could be reduced to two fundamental propositions:

> 1. that there is an Omnipresent Father of infinite power, wisdom, & Goodness, in whom we all of us move, & have our being & 2. That when we appear to men to die, we do not utterly perish; but after this Life shall continue to enjoy or suffer the consequences & [natur]al effects of the Habits we have formed here, whether good or evil.[8]

The central tenet of Unitarianism was that Christ was merely the 'adopted' son of God. He was a human model for other humans to copy and not, as Trinitarians believed, an object of worship. Unitarians rejected the doctrine of the Atonement (whereby Christ's death was seen as a sacrifice necessary to the salvation of mankind by virtue of its propitiatory effect on God) and denied the Christian value of the idea of redemption. They thought that Christians could develop attitudes and feelings that would allow them to enjoy the afterlife by following the moral example of Jesus. The rejection of the necessity for redemption was connected to a denial of inherited original sin. In general, Unitarians thought that good conduct rather than correctness of belief was the key to salvation, and they viewed human beings as creatures who had a high natural capacity for virtue and benevolence.

Coleridge's Unitarian connections and sympathies aligned him with a group whose unorthodox religious views gave rise to a radical perspective on political questions.[9] Unitarians firmly supported attempts to break the Anglican monopoly on important political offices by abolishing the doctrinal tests enforced under Test and Corporation Acts, and regarded the Church of England as the coercive purveyor of corrupt doctrines. In addition, they claimed that religious freedom was precarious without political rights, and therefore favoured some measure of parliamentary reform. Perhaps more important, however, was the fact that leading Unitarians were inclined to reject traditional views on the functions and justification of government. Joseph Priestley (the 'Patriot, and Saint, and Sage' of *Religious Musings*), whom Coleridge later described as 'the author of modern Unitarianism'[10], argued that the purpose of government was to secure the happiness of the subject and that 'if it fail in this essential character . . . no other property or title . . . ought to shelter it from the generous attack of the noble and daring patriot'.[11] The radical implications of Unitarianism became clearly apparent after the onset of the French Revolution in 1789. It was no accident that the primary target of Edmund Burke's *Reflections on the Revolution in France* was Richard Price, a famous Unitarian divine, or that Samuel Horsley, Bishop of St David's, Rochester, and then St Asaph's, combined a fulsome welcome to émigré Catholic priests from France with vilifications of English Dissenters.[12]

The overt radicalism of Unitarians such as Price, Priestley and Frend helped cement the orthodox view that Dissent provided the warmest sympathisers with the Revolution in France, and the most likely source of English imitators. Priestley, for example, had a penchant for millenarian and prophetic speculations and now applied these to the interpretation of events in France.[13] This gave his pronouncements a menacing edge that did not escape the attention of those who already saw Unitarianism as a subversive force. In his reply to Burke's *Reflections*, Priestley described the Revolution as 'unparalleled in all history', and treated it as the first act in a transformation that would inaugurate a change from 'darkness to light, from superstition to sound knowledge, and from a most debasing servitude to a state of the most exalted

Freedom'.[14] The millennium would see the separation of Church and state, and the abolition of the archaic and oppressive system of government which Burke defended. Frend's original plan for *Peace and Union* was radical enough, since he intended to promote legal, parliamentary and religious reform. However, the outbreak of war with France in late January 1793 led him to add a virulently antiwar appendix. As his biographer notes, the effect of this was to reveal Frend as a 'Jacobin' as well as a 'non-conformist'.[15]

Coleridge's Unitarianism and his willingness to identify publicly with such a figure as Frend, aligned him with forces in English politics that were hostile to the *status quo*. His early political writings confirmed this identification. They advanced millenarian interpretations of the French Revolution, rejected the theological soundness of Trinitarianism and attacked many of the political features of the Anglican Church–state.[16] However, if Coleridge's association with Unitarianism is important in understanding his early lectures, so too is the plan for a utopian settlement which he and Robert Southey formulated during the summer and early autumn of 1794.

Although Coleridge's conversion to Unitarianism was politically significant, his letters and notebooks from his Cambridge years suggest that political interests were not infrequently displaced by personal and financial worries. For example, in February 1793 he spoke warmly of William Paley's *Reasons for Contentment*. The context of this recommendation was Coleridge's unsuccessful candidature for the Craven, a prestigious scholarship, awarded after an exhausting set of examinations, and in any case, he seems to have valued the Archdeacon's help in warding off depression ('my hypochondriac gloomy Spirit *amid Blessings* too frequently warbles out the hoarse gruntings of discontent – !'[17]) and did not necessarily endorse his complacent social theory. Still, even allowing for that, the use of Paley was rather odd for someone of Coleridge's leanings.

In June 1794 Coleridge met Robert Southey, a young Oxford undergraduate; his influence revived and deepened Coleridge's already heterodox interests, and fostered his development as both a political activist and a political writer. Coleridge's correspondence with Southey over the summer of 1794 abounded with the rhetorical froth of his regenerated political enthusiasm. The first letter, for example, carried the motto 'S. T. Coleridge to R. Southey – Health & Republicanism!' Coleridge commented on the poverty of the common people, deplored the arrogance of 'aristocrats', and related both to the shortcomings of English social and political institutions.[18] These criticisms accompanied the development of an alternative model of social organisation in the form of an ideal society to be established in the United States.

The settlement was to be known as 'Pantisocracy' (a Coleridgean coinage that Southey glossed as 'The equal government of all'), but it also incorporated the principle of 'aspheterism' or 'the generalisation of individual property'.[19] There are no surviving first-hand details of the way in which the proposed settlement was to be regulated, but the general intention was to create an environment which avoided personal subordination.[20] This was to be achieved by means of fixed, mutually agreed rules which would avoid the need for personal forms of authority. In any case, since the pantisocrats were very optimistic about the potentialities of a situation where human interaction was structured by the demands of rational benevolence, regulations of any kind were likely to play a minimal role in their lives. The importance that Coleridge attached to avoiding personal authority can be seen in his unease at Southey's suggestion that children and servants should be included in the party. He feared the effects that children partially raised in England (and thus tainted by civilisation yet lacking the rational faculties to rise above it) would have on the children of pantisocracy, and thought that the presence of servants would import habits of dominance and subservience into an environment where rational benevolence was supposed to reign supreme.[21]

Pantisocracy was based upon the expectation that in the absence of political institutions and social conventions which generated subservience and oppression, it would be possible to live according to the dictates of rational benevolence. However, the structure of the proposed settlement indicated that Coleridge and Southey believed that private property would impede the attainment of this goal. They, in common with a number of their contemporaries, believed that there was a close connection between gross inequalities of wealth and the existence of oppressive social and political relationships that were institutionalised in Church and state. Other contemporary solutions to these problems rested on the establishment of equal property by dividing and redistributing land, or on schemes of nationalisation that took advantage of the productive benefits of differential holdings, but allowed for them to be distributed throughout the community by welfare payments.[22]

Under pantisocracy, however, land was to be held in common, and the fruits of the very limited amount of necessary daily labour were, as Thomas Poole wrote, to be for the 'common use of all'.[23] The expectation that daily labour could be greatly restricted accorded with views found in William Godwin, and reflected a belief that the need for unnecessarily large amounts of onerous labour was generated by a thirst for luxury in societies where material possessions played a crucial role in the estimation of personal worth.[24] However, the communistic features of aspheterism rested on a belief that the excessive attention paid to property in contemporary societies was merely an extreme example of the generally deleterious effect of exclusive, private possession on human interaction. As we shall see, Coleridge thought that private property was the source of avarice and domination and that it thus lay at the root of inequality, oppression and government.[25]

To some extent, Southey and Coleridge's pantisocracy involved a search for personal contentment, but it also reflected their disillusionment with the moral condition and political structure of contemporary England.[26] The scheme may thus have been intended to have a wider social bearing. To the extent that this was the case, the pantisocrats' motivation differed from that of Joseph Priestley, who was once mooted as a possible ally. Priestley's interest in emigration was largely conditioned by a desire to avoid the mistreatment he had suffered at the hands of Church and King mobs in Birmingham in 1791, and his ideal community merely required the congenial company of what he called 'friends of liberty'.[27] The pantisocrats thought, however, that their settlement would help demonstrate the validity of their claims about the connection between property and domination, and point to the potentialities of a society that avoided these pitfalls and gave free scope to rationality and benevolence.[28]

Aspects of the pantisocratic impulse also related to the contemporary interest in millenarian speculations. This tradition stressed that fulfilment would take place on earth, and not infrequently made equality and communism central features of this process.[29] These goals were to be features of pantisocracy, and the combination of millenarianism and utopian communism played an important role in Coleridge's *Religious Musings* of 1794. In this poem, millenarian images ('Yet is the day of Retribution nigh: / The lamb of God hath opened the fifth seal; / And upward rush on swiftest wing of fire; / The innumerable multitude of wrongs; / By man on man inflicted!'[30]) were juxtaposed with glimpses of a reborn world that had many pantisocratic features.

In the event, the financial requirements of a move to the New World were such that neither the personal nor the universal expectations connected with pantisocracy were ever put to the test. Southey's suggestion that the scheme be tried on an experimental basis on a rented farm in Wales marked the beginning of the end for the full-blown project. One result of the curtailment of the original scheme was that financial problems became less daunting but no less pressing; it was no longer necessary to meet the costs of settling in America, but working capital had still to be raised for the Welsh experiment. Coleridge and Southey planned to earn their shares through writing and lecturing, using Bristol as a base.

The lectures that Coleridge gave in Bristol in 1795 provide the sources for his earliest essays in political theory. They are of considerable importance in relation to the ideas lying behind the pantisocratic scheme, and exhibited features that could be found in both religious and secular forms of contemporary radical argument.

1
Coleridge and Contemporary Radicalism: The Bristol Lectures (1795) and *The Watchman* (1796)

Coleridge began lecturing in Bristol in late January or early February 1795. Over the course of the year he gave eleven lectures, five of which were published. The first of these, *A Moral and Political Lecture*, appeared in print almost immediately, but, although the next two were given at about the same time, they were not published until December 1795, when they appeared together under the title, *Conciones ad Populum. Or Addresses to the People*. This work contained a revised version of *A Moral and Political Lecture*, and another piece entitled 'On the Present War'. The immediate context of all three lectures was the buoyant reformist atmosphere produced by the acquittal of Thomas Hardy, John Thelwall, Horne Tooke and their associates in the treason trial of November 1794, the scarcity and hardship attributed by many writers (including Coleridge) to an unjust and unnecessary war, and the government's growing nervousness about popular unrest, which led it to continue the suspension of *Habeas Corpus* in February 1795. Coleridge's three lectures advocated the combination of reform and enlightenment that was a common feature of radical argument in the 1790s. In later lectures and in parts of *The Watchman*, he added a new dimension to his radicalism by stressing the moral, political and social significance of private property.

I MORAL ENLIGHTENMENT AND POLITICAL REFORM

The published version of *A Moral and Political Lecture* used some of

Akenside's verse as a motto. These soothingly offered

> To calm and guide
> The swelling democratic tide;
> To watch the state's *uncertain* frame;
> To baffle Faction's *partial* aim;
> But chiefly with determin'd zeal
> To quell the servile Band that kneel
> To Freedom's jealous foes;
> And lash that Monster, who is daily found
> Expert and bold our country's peace to wound;
> Yet dreads to handle arms, nor manly counsel knows.[1]

Akenside's imagery was taken up in Coleridge's initial paragraph: 'in the present agitations of the public mind, every one ought to consider his intellectual faculties as in a state of immediate requisition'.[2] Coleridge's lecture reflected the dual concern with caution and activism found in Akenside, but the opening passages also suggested that the ship of state might be undermanned: 'When the Wind is fair and the Planks of the Vessel sound, we may safely trust everything to the management of professional Mariners; but in a Tempest and on board a crazy Bark, all must contribute their Quota of Exertion.' It was the vessel that was crazed, not the personnel, although given the gravity of the situation it was especially important for the latter to remain calm, for the salvage operation to utilise the 'intellectual faculties' of both passengers and crew, and for it to be bottomed on 'fixed Principles'.[3]

Coleridge's reference to 'fixed Principles' combined with the cautious message of Akenside's verse, superficially resembles his later search for the 'permanent' forces in human existence. This conception has strong Burkean overtones, and can be given a conservative gloss. However, Coleridge's position in 1795 had more to do with William Godwin than Burke, and reflected a concern found in much of the radical pamphlet literature of the 1790s. Coleridge contrasted 'fixed Principles' with the instability of 'Passion or Accident', with the acceptance of notions not fully understood nor subject to a thoroughgoing assessment of their consequences.[4] This was quite consistent with the rationalism of writers such as Godwin, who started from the 'grand and comprehensive Truth'[5] of universal benevolence. Coleridge believed that criticism based on this criterion should be applied to all human actions and institutions. Behaviour that would promote rather than frustrate human happiness must be grounded on an uncontrovertible principle. This concern was quite different from that implied by Burke's talk of the virtues of 'opinion . . . bottomed upon solid principles of law and policy', since these were historical entities which generated value, not rationally deduced derivatives of an external criterion.[6] Burke condemned the French Revolution because it sought to substitute universal principles for the 'solid principles of law and policy'. Coleridge was far more sympathetic. He claimed that the extreme reaction to the Revolution often used concern for humanity as a mask for 'malignant passion'. In so doing, it exhibited the absence of the fixed principles which he wished to promote. The French experience was Janus-faced. The Revolution had succeeded in achieving some of the negative requirements of human freedom (in Akenside's words, it quelled 'the servile Band that kneel / To Freedom's jealous foes'), but it also exemplified the dangers of attempting widespread reform among an ignorant population incapable of granting rational acceptance to fixed principles. 'The annals of the French Revolution have recorded in Letters of Blood, that the Knowledge of the Few cannot counteract the Ignorance of the Many; that the Light of Philosophy, when it is confined to a small Minority, points out the Possessors as the Victims, rather than the Illuminators, of the Multitude.'[7] Coleridge believed that illumination was crucial if the benefits of the revolution were to be attained without the bloodletting which had marked its progress in France. Given this consideration, the question of the moral and intellectual calibre of would-be reformers and their capacity to lead the population to a rational acceptance of fixed principles was of great importance. Consequently, Coleridge devoted the remainder of *A Moral and Political Lecture* to developing a taxonomy of reformers based upon the stipulations laid down in the early part of the lecture.

He identified four classes among the 'Friends of Freedom'. The first was characterised by an unstable combination of humane sensibilities and indolence which made them fair-weather friends of reform: 'On the report of French Victories they blaze into Republicanism, at a tale of French Excesses they darken into Aristocrats.' These men lacked commitment because they did not start from a principled opposition to oppression. Their moderation was a function of intellectual indolence, not of rational deliberation; stunted intellects produced only lukewarm passions whose one virtue consisted in avoiding excess.[8]

The second class of the 'Friends of Freedom' differed from the first in having an overabundance of passion directed to the overthrow of oppressive institutions, and to the ruthless punishment of those associated with them. Their guiding motive was revenge, and their zeal for this prevented them from seeing that many who appeared to benefit from oppression were as much the victims of it as those who suffered more directly. Although Coleridge treated the second class as one, he included within it those whose want of humanity could be ascribed to the harshness of their existence and a lack of education, and those whom 'Plenty has not softened, whom Knowledge has not taught Benevolence'.[9] These groups posed an obvious threat to any attempt to imitate Poland's bloodless revolution, but they also fostered a political climate in which the activities of *agents provocateurs* provided pretexts for government repression.

The indolence of the first class, and the misdirected heat of the second, contrasted strongly with the cool consistency of the third. In delineating the third class, Coleridge drew upon traits associated with Nonconformists whose main concern was the removal of religious tests. He commented favourably on their opposition to 'privileged orders', and 'mouldering establishments', but was critical of their obsession with the 'childish titles of aristocracy', which completely overshadowed any appreciation of the need to elevate the lower orders. They failed to see that the oppressed condition of the people had deeper causes than the disabilities which only lightly touched the comfortably-off members of the Dissenting middle classes: 'It is a mockery of our fellow creatures' wrongs to call them equal in rights, when by the bitter compulsion of their wants we make them inferior to us in all that can soften the heart, or dignify the understanding.' Coleridge may once have appreciated the personal value of Paley's 'Reasons for Contentment', but he now implied that such arguments militated against an interest in the welfare of the lower classes, and ignored the fact that their intellectual and moral enlightenment was closely related to their material improvement.[10]

The fourth class of the 'Friends of Freedom' represented an idealisation of Coleridge's view of his own role in contemporary politics. 'Thinking and disinterested Patriots' exhibited a calm and intellectually informed passion for the spread of knowledge. They aimed to establish the preconditions for beneficial social and political change by 'illuminating' the population and inculcating in them an understanding of the central role of circumstances in determining human conduct. An appreciation of the role played by the intellectual and moral environment was one of the 'fixed Principles' whose acceptance Coleridge wished to encourage. It necessitated the propagation of 'general information' as part of the process through which widespread benevolence would become the guiding principle of human conduct. True reformers would disseminate such information and prepare the population for a peaceful but far-reaching reform of social and political institutions.[11]

Although Coleridge was critical of the conduct of some radicals, this did not mean that his own position was antithetical to radicalism in general. Indeed, he adhered to a perspective on the relationship between individual enlightenment and political and social reform that was common in contemporary radical or 'Jacobin' literature.[12] In his first lecture Coleridge argued that enlightenment was a necessary condition for an advance to political freedom, and claimed that 'thinking and disinterested Patriots' were entitled to hasten this process by addressing themselves to public issues in public forums. He was obliged to make this claim because defenders of the existing political and religious establishment were suspicious of the effects of widespread public discussion of political issues. To Bishop Horsley, and to John Reeves, the founder of the original 'Association for the Protection of Liberty and Property', the 'Quota of Exertion' which Coleridge urged was wrecking, not salvaging, the ship of state. He described 'French freedom' as a 'beacon' which would guide the English to freedom; in the eyes of the conservative critics of the Revolution it was a dangerous conflagration that English radicals intended to use for incendiary rather than illuminatory purposes.[13]

Writers such as William Godwin, John Thelwall and Thomas Holcroft were frequently portrayed as disseminators of ideas which had produced bloodshed and chaos in France. But they, like Coleridge, went to considerable lengths to disprove the accuracy of this characterisation, and argued that the excesses of the French revolutionaries owed much to the blinkered and blinkering tactics employed by the adherents of the *status quo*. The radicals claimed a right to speak out on the grounds that ignorance produced a crisis in the state that could only be resolved by substituting knowledge for error. In his *Enquiry Concerning Political Justice* William Godwin had argued that habits of thought, social conventions and institutions which mystified human relationships should be abandoned in order to facilitate benevolent, enlightened social interaction. Similar arguments appeared in a wide range of works by authors who did not share Godwin's dislike of political organisations, and who grafted political activism onto radical theorising.[14] Their activities were directed to the propagation of the fruits of enlightened rationalism, but an essential element in this was a stress upon enlightenment itself, a concern which was, as we have seen, a major theme of Coleridge's *Moral and Political Lecture*. John Thelwall, for example, told his audiences (and those who later read his lectures in *The Tribune*) that rational assent was all important: 'You must have your knowledge not as the parrot has his by rote; but from the labour of your own minds; from the feelings and convictions of your own hearts.'[15] The reformers' primary duty was to illuminate the population, not to incite them to premature, reckless political activity. Thelwall was not alone in making this point; in this respect he shared common ground with such people as Horne Tooke, another defendant in the famous trial of November 1794; Daniel Eaton, the radical newspaper proprietor; and Joseph Gerrald, who was sentenced to transportation.[16]

Most of *A Moral and Political Lecture* was republished in *Conciones ad Populum* under the title 'Introductory Address'. In this version Coleridge added passages which praised the personal qualities and principles of the Girondists and criticised the intolerance of Robespierre. He did not, however, reject Robespierre's goals out of hand; the wickedness of these had 'by no means been proved'.[17] Coleridge also offered some general remarks on what he now saw as the characteristic weaknesses of the first three classes of the supposed 'Friends of Freedom'. Their knowledge was abstract, or one-sided – they had 'attained that portion of knowledge in politics, which Infidels possess[ed] in religion' – and their abstract criticisms were particularly ill-suited to the capacities of those whom they addressed. As an alternative, Coleridge urged true reformers to 'plead *for* the Oppressed not *to* them'; they should imitate the Methodists in being '*personally* among the poor', teaching them 'their *Duties* in order that [they] may render them susceptible of their *Rights*'. He claimed that the Bible was the most effective vehicle of popular reformation: 'By its Simplicity it will meet their comprehension, by its Benevolence soften their affections, by its Precepts it will direct their conduct, by the vastness of its Motives ensure their obedience.'[18]

Coleridge regarded religion as a *vehicle* of popular enlightenment, not a substitute for it.[19] Religion was necessary for the implementation of political and social change – it cleared the individual's 'gloom', and 'by habituating his mind to anticipate an infinitely great Revolution hereafter, may prepare it even for the sudden reception of a less degree of amelioration in this World'[20] – but moral reform was not seen as an alternative to social and political change. It was, in fact, part of the same process. Coleridge's views on this point reflected a belief, common among radicals (and later criticised in *The Friend*[21]), that there should be no separation between the dictates of morality and the structure and practice of politics. At the same time however, his claim that religion should prepare the way for social and political change challenged the regime-supportive role assigned to it by defenders of the Anglican–aristocratic establishment.

The stress upon moral reform in Coleridge's early political writings did not distinguish his position from that of contemporary radicals. Although writers such as Thelwall thought that the promotion of human happiness required the reformation of political institutions – 'the restoration of our natural and constitutional rights – our annual parliaments, and our universal suffrage, which corruption has secretly and gradually stolen away' – these aspirations were not divorced from a concern with moral reformation. The stress upon enlightenment and education was meant to promote change without chaos – 'Men ignorant and uninstructed become mad and frantic with their wrongs' – by showing that the success of political reform depended on the moral and intellectual development of the population at large. If men remained steeped in ignorance, rational benevolence could not become the guiding principle of human life. The claim that political change alone would not alleviate human misery, a central tenet of the Godwinian perspective on the relationship between virtue and knowledge, was one that Coleridge shared with Unitarians such as Price and Priestley, and with such secular radicals as Godwin himself, Holcroft and Thelwall. At times the question of the form government took seemed relatively unimportant, even for such a 'political' radical as Thelwall:

> It is not the external structure of government that I find fault with . . . It is . . . the principle that actuates the government, and if this is sufficiently pure . . . I will hail and venerate that country as my own, and rejoice in the establishment of such principles, whatever may be the exterior encumberances, with which accident, or choice, may happen to have surrounded it.[22]

Of course, political institutions played an important role in shaping the environment in which human character developed, but the persistence of oppressive forms of political authority owed a great deal to the ignorance and immorality of the population. The line of argument underlying this complex picture of the interrelationship of moral character and social and political institutions is circular, but it is intelligible if social progress is seen as taking place through mutually supporting advances in popular enlightenment and political institutions.

In any case, the stress on political reform *and* individual enlightenment which appeared in radical literature of the 1790s means that the moral–political dichotomy cannot serve to distinguish Coleridge from other contemporary radicals.[23] The concern to ground reform on fixed principles, and to instruct rather than inflame the common people, was quite compatible with the promotion of radical political change and was, indeed, often regarded as a prerequisite of it. The illuminatory function that Coleridge ascribed to the true 'Friends of Freedom' was meant to encourage action based on clearly formulated principles, a position which was derived from a view which related ignorance and evil. However, the ennunciation and defence of the principles in question played only a minor role in Coleridge's earliest Bristol lectures. Benevolence was upheld as the guiding light of human conduct; it condemned oppression at home, and the sacrifice of the victims of the slave trade to the dehumanising greed of those engaged in the trade and those who consumed its exotic fruits. But in his earliest political writings Coleridge did not explain the basis upon which the principle rested. His argument thus involved a significant lacuna: if goodness depended upon intellectual clarity, then one should be able to provide a rational explanation of the primacy of enlightened benevolence; this would help to enjoin acquiescence in benevolence as a goal.

Matters relating to these issues were raised in Coleridge's 'Lectures on Revealed Religion', given in May and June of 1795.

These lectures showed that he regarded politics as a sphere for realising Christian goals, one where moral and religious injunctions played a direct role. They were significantly influenced by a Unitarian perspective on religious establishments and Trinitarianism, but they combined this with a detailed analysis of the relationship between property and political power, and related closely to the system of non-private property that lay at the heart of the pantisocratic scheme.

II RADICAL RELIGION: THE CRITIQUE OF PROPERTY AND GOVERNMENT

The full title of Coleridge's six lectures, 'Lectures on Revealed Religion, Its Corruptions and Political Views', provides a succinct summary of their subject matter. In particular, it points to a direct connection between religion and politics; as the 'Prospectus' notes, the lectures deal with the 'political applications' of Trinitarian corruptions of Christianity.[24] They contain an attack on the doctrines and practices of the Established Church, and portray it as the purveyor of a corrupt and oppressive form of Christianity. This critique of the Church of England linked Coleridge's position to that of many contemporary radicals, but the fact that his argument depended upon an appeal to revealed religion distinguished his position from that of writers who were radicals *and* atheists. Indeed, the six lectures were, in part at least, a response to those who identified liberty with a rejection of Christianity.[25] This point was emphasised in the 'Allegoric Vision' with which the lectures began. Coleridge conjured up images of individuals whose 'Foreheads spoke Thought', but who were 'indignant at religion' and were attracted by the facile inanities of atheistic materialism. They were blind to the 'mild majesty' of adherents of true religion, whose countenances 'displayed deep Reflection animated by ardent Feelings'.[26]

The lectures' 'political views' applied the implications of revelation to political and social matters. Coleridge claimed that the existence of church establishments was a consequence of a departure from the original, simple and true basis of Christian doctrine. The single most important article of Christian faith, 'Immortality made probable to us by the Light of Nature, and proved to us by the Resurrection of Jesus', entailed a religion 'of which every true Christian is the Priest, his own Heart the Altar, the Universe its Temple, and Errors and Vices its only Sacrifices'.[27] Religious establishments only developed when true Christianity was corrupted by the introduction of mysterious sophistications such as Trinitarianism and Redeptionism. By their very implausibility and lack of connection with true, simple Christianity, such doctrines necessitated the growth of a priestly cast to interpret and expound what should be 'so obvious to the meanest Capacity, that he who runs may read. He who knows his letters may find in [the Gospels] everything necessary for him.' Coleridge claimed that there was, in fact, little to choose between the Church of England and that of Rome. Both carried 'the mark of antichrist'. Both had 'an intimate alliance with the powers of this World, which Jesus positively forbids', and both were purveyors of mystery.[28]

The alliance with the powers of the world was the second reason for rejecting church establishments. Coleridge regarded this alliance as contrary to Christ's declared intention – 'My Kingdom is not of this world' – but it also had the effect of reinforcing and legitimising unjust features of temporal institutions, and tainting the practice of Christianity with their evils. 'This dear-bought Grace of Cathedrals, this costly defence of Despotism, this nurse of grovelling sentiment and cold-hearted Lip-worship . . . inspires Oppression, while it prompts Servility.'[29] The bishops' support for the bloody and unjust war against France epitomised the depravity of Christian sentiment engendered by the Church-state alliance.

> It is recorded in the shuddering hearts of Christians, that while Europe is reeking with Blood, and smoking with unextinguished Fires, in a contest of unexampled crimes and unexampled calamities, every Bishop but one voted for the continuance of the War. They deemed the fate of their religion to be in the contest! – Not the Religion of Peace . . . not the Religion of the meek and lowly Jesus, which forbids his Disciples all alliance with the powers of this World – but the Religion of Mitres and Mysteries, the Religion of Pluralities and Persecution, the Eighteen-Thousand-Pound-a-Year Religion of Episcopacy. Instead of the Minister of the Gospels, a Roman might recognise in these Dignitaries the High-priests of Mars – with this difference, that the Ancients fatted their Victims for the Altar, we prepare ours for sacrifice by leanness.[30]

Coleridge's critique of established religion rested upon a Unitarian view of the political and social implications of the Christian faith. He believed that the essential meaning of the Gospel could be summarised in the demand that 'Christians must behave towards the majority with loving kindness and submission preserving among themselves a perfect Equality'.[31] Christian precepts enjoined equality and freedom and thus condemned the theological and political features of the Established Church: it was a barrier to theological clarity, an obstacle to religious freedom, and an important adjunct of oppressive social and political structures.

The treatment of revealed religion in the lectures on the subject was heavily dependent upon standard sources of both orthodox and Unitarian origins. However, Coleridge used these arguments as the basis for statements about the *political* implications of Christianity, a religion which was, he claimed, the 'Friend of Civil Freedom'[32], and developed a stance that was more extreme than that of other Unitarians such as Joseph Priestley. While Priestley thought that civil liberty was necessary for religious freedom, Coleridge treated freedom *and* equality as mandatory implications of Christianity.[33] As a result, many of the arguments of the lectures are closely related to Coleridge's pantisocratic preoccupations, and in this and other respects they involve a trenchant critique of government and society. The sixth lecture (which survives in only a fragmentary form) appears to have included speculations about the 'probable State of Society & Government if all men were Christians', a state of affairs that was to be produced in miniature in the pantisocratic settlement.[34] Coleridge focused in particular on the relationship between private property, government and the egalitarian demands of Christian doctrine.

Coleridge argued that the development of private property inevitably gave rise to political and social institutions, and to psychological and moral dispositions, which frustrated the quest for 'Universal Equality' that was the 'object of the Messiah's Mission'. These institutions and dispositions reinforced each other, hastened the movement away from equality, and produced wretchedness and servitude. 'Where the Causes of evil exist, Good cannot be – In the moral world there is a constant Alternation of Cause and Effect – and Vice and Inequality mutually produce each other.'[35] The beginnings of inequality corresponded with the development of fixed settlements and commercial and trading activity, which endowed land in the vicinity of towns with a value it had not had for nomadic herdsmen and encouraged the recognition of property rights in land. Coleridge regarded these rights as a means of securing justice to individuals in circumstances where there was a weak natural sense of what was due to each. Property was originally intended, as Coleridge remarked in a notebook entry of a slightly later date, 'to secure to every man the produce of his Toil',[36] but it was necessary only because a growing fascination with material objects, a symptom of self-interest and avarice, had already begun to undermine both equality and the social harmony which equality fostered. The development of manufactures, a cause and consequence of the growth of 'artificial wants', provided further opportunities for enrichment and quickened the movement away from equality. This process reached its logical conclusion in the horrors of the slave trade. Coleridge thus traced the origin of property to the growth of avarice, and claimed that, once God-ordained equality had been abandoned, property became an unavoidable feature of human life; it was 'absolutely necessary for the quiet of mankind'. As such, it predated the foundation of government, but, because property was a necessary condition of activities which generated further, and more profound, inequalities, it created an environment in which government itself became a necessity. The state came into being to defend previously established but poorly defended rights. However, the development of such rights and the need to defend them were aberrations to which all future injustices could be traced. 'Thus the jarring Interests of individuals rendered Governments necessary', and since governments were the offspring of inequality and vice they produced further evils: 'like quack Medicines . . . they have produced new diseases, and only checked the old ones – and the evils which they check, they perpetuate'.[37]

Coleridge's critique of the formation and intrinsic character of government had strong anarchistic overtones, and paralleled the arguments of Godwin's *Enquiry* and also the less rigorous views of Thomas Paine in *Common Sense* and *The Rights of Man*. It rested upon a contrast between the evil character of government and humane, mutually advantageous social co-operation. As Paine put it, in a formulation adopted by both Godwin and Coleridge, 'Society is produced by our wants, and government by our wickedness. . . . Society in every state is a blessing, but government even in its best state is but a necessary evil.'[38]

Having related the need for government to the development of vice, Coleridge then listed the harm which government itself engendered. It generated wars, attributable to no better causes than the 'Folly and Prejudices of our Monarchs and the wretched compliance of Ministers'.[39] Wars burdened those who were already weighed down by heavy taxes; these supported corrupt administrations that were both an effect of depravity, and a mechanism through which equality and freedom were undermined: 'Selfishness is planted in every bosom, and prepares us for the Slavery which it introduces.'[40] Government produced no benefits to mitigate these evils. It provided for neither the material nor the educational needs of the population, and only inadequately protected individuals from the consequences of the brutality and ignorance which government itself generated. The close relationship between government and commerce was symptomatic of this tendency. The growth of commercial activity stimulated artificial wants which could only be satisfied by sacrificing the material and moral well being of the bulk of the population. Government encouraged commerce and then used its coercive power to control the depressed and disgruntled populace. Coleridge thought that inequality lay at the root of all these evils: 'as long as anyone possesses more than another, Luxury, Envy, Rapine, Government & Priesthood will be the necessary consequence, and prevent the Kingdom of God – that is the progressiveness of the moral world'.[41]

But inequality could not be avoided merely by instituting equal property. The equalisation of property would be difficult to attain because of the difficulty of balancing complex qualities and appropriate quantities of different things. In any case, if equal property were established in an environment where individuals lacked enlightened benevolence, it would be short-lived. In the face of these difficulties Coleridge urged the need for moral reform. It was necessary to 'exert over our own hearts a virtuous despotism, and lead our own Passions in triumph, and then we shall want neither Monarch nor General. If we would have no Nero without, we must place a Caesar within us and that Caesar must be Religion!'[42] This should not be seen as a purely 'moral' or 'religious' response. It was in fact part of a political solution, a forceful restatement of one of the central themes of the earlier Bristol lectures: namely, that political change was an element in a process which necessarily involved moral enlightenment. In *A Moral and Political Lecture*, however, religion was a vehicle of reform; in the 'Lectures on Revealed Religion' it was also seen as the substance of such a process. But, if the egalitarian doctrines of the gospels were to bear fruit, they had to be instilled into political practice. Religion was the basis of politics, not a substitute for it.

Coleridge considered the political ramifications of the Christian message by discussing the constitution of the ancient Jews. This approach was common in contemporary treatments of revealed religion.[43] The laws of Moses were seen as having the joint and related aims of preserving the Jewish nation against idolatry and its temporal enemies; the miraculous survival of monotheism and national freedom was proof of the fulfilment of the prophecies which were essential to Christianity. The Jews' partiality for idolatrous practices, and their relatively low level of spiritual and intellectual enlightenment, strengthened the force of their example, since it made the existence of the dispensation even more remarkable than it might otherwise have been. In political terms, the divine origin of the constitution was established by comparing its qualities with other possible worldly models, such as that of the Egyptians.[44]

The hallmark of the Jewish constitution was its institutionalisation of liberty through equality. Its liberal character reflected the requirement that all men should be acknowledged as God's creatures, and should be subject to Him alone. Freedom was the natural condition of those who were the recipients of 'the infinite Love of the true Deity',[45] but the demand for liberty entailed a demand for equality also. This part of Coleridge's argument depended upon a general claim about the relationship between property and political power and the resulting incompatibility of liberty and inequality. 'Property is Power and equal Property equal Power. A Poor Man is necessarily more or less a Slave. Poverty is the Death of public Freedom – it virtually enslaves individuals, and generates those Vices, which make necessary a dangerous concentration of power in the executive branch.'[46] The Jewish constitution was excellent because it recognised this relationship and attempted to avoid slavery by instituting and maintaining a strict system of equality. The land was divided equally, and indebtedness was curtailed by a prohibition against lending money at interest and by a requirement that all debts be remitted every seventh year. As commerce and manufactures were strongly discouraged, land provided the main means of subsistence. It was also the basis of the state because it provided maintenance for the militia. Independent landholders served in the militia in rotation for a month at a time, and while in service they also acted as the legislative arm of the constitution, ruling with the help of a senate comprised of seventy elders. This system ensured the defence of the nation, and guarded against the despotism which could result from a permanent ('standing') army or a long-serving legislative body. Transfers of land were subject to stringent conditions which precluded the erosion of the popular basis of the government. Land could not pass out of the tribe to which it was originally allotted, nor could it, in the long run at least, accumulate in the hands of particular members of the same tribe. The half-century 'Jubilee' restored men to their original possessions and thereby protected the basis of the state and weakened the incentive to accumulate. The Jewish state was thus designed to secure universal liberty by maintaining equality. The political personalities of its members were a function of their possession of equal lots of land; these provided the basis for participation in a protective and legislative system which was circumscribed by an immutable body of law derived from God via Moses.[47]

One of the contexts of Coleridge's account of the excellence of the Jewish constitution was a tradition of theologically oriented arguments about the Mosaic dispensation.[48] But the guiding principles of the 'Lectures on Revealed Religion' was that theology and political theory were closely interrelated, and so these arguments were given a political bearing. This had important implications for the anti-property and anti-political-authority features of Coleridge's early theory. As we have seen, a central point about the divine source of the Mosaic code was that it was successful among a people who were neither more enlightened nor more virtuous than their neighbours. The character ascribed to the Jews helped to make the case for the dispensation a very strong one; it also lent credence to claims about its actual role in the fulfilment of God's purposes. Coleridge pointed out, however, that Christians could not regard the Jewish constitution as perfect. If it were, there would be no reason for it to be superseded by the new dispensation instituted by Christ. The most important imperfection in the Jewish constitution lay in the system of property that it instituted. Coleridge regarded this as a fatal necessity; necessary because of the character of the Jews, it was fatal to the long-term survival of the Jewish commonwealth.

The constitution maintained equal individual property rather than equal claims to a commonly held stock. A system of non-property (of the kind which Coleridge and Southey wished to establish in the United States) was not possible in ancient Israel because of the flawed moral character of the Jews. They were imbued with childish selfishness and were 'too ignorant a people, too deeply leavened with the Vices of Ægypt to be capable of so exalted a state of Society'.[49] Their selfishness could only be prevented or checked through a strictly regulated system of equal, but individualised, property. Without the capacity for enlightened benevolence made possible by the advent of Christianity, the Jews lacked the attributes necessary to maintain a system of non-property. The imperfections of the Jewish constitution were necessary in relation to the character of those for whom it was designed, and thus helped to ensure the longevity of the Jewish state. But, because the constitution was imperfect, the Jewish state could not be permanent. Its recognition of individualised property rights provided the seed-bed for the self-seeking and avarice which finally destroyed it. In the time of Samuel, the Jews succumbed to the temptations which individualised property had built into their constitution: 'seduced by the splendor of monarchical Courts around them the people of Israel petitioned for a King. . . . Their crime was the foulest of which human nature is capable – they were weary of independence, and their punishment was the heaviest. They had their Request granted.'[50]

Coleridge denied that the original Jewish monarchy was despotic – it could not therefore serve as a model for divinely ordained despotism – but he claimed that the departure from republican equality set in train a course of development which encouraged displays of 'Vain Splendor and unnecessary Luxuries'. These generated envy and a desire for emulation which eroded economic and political equality: 'so . . . Avarice in some and Profusion in many introduce Poverty into the State and with it every vice that debases human nature'. The Mosaic dispensation was important because it helped create the conditions for the Christian revelation, but the history of the Jewish state provided a warning to those who followed. In its years of stability, and in those of decay, it represented 'one strong proof among very many others, that the Dispensations of God have always warned Man against the least Diminution of civil Freedom'.[51]

There are interesting parallels and contrasts between Coleridge's treatment of the Jewish constitution in the 'Lectures on Revealed Religion' and the details of the pantisocratic scheme. Both condemned property on the grounds that it provided an insuperable barrier to freedom and equality. Pantisocracy, however, was a system which avoided property, not one based on legally regulated equality. Enlightened benevolence allowed for equality without property, but this could only exist if care were taken to exclude those whose minds had already been formed on non-benevolent lines. These considerations explain why Coleridge reacted so strongly against Southey's plans to include servants and children in the scheme.[52] The former had already been inculcated in relationships of subservience and superiority which would counteract natural inclinations to benevolence, while the latter suffered from the same disabilities as the Jews. They were both vicious and ignorant, and would either pervert the children born under pantisocracy, or necessitate a system of rigid regimentation that was incompatible with the principles of disinterested voluntarism upon which the settlement was to be based. The character of the pantisocrats, the scale of the settlement, and the absence of private property meant that the settlers would not require political institutions. However, some mutually agreed rules would be needed to structure benevolent interaction within the settlement. According to Tom Poole, these regulations were to be fixed, and were to be decided upon, before the settlers left England.[53] They thus bore an at least formal resemblance to the immutable laws of Moses which provided the legislative basis of the Jewish state. In both cases, the government of men was to be largely avoided by instituting a government of laws. Under pantisocracy, no less than in ancient Israel, a concern with equality necessitated the minimisation of the exercise of authority by some individuals over others. Because the Jews lacked the moral qualities necessary to support a system of non-property, inequality could be avoided only through a complex and rigid system of law. Pantisocracy would ensure equality without individualised property, so there would be no need for political structures, or for extensive systems of regulation. These were either a function of inequality, or reflected the possibility of such a state developing. Neither of these problems would be faced by those who were so enlightened that property became unnecessary.

III RADICAL RELIGION AND 'CIVIC HUMANISM'

Much of the interest in the 'Lectures on Revealed Religion' has focused on the relationship between Coleridge's ideas and those of

Godwin, Priestley and Hartley.[54] The fullest accounts suggest that Coleridge shared Godwin's anarchistic perspective on government, and followed him in ascribing human misery to the inflation of wants consequent upon the widespread development of commercial activity. Coleridge adopted a view of the political and social importance of moral and intellectual enlightenment which can be identified with Godwin, but which was common to a number of contemporary writers. However, Godwin's understanding of enlightened benevolence was secular, while that of Coleridge was based upon a distinctly Christian perspective. This relied heavily on Coleridge's contemporary interest in Priestley and Hartley, who are likely sources for such general features of Coleridge's position as his belief in human perfectibility and progress. They also contributed an alternative, and specifically religious, set of justifications for positions which Godwin advanced without the aid of theology. The distinctly theological parts of the 'Lectures on Revealed Religion' depended upon arguments and illustrations which were the stock-in-trade of Unitarians such as Priestley. Priestley's writings also provided a likely source for Coleridge's initial introduction to the ideas of David Hartley. Hartley's theory of association was particularly important. It explained the psychological basis of benevolence and showed how it developed from selfish and private roots to become a public, and indeed universal, goal that was located in a process of association which led to God. Coleridge's belief in the afterlife explained his hostility to atheism, while his understanding of the process of association led him to reject the parts of Godwin's argument which portrayed particular, and especially familial, affection as harmful to the growth of widespread benevolence. In belittling such affections Godwin was cutting off the root from which universal benevolence grew.

These accounts of the sources of Coleridge's ideas are important in understanding the Bristol lectures and the aspirations underlying the pantisocratic experiment. Some important loose ends remain, however, especially with regard to Coleridge's radical political and social egalitarianism. Godwin, for example, was a strong critic of communitarianism, while Priestley denied that there 'was any obligation on Christians . . . *To throw their goods into common*'.[55] His conduct in America, where he engaged in large-scale land speculation, bore witness to this, and illustrated the gap between his views of the benefits of immigration and those of

Coleridge.[56] Priestley was also enthusiastic about the benefits of commerce, in spite of his acknowledgement of its inegalitarian outcomes, and was not wedded to the idea of political equality. Civil liberty was all-important, but Priestley thought that this could be ensured by a system of representation which related political influence to property. Finally, Priestley's American settlement was patriarchal, not egalitarian, in its political structure.[57]

Leonard Deen has argued that Coleridge's egalitarianism rested largely on a radical interpretation of passages in the Bible. It provided a model of an innocent pastoral state, and an account of Jewish history which Coleridge used to exemplify a decline in the moral and material condition of man resulting from an abandonment of political and social equality.[58] What Deen does not make clear, however, is how Coleridge came to interpret the Old Testament in this way. The point is, that the history of the Jewish people was neither theologically nor politically unproblematic. The incomplete early sections of Coleridge's third lecture probably originally contained a critical treatment of Paine's deistic attack on the Old Testament evidences for revealed religion,[59] but Coleridge also noted with approval Paine's condemnation of the Jews' hankering after monarchy. This was important because the history of the Jews was often used by conservative writers to buttress claims about God-ordained, absolutist monarchy which were essentially, and in some cases overtly, Filmerian.[60] By contrast, Coleridge's treatment of the history of the Jews, like that of Paine, generated radical political conclusions. These were dependent in part on his use of Scripture, following Unitarian practice, as a tool of social and political criticism, but were also the result of the way he used seventeenth- and eighteenth-century arguments about the relationship between property and political power.

In the 'Lectures on Revealed Religion' Coleridge frequently drew upon Moses Lowman's *Dissertation on the Civil Government of the Hebrews*.[61] Lowman's book was a standard source for defenders of the Jewish constitution, one which appealed particularly to Dissenters because of its liberal perspective on civil and religious freedom. Coleridge depended upon it for details of the constitution and for his account of the significance of the Mosaic dispensation. In addition, his claims about the relationship between property and power, poverty and servitude, were adapted from Lowman's book. However, these ideas did not originate with Lowman, but were taken by him from James Harrington's *Oceana*. This work, first published in 1656, contained a model of a free commonwealth which was intended to promote a republican form of government in England based upon an extensive body of independent freeholders.[62]

Harrington was one of a galaxy of seventeenth-century upholders of republican and/or democratic values who were called upon in the 1790s to support the aspirations of contemporary radicals.[63] Coleridge made a couple of hortatory references to Harrington in the Bristol lectures, and the pantisocratic scheme and his analysis of the Jewish constitution included a number of features which also appeared in *Oceana*. Fixed laws, the rotation of office-holders, and the importance of a militia were common Harringtonian themes.[64] Moreover, Coleridge's treatment of the Jewish constitution was based upon a conception of the relationship between property and political power which came from Harrington.

Harrington applied the connection between 'the proportion or balance of dominion or property in land' and 'the nature of Empire' to a situation where the dispersal of property seemed to make a free, equal commonwealth a feasible and desirable possibility.[65] In a republican framework a citizen body of independent proprietors could pursue the universal values that would ensure the commonwealth's continuance, and their freedom. In this model, the active pursuit of the universal prevented the intrusion of particular, destructive values into the political life of the state; it was strongly and necessarily participatory. The same mode of analysis could, however, also be applied to a society with marked differentials of property-holdings, although in this case it would justify an *unequal* commonwealth. In the late seventeenth century it began to be used in this way to justify the traditional constitution, in which political rights were, of course, far more restricted than in a popular republic. In both cases, however, the possession of landed property was seen as the basis of participatory claims. This requirement led to the development of a tradition of political argument which concentrated on a perceived threat to tha landed classes and the constitution from those who possessed new forms of wealth derived from credit financing of government. It raised the spectre of an independent executive who would be able to maintain their position by producing a corrupt and servile legislature. This possibility formed the basis of a Country Party ideology espoused by 'Old Whig' and Tory opponents of the Whig regimes that dominated English politics after 1715. Its principal targets were financiers and the ministers who supported them, and office-holders, pensioners and standing armies whose slavish, self-interested loyalty was purchased through the funds generated by credit financing.[66]

Harringtonian and Country Party assumptions about the correspondence between property and political effectiveness played an important role in Coleridge's analysis of the Jewish constitution. However, Coleridge used these assumptions in a way which seriously challenged the political implications usually deduced from them.[67] He argued that individual property was inherently unstable, and that, where it existed, political freedom was precarious. Indeed, the appearance of private property marked the beginning of a process that produced economic and political inequality. Thus, while Coleridge could be said to accept the Harringtonian maxim that 'rights exist for the sake of equality and the virtue which is its expression',[68] he believed that rights to private property were incompatible with equality. He therefore rejected the idea of an equal commonwealth based on independent proprietors in favour of one with a communitarian basis, and did so because of his literal acceptance of biblical injunctions about Christian equality. In other words, Christian egalitarianism necessitated the abandonment of the independent-property-holder myth that lay at the heart of Harringtonian discourse.

At the same time, however, Coleridge's understanding of the requirements of a free society were radicalised by his acceptance of the Harringtonian conception of the relationship between property and political power. In this respect, his position differed significantly from that of both Christian and non-Christian critics of existing social and political structures. As we have seen, Priestley took a generally complacent attitude towards economic inequality, and assumed that the existing distribution of property was perfectly compatible with the exercise of civil liberty. The same was true of Richard Price.[69] William Godwin, on the other hand, was critical of the status associated with property-holding, but nevertheless regarded property as a fundamental right which individuals recognised in others, and which provided the basis for moral relationships between them.[70] Neither Godwin, Priestley nor Price thought that the end of oppression required the abolition of property rights, but this was the conclusion which Coleridge drew from the Harringtonian theory of the relationship between property and political power.

IV CORRUPTION AND PARLIAMENTARY REFORM: COLERIDGE'S CRITIQUE OF THE TWO BILLS

In his treatment of the Two Bills, Coleridge maintained the interest in contemporary affairs that had marked his earliest political writings, and which he continued to promote in his poetry:

> O abject! if, to sickly dreams resign'd
> All effortless thou leave Life's commonweal
> A Prey to Tyrants, Murderers of Mankind.[71]

These efforts were now focused on the contemporary political scene, rather than on a distant settlement. Pantisocracy was designed for the rational and reasonably virtuous, and was not feasible in an environment where ignorance and vice, reinforced by oppression and poverty, were major problems. As an alternative, Coleridge argued in favour of a combination of parliamentary reform and a modification of property rights. In so doing, he continued his identification with radical elements in contemporary politics.

The 'Lecture on the Two Bills' and *The Plot Discovered* were produced in response to acts introduced into the House of Lords by Lord Grenville, and into the Commons by William Pitt, on the sixth and tenth of November 1795. Lord Grenville's Bill (or the 'Treason Bill' as it was also called) was meant to ensure the 'Safety and Preservation of His Majesty's Person and Government against Treasonable and Seditious Practices and Attempts', while Pitt's Bill (also known as the 'Convention Bill') was designed to 'More Effectually Preventing Seditious Meetings and Assemblies'.[72] These Acts widened the definition of treason and sedition to include criticisms of the Constitution, and placed public meetings and petitioning under the effective control of local elites, particularly Justices of the Peace and Lord Lieutenants of Counties. Their critics claimed that these Acts would produce severe and unwarranted restrictions on liberty of speech, publication and assembly.

Coleridge began his critique of the Two Bills by asserting the right, indeed the duty, of private individuals actively to oppose the government when the public interest was at stake. This claim was also made in the earlier lectures, but it was particularly relevant to the Two Bills, since they were intended to prevent the exercise of such a right. In the 'Lecture on the Two Bills' Coleridge supported his claim by quotations from Bolingbroke which were culled from James Burgh's *Political Disquisitions*.

> True political moderation . . . consists in not opposing the measures of Government, except when great and national Interests are at stake: and when that is the case, in opposing them with such a degree of warmth as is adequate to the nature of the evil. . . . The Question, in a season of . . . extremity . . . ceases to be who has a *right* to do this or that? Every man has a *right* to save his Country from Slavery.[73]

Those who opposed the Two Bills were acting responsibly. Their conduct contrasted strongly with the view epitomised by Bishop Horsley's dictum 'THE MASS OF THE PEOPLE HAVE NOTHING TO DO WITH THE LAWS BUT TO OBEY THEM', and with that of the government and its supporters, who had 'annihilated the Constitution . . . hunting & goading . . . Freedom . . . now she runs mad / – and recalled Anarchy!'[74]

The fact that Coleridge's responses to the Two Bills leaned heavily upon Burgh's *Disquisitions* is important in terms of his relationship with the Commonwealth tradition. Burgh's work was, as Lewis Patton says, 'a popular Whig sourcebook',[75] but it was one which contained a compendium of views from Commonwealth and Country Party sources. As we have seen, the idea of corruption was central to this perspective, and it also played an important role in Coleridge's critique. He argued that the restrictions imposed by the Two Bills would undermine the Constitution by corrupting it into a despotic form. Coleridge elucidated this claim by reference to a tripartite classification of constitutions which he probably borrowed from Burgh.[76] Government '*by* the people' existed where the people were '*actually* present' or where they were '*morally* present' – that is, represented by delegates who acted on the instructions of their constituents. The second mode of government, government '*over* the people', was despotic: 'the people at large have no voice in the legislature, and possess no safe or established mode of political interference: in few words . . . the majority are always acted upon, never acting.' The type of government which had existed in England was representative of the third mode, government '*with* the people'. Coleridge described this as a 'mixed' mode of government, one which combined elements from the other two. It was essentially transitory. 'This ought to be a *progressive* Government ascending from the *second* mode to the first: at least, it is bad or good according to its distance from, or proximity to, the first mode.'[77] Although Coleridge's analysis drew upon ideas of the constitution as a balanced mixture of elements, the logic of his argument implied that such notions were applicable only to certain stages in a progression that would eliminate the need for balance since there would eventually be only one estate, 'the people'.[78]

Coleridge refused to accept that the people were 'virtually' represented in existing parliaments. The House of Commons contained large numbers of military and naval officers, placemen, and merchants and financiers who depended upon the executive and therefore could not be relied upon to act as the 'virtual' representatives of those who had no role in its selection. The key issue was to secure representation of the peoples' interests, and this would not be possible 'unless . . . the legislative power is in the hands of those, whose worldly self-interests manifestly preponderate in favour of the incorrupt use of it'. Coleridge pictured the British system of representation as potentially corrupt and argued that it would be actually corrupt, and would shut off the possibility of improvement, if it excluded a degree of popular participation through freedom of speech, publication, assembly and petitioning:

> The Liberty of the Press, (a power resident in the people) gives us an *influential* sovereignty. By books necessary information may be dispersed; . . . and by right of petitioning that will may be expressed. . . . This unrestricted right of over-awing the Oligarchy of Parliament by constitutional expression of the general will forms our liberty; it is the sole boundary that divides us from Despotism.[79]

The Two Bills threatened both the 'unrestricted right' and the 'sole boundary'.

Coleridge's defence of a free press and of rights of assembly and petitioning was part of a broader concern with constitutional improvement.[80] He was favourably disposed to the development of representative government in France – 'Such, I trust will be the Government of France. France! whose crimes and miseries posterity will impute to us. France! to whom posterity will impute their virtues and their happiness'[81] – and claimed that an improvement in the 'mode' of representation would avoid the 'accidental benefits' of 'virtual representation'. The free dissemination of information and the concerted expression of political ideas were important because they provided opportunities for political enlightenment, and for the expression and consideration of ways in which the constitution could be improved:

> if . . . ministers believe . . . that the constitution as it at present exists is the best possible, they must likewise believe either that there is no God, or . . . that he is not all-powerful or not benevolent. For this said summum bonum as it at present exists, doth evidently prevent little evil and produce much. . . . But if the present Constitution be progressive, if its only excellence, if its whole endurableness consists in motion; if that which it is be only good as being the step and mode of arriving at something better; . . . then are our ministers most unnaturally dwarfing what they dare not at once destroy.[82]

The defence of the existing constitution was merely a means to its *improvement*. Constitutional improvement involved movement towards 'government by the people', towards a participatory system whose comprehensiveness guaranteed liberty through active self-rule.

V POLITICAL PROGRESSION AND THE DIFFUSION OF PROPERTY: COLERIDGE, THELWALL AND *THE WATCHMAN*

The 'Lecture on the Two Bills' was the last of Coleridge's Bristol series. It was followed by an experiment in political journalism which occupied him for the early months of 1796. In some respects, *The Watchman* took over where *The Plot Discovered* left off. The prospectus for the journal made it clear that it was to be a vehicle for the opinion-forming diffusions of information which were threatened by the Two Bills: 'In the present perilous state of our Constitution the Friends of Freedom, of Reason, and of Human Nature, must feel it their duty by every means in their power to supply or circulate political information.' *The Watchman* was to provide support for the Whig Club (a body whose founding declaration was overridingly concerned with the Two Bills), and for what Coleridge called the 'PATRIOTIC SOCIETIES, for obtaining a Right of Suffrage general and frequent', a goal which was significantly wider than that of the Whig Club itself.[83]

In its original articles, and in the material culled from other newspapers, *The Watchman* reiterated arguments advanced in the Bristol lectures. These dealt with the diffusion of knowledge, corruption, the war, the Established Church and the slave trade.[84] At times, Coleridge turned some of the weapons used against the British government on France. He criticised the French for prolonging the war by setting unrealistic terms, and he objected to limitations on freedom of speech, publication and assembly on grounds that were similar to those used in his critique of the Two Bills.[85] These remarks showed a willingness to criticise the policies of the French administration, but did not signify a rejection of the aspirations underlying the Revolution. Much the same may be said of Coleridge's essay 'On Modern Patriotism'. The main target here was Godwin, especially his attitude to 'filial affection' and marriage, and his belief that a sense of justice could develop out of self-interest. Coleridge's response – asserting that under existing circumstances benevolence could only develop from religious beliefs[86] – was quite consistent with the doctrines of the Bristol lectures.

However, the very radical views on property which had appeared in the 'Lectures on Revealed Religion' did not play a direct role in Coleridge's treatment of the political aspects of reform in his consideration of the Two Bills, or in *The Watchman*. In the 'Lectures on Revealed Religion' Coleridge had attempted to work out the implications of radicalised Christianity for property and government. The stress was on the interrelationship between equality and freedom, and the solution proposed was not, strictly speaking, a political one, since it tended to question the legitimacy of authoritative relationships. However, it established the sorts of considerations that needed to be taken into account if freedom and equality were to be advanced in a political context. One set of considerations was largely negative, since it warned of the dangerous effect of corruption on constitutional progression; others were, however, more positive. They focused upon the prerequisites of extensive participation, one of which was the avoidance of wide property differentials. Since the goal was progressive reform, the radical egalitarianism of pantisocracy had to give way before a treatment of property that was located within the existing political context and looked to the *modification* of property rights rather than their abolition. This can be seen in correspondence between Coleridge and Thelwall and in fleeting references in *The Watchman*.

Coleridge wrote to Thelwall on 13 November 1796 expressing general approval of his ideas on the 'origin of Property & the *mode of removing it's* evils'.[87] Indeed, Thelwall's treatment of private property was similar in some respects to that which Coleridge had sketched in the 'Lectures on Revealed Religion'. He claimed that property '*is the fruit of useful industry; but the means of being usefully industrious are the common right of all*', and went on to point out that, 'though *Liberty and Property* are so frequently joined together, in popular exclamations, the very basis of the latter, by a sad necessity, furnishes the foundation of an altar upon which the former is too frequently sacrificed'. The reason for this 'sad necessity' was that private property rights in the means of useful industry were due to moral injustice, and could only be justified subsequently by reference to what Thelwall called 'general expediency'. Property facilitated cultivation, but in advanced stages of development it generated significant inequalities, which negated any rationale based on expediency; these inequalities, were aggravated by politically derived privileges. A return to rude equality would not provide a solution, however; it would merely 'plunge the world in yet unheard of horrors', the most favourable outcome of which would be a *'new "Gothic Customary"* – a new order of proprietors and nobility'.[88] The remedy which Thelwall proposed – the removal of artificial, politically fostered institutions (such as primogeniture) which generated monopoly, and the establishment of exchange relationships between proprietors and labourers, reflecting the character of property as 'the fruits of useful industry' – responded to Burke's claim that the radicals wished to enjoy the benefits of natural primitive rights in a framework structured by developed rights. Thelwall appreciated that the restoration of natural or aboriginal rights would merely provide an opportunity for the re-enactment of a historical process marked by oppression and injustice.[89] His theory of property rights therefore took account of historical processes but still sought to realise the purposes lying behind the original right. Thelwall demanded that labourers be granted 'adequate rewards', not those forced on them by monopolising proprietors whose exercise of their rights was incompatible with the function of property. This claim was grounded on a tripartite basis of men's natural rights as 'joint heirs to the common bounties of nature', 'implied contract' which called 'upon us to appreciate, with impartiality, the comparative values of capital and labour', and the 'principles of civil association', the object of which was 'general benefit'.[90]

Coleridge thought that Thelwall's theory of property was basically sound, even though it lacked a religious basis. 'We run on the same ground, but we drive different Horses. I am daily more and more a religionist – you, of course, more & more otherwise.'[91] He endorsed Thelwall's views on removing the evils of property and described these evils in similar terms. In an extract from *Religious Musings* published in *The Watchman* as 'The Present State of Society', Coleridge described the property of the rich as ill-gotten gains from plundering the labouring population:

> The Wretched Many! Bent beneath their loads
> They gape at PAGEANT POWER, nor recognise
> Their cot's transmuted plunder . . .
>   Whence that cry?
> The mighty army of foul spirits shriek'd
> Disherited of earth! . . .[92]

In a slightly later discussion of proposals for improving wastelands, Coleridge brought together the idea of the unavoidable nature of property in present circumstances, and the need to modify it to secure justice for the poor:

> We hope they will adopt and pursue the principles so often recommended, of using all prudent means for restoring each individual, willing to labour, to his share of the earth (unavoidably alienated by the involved relations and bearings of society); and raising the industrious day-labourer to the comfortable and dignified situation of an independent cultivator. . . .[93]

This was not, of course, the language of the radical egalitarianism found in the Bristol lectures. It reflected, however, a continuing concern with the material preconditions of liberty, and a willingness to modify existing property relationships for the sake of the realisation of other values, especially political equality.

VI CONCLUSION: RADICAL CHRISTIANITY AND 'CIVIC HUMANISM'

The political theory espoused by Coleridge in the mid-1790s is best characterised as a variety of Christian radicalism in which the radical element was as important as the Christian.[94] In common with other Unitarians, Coleridge thought that the message of revealed religion could be applied directly to politics. Moreover, the Christian belief in the benevolent example of Christ, and the idea of a future state, played an important role in encouraging men to virtuous action. In some of the Bristol lectures, Christianity was seen as particularly valuable for those whose ignorance inhibited a rational assent to the dictates of benevolence, but, in Coleridge's critique of Godwinian rationalism and sensualism in *The Watchman*, Christianity was portrayed as a *universal* alternative to rational self-interest:

> Your *heart* must believe, that the good of the whole is the greatest possible good of each individual: that *therefore* it is your *duty* to be just, because it is your *interest*. In the present state of society, taking away Hope and Fear, you cannot believe this – for it is not true; yet you cannot be a Patriot unless you do believe it. How shall we reconcile this apparent contradiction? You must give up your sensuality and your philosophy, the pimp of your sensuality; you must condescend to believe in a God, and in the existence of a Future State![95]

If Coleridge had merely adopted the political views of leading Unitarians such as Priestley, this would have been sufficient, in terms of contemporary usage at least, to make him a 'radical'. Coleridge, however, advanced beyond such a position and was critical of its shortcomings. His early political thought contained a far-reaching critique of contemporary political and social institutions, and demands for their reformation. In the context of the pantisocratic settlement, Coleridge proposed a restructuring of social and political relationships, necessitating the end of private property and the substitution of benevolent interaction for governmental regulation. In the context of contemporary English society, his proposals were similar to those of other radical reformers such as John Thelwall, with whom he also shared a concern to avoid rabble-rousing and bloodletting. However, it is a mistake to confuse the moderate procedures that Coleridge recommended with the radical character of his analysis and goals. Recklessness was imputed to radical reformers by their opponents, and was a characterisation which clearly applied to some groups and individuals. But it was neither a necessary feature nor a barometer of reforming intentions.

Although Christian in inspiration, and depending upon the character of Christianity for its success, Coleridge's radical analysis and programme owed much to the language of English, quasi-republican, civic humanism which had survived into the eighteenth century in the form of the ideology of the Commonwealthsmen. These conceptions provided a political leverage to the somewhat diffuse objections to political inequality and private property which underlay the pantisocratic scheme. The political implications of civic humanism were generally republican, although in eighteenth-century British political argument this was transmuted to a concern for maintaining a mixed constitution by preserving the republican element against the improper, and hence corrupt, influence of the executive branch.

This concern appeared in Coleridge's early political writings, where it was expressed in a form (common also among some of the 'patriotic associations' in London) of support for parliamentary reform as a means of lessening corrupt influence by broadening the electoral base of the House of Commons. That Coleridge supported parliamentary reform in the 1790s seems clear from his lectures and from *The Watchman*; the details of his position are less clear. Favourable references to France that postdated the Constitution of the Year III (which effectively excluded the propertyless) suggested a willingness to accept something less than universal suffrage.[96] It is likely, however, that a restricted franchise was regarded as a step in a progression culminating in 'government by the people', a state of affairs which would necessitate a modification of property rights to ensure a greater degree of independence for the population at large. The terms of Coleridge's discussion – especially the treatment of political freedom in relation to property rights – reflected the impact of the Commonwealth ideology; indeed, this added an important dimension to his Christian radicalism. It provided a structural account of social and political relationships which elevated Christian moralising into political theorising. It must be acknowledged, however, that there were some significant peculiarities in Coleridge's relationship to civic humanism which are attributable to his Christian perspective.

In the civic-humanist paradigm the idea of virtue was usually, although not exclusively, associated with the practice of citizenship, with the performance of those actions necessary to maintain the republic against corruption. Coleridge's early political writings exemplify this use of the notion of virtue, especially in his identification of certain practices as potentially or actually corrupt. At the same time, however, the stress upon enlightenment suggested that virtue was a prerequisite of political participation, not just a concomitant of it. That aspect of Coleridge's position implied a weakening of the ideal of man as an active political creature, one which may, as was the case with James Mackintosh, shade over into a form of gradualism that cannot usefully be included within the civic-humanist paradigm.[97] There are, however, features of Coleridge's early position which indicate a far closer and more important affinity to civic humanism than the diffuse, rhetorical use found in Mackintosh.

Coleridge's support for parliamentary reform, and his identification of *The Watchman* with reform societies, provides evidence of links with contemporary groups who harnessed political reform to a civic-humanist perspective and redefined notions of economic independence and moral autonomy so as to justify a more extensive franchise.[98] At other times, Coleridge went beyond this fairly moderate position and argued for economic reform. While accepting inequality, he wished to restore or extend property rights with a view to extending the scope for morally autonomous independent action. Coleridge's overriding concern was with a conception of freedom and equality derived from Christian sources, but his argument depended upon a perspective on property, independence and political personality that was essentially Harringtonian. It represented a fairly radical restructuring of the neo-Harrington paradigm (which was essentially nostalgic: it defended what was, and sought the recovery of the past) in the interests of political and social goals that were located in the future. In other words, Coleridge's Christian moralism had the effect of radicalising civic humanism, and in that respect his early political thought was based upon a conception of morality which generated political radicalism rather than eliminated the need for it.

As we have seen, Coleridge's remarks about moral reformation have led a number of commentators to treat his early thought as moral rather than political in focus.[99] The problem is that these interpretations ignore the context of Coleridge's argument, make it difficult to account for the political content of the early lectures, and rest on a misunderstanding of the relationship between the moral and the political in Coleridge's thought. There still remains, however, the problem of the way in which Coleridge's concern with moral reformation is related to the civic-humanist aspects of his early thought. One solution is to regard individual morality as a necessary, but not a sufficient, condition for the exercise of Christian virtue. Other conditions were the progressive reformation of the political and social environment, especially those features touching on political and property rights. It was these aspects of Coleridge's theory which were informed by a civic-humanist perspective; they therefore coalesced with his Christian moralism rather than contradicted it. As we shall see, the interaction of these two perspectives played an important role in Coleridge's later political thought, providing a continuity of theory which survived shifts in his political position.

2

Constitutions, Concordats and Country Party Ideology: The Realignment of Coleridge's Political Theory, 1799–1802

After the collapse of *The Watchman* in May 1796, Coleridge's career as a political writer was in abeyance until early 1798, when he was engaged to write for Daniel Stuart's *Morning Post*. At this time, Stuart's paper was generally anti-ministerial, anti-war and liberal on issues such as freedom of the press and parliamentary reform, and Coleridge's early prose efforts for the paper sat comfortably enough with the position of its proprietor. These articles (a series of six appeared between 1 January and 8 March 1798) represent, as David Erdman writes, 'in their intensity and in their irony and in the radicalism of their themes – advocacy of parliamentary reform, opposition to the war with France, opposition to the new war taxes after the collapse of the peace negotiations – a recrudescence of the fervour that was evident in Coleridge's earlier political utterances . . . heretofore assumed to have faded away'.[1] Over the course of the next year, however, both Coleridge and the *Morning Post* became increasingly hostile towards France and towards the forces of reform at home.[2] In Coleridge's case, this shift in political sympathies culminated in the development of a more favourable perspective on established churches, at least in the English form, a perspective which was anathema to the radical, anti-establishment non-conformism of the Bristol period.

Disillusionment with the course of events in France is apparent in Coleridge's 'France: An Ode', the immediate context for which was the French invasion of Switzerland.

> Forgive me Freedom! O forgive those dreams!
>   I hear thy voice, I hear thy loud lament,
>   From bleak Helevetia's icy caverns sent –
> I hear thy groans upon her blood-stain'd streams!
>   Heroes, that for your peaceful country perish'd,
> And ye that, fleeing, spot your mountain-snows
>   With bleeding wounds; forgive me, that I cherish'd
> One thought that ever bless'd your cruel foes!
>   To scatter rage and traitorous guilt,
>   Where Peace her jealous home had built;
>   A patriot-race to disinherit
> Of all that made their stormy wilds so dear;
>   And with inexpiable spirit
> To taint the bloodless freedom of the mountaineer –
> O France, that mockest Heaven, adulterous, blind,
> And patriot only in pernicious toils
> Are these thy boasts, champion of human kind?
>   To mix with kings in the low lust of sway,
>   Yell in the hunt, and share the murderous prey;
> To insult the shrine of Liberty with spoils
>   From freemen torn; to tempt and to betray?

In this poem Coleridge expressed his determination to 'disengage' (as Erdman puts it) from oppositional and reformist politics in England.[3] Developments in France played a role in this process, but it is also important as E. P. Thompson argues, to take account of the psychological strains placed on Coleridge and his associates at Nether Stowey (principally William Wordsworth and John Thelwall) by the attention of government spies and the hostility of the local population.[4] Coleridge had expressed his nervousness to Thelwall in August of the previous year. Having recounted the ill-feeling engendered by Wordsworth's arrival, he went on to warn that 'If *you* too should come, I am afraid, that even riots & dangerous riots might be the consequence. . . .'[5] By March of the following year, when conscription into the militia seemed a distinct possibility, the situation had become intolerable, and Coleridge and the Wordsworths resolved to take themselves off to Germany.[6] In the event, the party did not leave until mid-September; they arrived back in England by July 1799. Early in November 1799, Stuart offered Coleridge a salary if he would undertake to live in London and write regularly for the *Morning Post*; this offer was accepted, and by November Coleridge had settled in the capital. Within a few days the release of preliminary details of the new French constitution began to filter through to London and provided the focus for Coleridge's first series of leading articles for Stuart.

The fact that the Constitution was the brainchild of a triumvirate led by Napoleon and that, as Coleridge said, it formed 'the mere ornamental outworks of a military despotism'[7] undoubtedly put another nail in the coffin of his pro-French sympathies. It thus reinforced the disillusionment engendered by his growing alarm at the expansive tendencies of French foreign and military policy. One possible response to the 1799 Constitution was to regard it as an important episode in a revolution betrayed.[8] This response can be discerned in some contemporary reactions to the new constitution, and weak echoes of it appeared in Coleridge's treatment. He referred to Napoleon and his collaborators as 'mountebank Liberticides' and claimed that the Constitution entailed 'enormous sacrifices to the wish of producing stability and preventing innovation'.[9] However, the theme of betrayal is very muted in Coleridge's treatment of the Constitution, the real significance of which lies in the fact that it formed the first clear political statement of a retreat from the radicalism of the Bristol lectures. While there can be little doubt that the psychological roots of Coleridge's disengagement from, and subsequent rejection of, radical politics were nurtured by developments abroad and by the increasing burden of repression at home, these factors do not fully explain the shift evident in the articles on the French constitution. They represented a theoretical reorientation, and must be discussed in these terms rather than seen merely as a retreat into conservatism. The development of a positive attitude towards private property played a crucial role in this process.

I THE CRITIQUE OF THE FRENCH CONSTITUTION OF 1799: PROPERTY AND POLITICAL PERSONALITY

In a notebook entry dating from early December 1799, Coleridge sketched details of the new constitution based on a report that had come from Paris on the first of the month. This note dealt largely with the complex system of indirect elections and the fact that the chambers would be selected by a 'Constitutional Jury' out of a pool of 5000 nominees produced by the electoral system. He also noted that electors' eligibility depended on the payment of a tax equivalent to twelve days' labour, and that, whereas one chamber was to discuss legislation, the other had the sole right to pass laws.[10] At this stage Coleridge's information was incomplete, especially on the crucial question of who would choose the Constitutional Jury. These details did not become available until after his first article had appeared. As a result, there was a marked change of focus in the second, third and fourth articles in the series.

Coleridge began his consideration of the Constitution by identifying property as the basis of modern governments. It had gradually, but not (as we shall see) completely superseded 'the prejudices of superstition, birth, and hereditary right'. The importance of property was historically conditioned, and might in the future give way before other forces, but

> For the present race of men Governments must be founded on property; that *Government is good in which property is secure and circulates*; that *Government the best, which, in the exactest ratio, makes each man's power proportionate to his property.*[11]

Circulating property tended to divorce political personality from hereditary right because such rights were related historically to non-circulating property. Security of property was essential because it made for a stable fit between proprietorial and political power. It ensured that the 'physical power' of the propertyless many would be balanced by the 'artificial' strength of governments representing property interests. If property were not secure, then the balance would be unstable, especially if such insecurity were due to the corrupt, capricious exercise of political power which manipulated, but did not ultimately depend on, property.

In the first of his articles Coleridge concentrated on the franchise. He thought that an indirect system of election was a good idea because it provided a way of 'filtering' the influence of the bulk of the population: it took away 'the artificial powers of the State from those who already possessed the physical strength, without, however, tearing from them the soothing idea of self-importance'. He later added a less cynical justification: a process of filtration which starts from a broad base takes from the people the all-unsettling power of acting from immediate and momentary impulses, while, at the same time, by the stimulation of hope, and the sense of personal self-importance, it impels every individual to be a *Citizen*, suffers no man to remain dead to the public interest. . . .[12]

However, the tax qualification would destroy the benefits of the filtering process and produce disorder and corruption. It would be burdensome to the poorer sections of the population, and, since it seemed to take away with one hand what it gave with the other, it would generate resentment. Moreover, the qualification was too low greatly to reduce the size of the electorate, and this, together with the fact that individuals who met the qualification would be both voters and potential candidates, meant that the new structure was likely to produce disorder. To these difficulties were added the danger of corruption of those who were willing to allow their tax qualification to be met by rich individuals. The price the poor would pay for such patronage would be their independence, and the price paid by the *body politic* would be its corruption. In one fell swoop the Triumvirate seemed set to replicate the two worst features of English elections – disorder and corruption – in the French political system.

When Coleridge wrote his first article he had no clear information on the way in which the members of the chambers would be chosen, although even at this time he suspected that the composition of the legislature and the checks and balances of the constitutional structure were not related to real interests.

> One error appears to us to pervade the whole, viz. the assumption, that checks and counter-checks can be produced in Legislative Bodies, merely by division of chambers and diversity of titles, where no real difference of interest exists in the Legislative, as individuals, except that transient one arising from their functions.[13]

When further details became available they confirmed these suspicions, and showed that the apparent divisions of the Constitution were not only vacuous but also corrupt.

Coleridge learned that the 'conservatory Senators' who appointed members of the legislature from the pool of popularly chosen nominees were to be selected and paid by the executive. In practice this meant that the legislative body would be made up of the Consuls' creatures.[14] Since there was no property qualification for members of the legislature, and since a place in a mute, servile body would not attract the rich, the chambers would be filled by those who were fundamentally dependent. Lacking means of their own, members of the chambers would depend on the executive for their livelihoods, as well as for their places. In British terms, a corrupt House of Commons was one in which a significant proportion of MPs held offices of profit under the Crown, and in which some of these people owed their seats to the Crown's electoral influence. Coleridge pictured the legislature produced by the new French constitution as a gross caricature of the British House of Commons. It would be filled by men whose dependence on the executive was total. Its members would be servants, liable to lose both their places and their means of support. Their subservience to the Consuls would therefore be complete and unwavering.

The hallmark of the new constitution was corruption. Since the legislature was so obviously dependent on the consuls, the wealthy would find it expedient to bypass the decision-making machinery and offer direct financial inducements to those who held the real reins of power: 'men of property will . . . buy laws of the Government *in prospectu*'. Having learned that the conservatory Senate would be government appointees, Coleridge dropped his earlier objection to the corrupt potential of the electoral process. He thought that the cipher-like nature of the legislature would discourage the rich from taking an active political role. 'It appears to us that the men of property will be too wise to buy, at any heavy sum, places in a silent legislature, empowered only to decide on laws proposed to them by a Commander in Chief; their very decisions to annulable by the Senate, their creators.' The role ascribed to the Senate ensured that the independent and able would not seek legislative office; such men would not, in any case be suitable material for the hack role that legislators were called upon to play: 'needy men will hire themselves as the mechanic-legislators, necessary in this business of Law-making to the government, only as the bellows-blower is to the organist. The work *must* be done; but any fellow may do it.'[15] Because the legislature was likely to be filled with the dependent and corruptible, those who wished for the legislature's favour would first have to corrupt its masters.

When Coleridge described the government which the new constitution would produce as 'an oligarchy, supported, and only supportable, by the military',[16] he used the term 'oligarchy' to signify that property was given a role which militated against good government, instead of providing a guarantee of it. In so doing, Coleridge not only appealed to the classifications of constitutional forms found in classical writings – especially those of Aristotle and Polybius – but also to the eighteenth-century discourses which he had used for very different purposes in his earliest political writings.[17] Different aspects of his critique of the French Constitution related to different parts of this tradition. When approving the 'filtration' mechanisms for potentially allowing publicly beneficial popular involvement while still retaining a leading role for the wise and able, Coleridge was making a point that related to the participatory aspects of the tradition.[18] For the most part, however, he stressed its more conservative aspects and focused on the corruption of the Constitution through the erosion of the close relationship between political power and the balance of social forces encapsulated in property. This perspective necessitated political activity by property-holders, but it was not participatory in any true sense since it was assumed that only a relatively small section of the population would possess politically significant property-holdings. Such a constitution would be corrupted from its true form if property-based representation gave way to oligarchy.

In eighteenth-century England, Country Party and oppositional elements portrayed oligarchy as a more or less pressing threat.[19] The new French constitution built this tendency into the very basis of the legislative structure. In an important sense the government was not based on property at all. The consuls appointed the conservatory Senate, who in turn controlled nomination to a paid legislature for which there was no property qualification. The property these men possessed was generated through their political role and was therefore a derivative of the political process, not the basis of it. Property was likely to be important outside the confines of the formal political and constitutional structure, however, since those with independent wealth would use it to obtain legislation which protected and furthered their *particular* interests. It was this feature of the new regime that gave it an oligarchic character, albeit one in which the influence of wealth had to be brought to bear on an executive founded on military, rather than economic, power. In Coleridge's view, the oligarchic potentialities of the new constitution were parasitic upon the military position of the Chief Consul, but this dependence did nothing to deflect the harmful consequences of a constitution which ignored the legitimate interests of property, and pandered to those of an illegitimate nature. If individuals bought the favour of the executive, there could be no checking and balancing of the proportional interests of a variety of property-holders. The Constitution established

> divisions and subdivisions even to superfluity; but how, under any circumstances these could be a check on each other, or on the Consulate, nowhere appears. It is indeed mere fraud and mockery. Checks and counterpoises can only be produced by real diversity of interests, of interests existing independent of legislative functions; but these chambers are all alike filled with the creatures of the Dictator, by him chosen, feeding on his stipends, and acting under his controul.[20]

The notion of the constitution as a balance was a feature of political debate in the eighteenth century, and was associated with views of the constitution as a mixture of powers located in King, Lords and Commons. Such debate was frequently confused because of a failure to specify which forces were actually balanced against one another, and in the years after the American Revolution the idea of balance was seriously challenged both by radicals such as James Burgh, who questioned the need for more than one estate (the people), and by High Church Tories, who thought the idea was incoherent, and incompatible with the requirement that systems of government needed one, unquestioned source of power.[21] Coleridge's approach avoided at least some of these problems, since it focused on proprietorial interests and did not require a balance between the various elements of the constitution. This was a markedly Harringtonian view, albeit one which could be related to the traditional institutions of English government. The House of Commons was made up of independent property-holders, and its deliberations were seen as reflecting the interests of the nation encapsulated in property. Because such interests differed in kind and extent, the legislative system checked and balanced interests, a process that not only went on within the House of Commons, but also between it and the House of Lords, which represented hereditary property. This system was often thought to be endangered by politically generated – and therefore dependent – forms of wealth; hence periodic outcries against the corruption of the House of Commons through the intrusion of growing numbers of placemen, dealers in government stocks, and military and civil contractors.[22]

These politically generated forms of wealth provided ministers with the opportunity for exercising a strong and constant control over Parliament, thus undermining its independence. There were, however, other ways in which wealth could become politically problematic. Property and political power were connected because virtue was thought to be associated with possession, particularly with the possession of landed property. Other forms of property were suspect, especially when they undermined the political position of the landed gentry. Attempts to enforce a land qualification for members of the House of Commons were designed to counter these threats, as were related attempts to prevent the grosser forms of electoral bribery.[23] These measures pointed to an ambiguity in perceptions of the function that property should play in the political process. The fear of oligarchy, in a system based upon property, may appear paradoxical, but it rested on a never very clearly articulated distinction between the possession and the use of property.

Arguments about the need for a correspondence between property and political power implied that, while the possession of property was crucial, the need to expend it was not. Property was, in other words a *qualification* rather than a resource. Of course, aspirants for office did bribe voters and so on, and 'independence' implied that one could both support oneself in the style, and provide the hospitality, expected of public figures. But the direct use of money as a political resource was illegal and improper and was not infrequently concealed by expenditure on public utilities (schools and assembly rooms, for example) or by 'treating' voters rather than openly bribing them. These devices explain why those who upheld the political role of property could describe those who sought to pervert it as 'oligarchs'. The 'due' as opposed to the 'undue', or corrupt, role of property was defended on the grounds that it allowed for the legitimate and publicly beneficial representation of property, the basis of civic existence. If the public interest was defined in terms of property, it was essential that proportionality be maintained within the legislative system. This was only possible when property was treated as a qualification rather than a resource. If political influence were too closely related to expenditure, then the very rich would outbid those with modest property and thereby transform a balancing of interests into an auction in which the highest bidder would take possession of the state. This would be an oligarchy: a government of the rich in their exclusive interest and in disregard of the commonweal.

By criticising the French Constitution for creating an assembly of 'needy . . . mechanic-legislators', and claiming that this would encourage the rich to seek the attainment of their particular ends by 'buying laws', Coleridge expressed concern about the *direct* influence of extensive material resources. He implied that the 1799 Constitution would produce an unmediated and socially indifferent correspondence between wealth and political effectiveness. It replaced the legitimate connection between *having* property and exercising political influence with the corrupt expenditure of resources necessary to gain the favour of a military clique and its tame, dependent legislators.

However, while the system established by the new constitution was oligarchic, it was parasitic on the military position of Napoleon. This was now to be elaborately formalised and screened by a mock republican framework. These republican trappings were part of a theatrical charade which extended even to the ceremonial dress of the Consuls, the 'Walking advertisement for a Farce'.[24] Such elaborations did not disguise the fact that the Constitution failed to provide the security of property, the proportionality, and consequently the protection of the public interest, realised by the English Constitution. The system of checks incorporated in the French Constitution could not effectively balance real interests, because these interests were not represented in the constitutional structure.

The parallels between eighteenth-century arguments directed at ministerial oligarchies and Coleridge's fears about the development of an oligarchy in France can also be discerned in his consideration of the qualities associated with particular forms of property. While Coleridge was unwilling to embark on a general assessment of the role of hereditary elites in English politics, he pointed out that certain social advantages were associated with aristocracies. Their extensive landholdings, and their survival over long periods, gave the aristocracy a significant stake in the country, and a deep-seated attachment to it.[25] Moreover, in societies in which the acquisition of wealth was becoming increasingly important, the aristocratic spirit had a generally beneficial impact on 'manners', on the regulation of human intercourse by conventions of civility. The 'delicate superstition of ancestry', as Coleridge called it, provided a means of counteracting the 'grosser superstition of wealth'. It helped balance the economically active, but politically docile, forces of productive property with the 'graceful, shewy, and energetic' but volatile genius of the forces of popularity. The result was a stable, civilised, yet active population which would not develop within the confines of the elaborate but empty charade of the new French constitution:

> We find ourselves . . . disposed to hail with astonishment . . . a Constitution, in which all Legislative Functions are places of Government, Legislature itself a lucrative profession, and preferment in it to be expected neither from the . . . privileges of rank, or the influence of property, or from popular favour; but, as it should seem, by secret intrigue in the palace of a military Dictator, or in the different Courts of the great all electing conservatory Senators, who are themselves that which they are by a species of organization, almost as mysterious as that of mushrooms and funguses.[26]

This statement related in part to Coleridge's ideas about the constitutional necessity for balancing property, but it also added a further dimension, pointing to the requirements of a stable equilibrium of intellectual, moral and natural powers. The balance was not therefore concerned solely with material forces.

Coleridge's articles on the 1799 Constitution signalled an abandonment of the radical political perspective that had informed both the Bristol lectures and *The Watchman*. Further signs of this are apparent in other contributions to the *Morning Post* in late 1799 and early 1800. For example, on 12 December he commented that, if the measures of the French government arose out of necessity, instead of being due to the quality of French statesmanship, then the system 'which involves such necessity is unfit for France, unfit for human nature. Thus, in proportion as we diminished our disapprobation of the Leaders, we should increase our aversion from the Republic.'[27] Such comments however, related principally to the stance that English friends of freedom should adopt towards France, or were part of a sustained attempt to show that the

Revolution had run its course, and that a refusal to come to terms with the French would merely harden their resolve and add the enthusiasm of a revived Jacobinism to the undoubted military skills of Napoleon.[28] Coleridge's consideration of the new constitution was far more important than these other articles from the same period. It pointed to the basis of his increasingly hostile attitude towards both French and radical politics, and provided links with a tradition of discourse that had been put to very different uses in his early writings.

In the Bristol lectures and in *The Watchman*, Coleridge had used a particular version of arguments about the relationship between property and political personality as a basis for pantisocracy, and in support of radical political and religious reform.[29] By late 1799 he appears to have accepted the prevailing distribution of property and based his analysis on the premise that, since property was unequally distributed, political power would have to follow this pattern. Consequently, Coleridge's critique of the French Constitution concentrated on the extent to which it failed to take account of the legitimate interests of property. This line of argument was clearly not one which could be used to support the sort of electoral reform which had interested him in 1795–6. Coleridge spelled out the implications of his revised position at the beginning of the French Constitution series when he contrasted the United States with Europe:

> In America, where the great mass of the people possess property, and where, by the exertion of industry, any man may perhaps possess it in its most permanent form, this principle may, perhaps, co-exist with universal suffrage; but not so in old and populous countries, in which land is of high value, and where the produce of individual labour can hardly be large enough to admit of considerable accumulation.[30]

When compared with his position in 1795–6, this statement seems to involve a complete *volte-face*, and in terms of political implications this is certainly the case. But another way of considering the relationship between Coleridge's 1795 lectures and his articles of late 1799 is to focus on the argumentative structure of these works. When considered in this light, the latter can be seen to involve an appeal to a different facet of the discourse in which the former were located.

Coleridge's comparative remarks on America and Europe and his claim that 'Governments must be founded on property'[31] were closely related to the more radical formulation which he had borrowed from Moses Lowman and used in the 'Lectures on Revealed Religion': 'Property is Power and equal Property equal Power. A Poor Man is necessarily more or less a Slave.'[32] By 1799 Coleridge had accepted inequality as a fact and reached the conclusion that, property being power, unequal property should be reflected in unequal power. He was reluctant to accept, however, as he had done in 1795, that 'Poverty is the death of Public Freedom'. Coleridge's treatment of the French Constitution attempted to explain how 'Public Freedom' could be maintained within inegalitarian societies. His solution was to argue that public freedom could be preserved if the distribution of political power followed the distribution of property.

To claim at one time that the poor are slaves and that poverty entails the death of public freedom, and then to argue that public freedom requires that political power be proportionate to property, may seen the height of paradox. In fact, Coleridge's differing applications of the Harringtonian notion of the relationship between property and political power closely paralleled the way in which this mode of argument developed from the mid seventeenth century through to the eighteenth. What began as a defence of republican institutions in what were seen as egalitarian conditions developed into a rationale for a particular form of non-republican government on the grounds that it alone could maintain legitimate interests (expressed, as the republican version accepted, through property) against both the propertyless and those who controlled politically generated wealth.[33] If it were prevented from doing so, then property, and all other 'goods' constitutive of human, as opposed to political, freedom, would be at the mercy of those whose improper use of wealth generated political control out of all proportion to their property. It was not property itself which was the death of public freedom, but the improper use of certain kinds of wealth.

II LANDED AND COMMERCIAL WEALTH

Coleridge's remarks on the relationship between property and political power involved a consideration of the role played by factors other than the mere possession of wealth. His arguments depended, in part at least, on the extent to which property-holding gave rise to the development of politically significant patterns of behaviour. They therefore raised questions about how different forms of property measured up to these standards. Thus, while Coleridge insisted that constitutional arrangements reflected the balance of proprietorial interests, he simultaneously expressed reservations about some of the implications of this. In a letter of 25 January 1800 he wrote, that

> Property will some time or other be modified by the predominance of Intellect, even as Rank & Superstition are now modified by & subordinated to Property, that much is to be hoped of the Future; but first those particular modes of property which more particularly stop the diffusion must be done away, as injurious to Property itself – these are, Priesthood & the too great Patronage of Government.[34]

John Colmer ascribes the gap between these 'daring and speculative opinions on the subject of property' and the views expressed in the articles on the French Constitution to the seriousness with which Coleridge approached his role as a responsible leader-writer concerned with the realities of the existing situation.[35] This may well be so, but Coleridge's reference to 'modes of property' is also important in light of his claims about the impact of different sorts of property on political systems. The manner in which he treated distinctions between forms of wealth was closely related to the tradition of discourse that underlay his remarks on the oligarchic character of the new regime in France.

Coleridge distinguished between societies embodying hereditary principles and those founded on what he described simply as 'property'. The material basis of heredity was land, while mere property came principally from trading, industrial, commercial and financial activities. In the unfavourable contrast which Coleridge drew between the new French constitution and the balance of interests found in the English, he described the qualities associated with hereditary, land-based aristocracies as counterbalancing the 'grosser superstition of wealth'.[36] The distinction used here was between landed and non-landed wealth, but at other times Coleridge focused on the direct constitutional implications of different sorts of property. In these cases, productive activity (whether agricultural or industrial) was contrasted with 'commerce', an expression which applied especially to the moneyed interests whose wealth was derived from the provision of financial and loan-broking services for government.[37] Commercial wealth was generated by, rather than a prerequisite of political activity. Debt-financing provided a way of enlarging government's capacity to retain the loyalty of paid officials and dependent legislators, and the profits to be made from arranging loans added a further inducement facilitating the subordination of the legislature to the executive. Coleridge alluded to this type of corruption in 'Advice to the Friends of Freedom' (which appeared in the *Morning Post* between the first and second articles on the French Constitution), where he referred to Pitt's 'body-guard of Loan-jobbers, contractors, Placemen and Pensioners, in and out of Parliament'.[38] The theme was taken up in a more developed and pointed form in an article published shortly after the French Constitution series.

In 'Our Commercial Politicians', Coleridge used the distinction between industrial and agricultural activity and commerce to point to the dubious public benefits of non-productive wealth. Although prepared to allow that commerce might have a stimulating effect on other, more intrinsically worthwhile activities, Coleridge doubted if there were a significant relationship between the buoyancy of commerce and the well-being of the general population. He also expressed grave reservations about the constitutional implications of a strong commercial interest. Since men of commerce depended upon the profits to be reaped from government loans, and contracts, they were open to temptations to which those who derived their incomes from land were immune:

> Has not the hereditary possession of a landed estate been proved ... to generate dispositions equally favourable to loyalty and established freedom? Has not the same experience proved that the moneyed men are far more malleable materials? that Ministers find more and easy ways of obliging them, and that they are more willing to go with a Minister through evil and good?[39]

Coleridge's discussion of the relative merits of landed and other forms of property in 1799–1800 was related to his perception of their constitutional implications. Over the course of the next two years his analysis was broadened to incorporate an account of the wider social impact of different sorts of property. This served to reinforce his earlier claims about the inappropriateness of republican constitutions for unequal societies and added a significant sociological dimension to his theory. These ideas first appeared in the *Morning Post* in 1802 in a series of articles entitled 'France and Rome'.[40]

The ostensible purpose of those articles was to show that apparent similarities in the histories of late republican and early imperial Rome and modern France were not deep-seated enough to support hopes or fears about the longevity of the Napoleonic regime. Coleridge's argument consisted of two parts – the first relating to the justifiability of French expansionism, the second to the domestic implications of an imperial policy. He claimed that, while there had been some justification for Roman imperialism, there was none for that of France. The Romans brought real and lasting benefits to Europe, – they 'spread civilisation, sciences, and the humanising comforts of social life, over amazing tracts of country' – but the French exercised a wholly military dominion over people who were in many respects their moral and intellectual superiors, and who thus had nothing for which to thank them. Furthermore, because the French Empire depended upon the military skills of Napoleon, it could only be maintained through a despotic system of government within France. In this it resembled the Roman Empire, but there despotism had been both necessary and justifiable. Dictatorship was necessary in Rome because the state was made up of disparate elements with differing histories and languages, or 'cultures'. The freedom which the city enjoyed in the time of the Republic had been purchased at the cost of the miserable oppression of the rest of the state. Military dictatorship was necessary to weld this 'gorgeous robe of patch-work' into a unified whole,[41] and it was justified because each part of the Empire obtained the benefits of peace and civilisation. The situation in France was markedly different: there the Empire was a liberty-destroying burden. France's

> *true* Empire exists in herself; it is, indeed, one and indivisible, because it is composed of men, who have the same manners, the same language. . . . The provinces were the very body and limbs of the Roman Empire, but they are only the *wens* and diseases of the French. Rome *could* not continue free, because she *consisted* of incongruous parts; the liberty of the people was sacrificed to the

life of the Empire. France *is* not free, because she has wilfully *incrusted* herself with an heterogeneous compound; in all the petty States, which she has bound to herself, she has bound chains and fetters *around* herself.[42]

Underlying Coleridge's contrast between the cultural make-up of the Roman and French empires and between those and France itself was the belief that the French military despotism was an aberration caused by the peculiar circumstances produced by the Revolution. He believed that France possessed not only the cultural, but also the social and material, preconditions for a form of government that would protect public freedom through means appropriate to a society with a very unequal distribution of property.

Late republican Rome needed non-republican institutions not only for the sake of its provinces, but also because the balance of property had been eroded by the influx of wealth from the Asiatic conquests. Agrarian laws, like those of the Gracchi, had failed precisely because the need for them showed that the balance of property necessary for a republic was no longer a reality. The attempts to restore a rough equality of wealth had merely undermined existing, deferential relationships between 'the people' and what Coleridge called the 'natural aristocracy' of the senatorial class. These measures had made all 'goodmen . . . despair of the Republic' and willing to 'submit to the sober despotism of any individual, rather than the mad tyranny of a multitide'.[43] The same sort of development had taken place in France, although there it was a change in the balance between hereditary and other forms of property that signalled the passing of the material basis of the *ancien régime*. However, the despotism to which France succumbed was neither sober nor, given the possibilities, necessary.

Before the onslaught of the Revolution, France had possessed an aristocratic class strong enough to fuse its ethos with the new forms of property and to replicate the freedom-preserving balance attained in England. While despotism was the natural outcome of the configuration of social, economic and geo-political forces at work in late republican Rome, this was not the case for contemporary France. She possessed 'those feudal institutions', that 'happy intertexture of the interests and property of the state, which was in vain to be sought for in the original Constitution of Rome, in which every rich proprietor was regarded as an illegal oppressor'.

Moreover, in the mechanisms of representative government (a device unknown to the ancients) France possessed, or could acquire, the means to institutionalise and regulate the socially beneficial interaction of interests based upon differing forms and amounts of property.[44]

Coleridge's comparative analysis of late republican and early imperial Rome, on the one hand, and contemporary France, on the other, reinforced his earlier discussion of the inappropriateness of republican political institutions in unequal societies. His treatment of the topic showed distinct signs of a more direct acquaintance with Harrington's work than is apparent in his earlier writings; this is particularly so in his accounts of the way in which political forms followed the distribution of property, and in his identification of the Roman Senate as a 'natural aristocracy' existing within the framework of a republican state and providing an aristocratic element in a constitution which was a mixture of qualities rather than a mixture of hereditary classes.[45] These elements of analysis were blended with others, drawn from the more diffuse traditions of eighteenth-century Country Party ideology, to produce general statements about the relationship between political and social structures. The differing internal structures of equal and unequal societies necessitated different political forms. Equal societies possessed a unity which sprang from the sameness or uniformity of their parts. By contrast, the unity of unequal societies depended upon the harmonious interrelation of unequal, and hence differing, elements. Thus, Coleridge claimed that agrarian laws were necessary for republics, but were fatal to 'societies'.[46] Coleridge's terminology is a little odd, but the point seems clear: where a differentiated social structure already existed, the society in question gained its stability and cohesion from the interrelationship of differing elements. Attempts to restore equality would weaken the social structure and give rise, as had the Gracchian land reforms, to social dislocation and civil war, which undermined deferential relationships. These developments were harmful because they produced the conditions from which dictatorship was the only means of escape.

Unequal societies would only remain free if three sets of conditions were met. First, political rights must be restricted to those whose possession of fixed property provided the basis for a system of representative government which balanced the interests of property. Secondly, a society needed 'defence networks' – that is, historically grounded and generally accepted patterns of extra-political subordination. The Roman Empire lacked the social gradations upon which deference networks depended and could only attain order at home through a total denial of political rights. The situation was quite different in pre-revolutionary France, and, by implication, in England also. Both societies possessed 'feudal institutions . . . links of social subordination'. In France these had been shaken by the Revolution and were still the 'objects of an hostile oath',[47] but Coleridge's belief in the short future of the Napoleonic regime suggested that they could still serve their social, and hence also their political, role.

However, Coleridge's analysis implied that a 'happy intertexture' of interests would not be sustained unless a third set of conditions were satisfied. These related to the existence of a shared history and language, or 'culture'. The importance Coleridge ascribed to culture – it made despotism inevitable in the polyglot Roman Empire, and unavoidable so long as the French attempted to subdue their neighbours – is sometimes used to identify him as a harbinger of consensus, a notion which plays an important role in some varieties of modern democratic theory.[48] The problem with this claim is that Coleridge's remarks about culture apply to societies which were not thought capable of maintaining democratic systems, owing to their high level of social differentiation. To imagine that governments could be constructed in disregard of a society's property relations, to ignore 'social rights, that is, hereditary rank, property, and long proscription' was, Coleridge claimed, to embrace the basic fallacy underlying 'Jacobinism'.[49] In unequal societies democracy was inappropriate because it conflicted with the social structure.

III INDEPENDENT PROPERTY AND CHURCH ESTABLISHMENTS

Coleridge's comments on French affairs in the years 1799–1802 marked a retreat from the radical position on property and political power that had been a feature of his earlier political writings, and the focus of his political activities. In the mid–1790s, Coleridge's political radicalism had included a marked hostility to church establishments, particularly that of the Church of England. As we have seen, this hostility had a theological dimension derived from Unitarian sources, but it also sprang from a belief (common in radical circles) about the role the Church played in buttressing the social and political *status quo*.[50] It is not surprising, therefore, that Coleridge's abandonment of a radical position in politics was closely followed by the development of a more sympathetic attitude to the Established Church; or that his support for such a position was closely related to the discourses which played an important role in his newly formulated political theory.

Coleridge's development of a justification for church establishments on English lines can be traced to the spring and early summer of 1802. It therefore predated his unequivocal acceptance of the Trinitarian basis of Church of England theology – a development that is generally thought to belong to 1805–6.[51] However, there were earlier indications that Coleridge had begun to distance himself from Unitarianism. In 1798 he had accepted the Wedgwood brothers' annuity in preference to a Unitarian pulpit, and in the same year he came to the conclusion that the doctrine of the Logos was philosophically acceptable. Coleridge attempted, however, to combine a philosophical Trinitarianism with an essentially Unitarian view of redemptionism:

> The admission of the logos, as *hypostasized* (i.e. neither a mere attribute or a personification) in no respects removed my doubts concerning the incarnation and redemption by the cross; which I could neither reconcile *in reason* with the impassiveness of the Divine Being, nor in my moral feelings with the sacred distinction between things and persons, the vicarious expiation of guilt. A more thorough revolution in my philosophic principles, and a deeper insight into my own heart, were yet wanting.[52]

Coleridge's growing interest in German 'higher criticism' helped flesh out his view of the Logos.

Ironically, Coleridge's earliest acquaintance with German biblical criticism was due to his Unitarian connections, although the implications of it were not apparent in his very Unitarian 'Lectures on Revealed Religion'. These, as E. S. Shaffer has pointed out, were Coleridge's 'last attempt at a defence of an optimistic and necessarian view of revealed religion based on standard Unitarian authorities'.[53] In the years after 1795, particularly during his stay in Germany in 1798–9, when he had access to notes of Eichhorn's lectures, Coleridge established the basis of what Shaffer calls 'a new apologetics' that allowed him to work towards a theological, as opposed to a solely philosophical, acceptance of the Trinity.[54] This process was not completed until 1805–6, but it must have advanced some way by mid–1802, and may have helped Coleridge look on the Church of England with a less jaundiced eye. However, doctrinal differences were not necessarily central to antiestablishmentarianism. Bishop Horsley pointed out in an attack on Dissenters in 1790, that their opposition to established churches did not depend upon the variety of theological views in a given community or on the relative numerical strength of different sects, but upon their rejection of establishments as such.[55] Coleridge's early opposition conformed to Horsley's pattern: it involved a rejection of Trinitarianism, but was independent of it. His acceptance of the Church of England *qua* established church could therefore predate his reacceptance of the Trinitarian basis of its doctrine.

Coleridge's reconciliation with the Church of England involved two phases. The first cleared the way for an acceptance of establishments in general; the second, for acceptance of the form establishment took in England. The first of these developments is harder to document than the second, so the account which follows is necessarily somewhat speculative.

In a notebook entry that Kathleen Coburn dates to April–May 1802 there is a reference to a projected work on Church government, which, as in a number of other potentially interesting cases, Coleridge never actually wrote. The salient part of the entry reads: '1. On Property. 2.   Luther & Lutheranism, Calvin & Calvinism. . . . 3.   Presbyterians & Baxterians in the time of Charles 1 & 2. . . .'[56] It seems likely that this entry points to some of the reading which helped convince Coleridge of the justifiability of church establishments. The conclusion of the process is apparent in a letter from Coleridge to his brother, the Revd George Coleridge, dated 1 July 1802. Referring to an earlier discussion in which George argued that 'Church Establishments had been prejudicial to Christianity', Coleridge commented, 'At that time I was wholl[y] of the same mind & so I remained till mor[e re]ading [and] Reflection removed that opinion.'[57] The problems of how and why Coleridge changed his mind about church establishments could perhaps be resolved if there were evidence of his understanding of the doctrines mentioned in the notebook entry. Unfortunately such evidence is lacking. Coleridge's annotations of a number of

Richard Baxter's writings and of Luther's *Table Talk* are extant, but they are of a much later date.[58]

Despite the lack of any hard evidence, the references to 'Popery' and the 'Baxterians' in the notebook entry suggest a partial answer to the question of why Coleridge abandoned his opposition to established churches. In *Of National Churches* Baxter wrote that he had 'Long known that Popery doth not essentially consist in . . . Errours about Doctrine or Worship. . . . The Essence is only the Opinion of Universal Humane Church Soveraignty, and a Church Universal Unified and formally Constituted thereby.' He argued that an established national church was the only effective barrier against Popery: 'For Popery is but the Invading of the power of all other Bishops and Kings: And for each to resume his own power, is but the direct Deposing of the Pope.' In *A Holy Commonwealth* Baxter linked the clergy's capacity to 'manage God's word' and to 'reform the people' to the provision of a fixed and regular means of material support: 'I am not pleading for Lordly greatness, nor Riches to the Ministry . . . but only that they may be Learned, judicious, Godly, able faithful men, provided with their daily bread or food or raiment.'[59] In light of Coleridge's later views on the Established Church, which included a sharp attack on what were seen as the universalistic pretensions of Popery and stressed also the close connection between the clergy's educational and moralising role and their material endowments, it is possible that Baxter provided part of the basis for his revised views on the legitimacy of religious establishments.[60] Another possible source for Coleridge's reappraisal of church establishments is James Harrington. In *The Art of Law Giving* Harrington laid particular emphasis on the educational and leadership role of officials of national churches: 'it is no wonder that men, living like men, have not yet been found without a government, or that government hath not been yet found without a national religion; that is, some orderly and known way of public leading in divine things, or in the worship of god'.[61] Given Coleridge's increasingly favourable attitude towards aristocratic leadership, the fact that Harrington treated members of the National Church in the same way as he treated members of a natural aristocracy – both were offered *to* the population but chosen *by* them – may be of some significance.[62] This suggestion must, however, remain speculative. We know that Coleridge had read Toland's edition of Harrington's *Works*,[63] which included *The Art of Law Giving*, but there is nothing from this period to indicate

Coleridge's response to Harrington's defence of national churches.

The reasons for Coleridge's willingness to look more favourably on the Church of England are easier to establish than those governing his changing views on church establishments *per se*. Coleridge's first favourable statements on the Church were made in the context of a consideration of the Concordat of 1802. In a letter to his brother George on 3 June 1802, Coleridge declared that he was surprised at the warm reception given to the Concordat by many Church of England clergymen. He described the agreement between the Papacy and Napoleon as 'a wretched business', but one that

> first occasioned me to think accurately & with consecutive Logic on the force & meaning of the word *Established* Church / and the result of my reflections was very greatly in favor of the Church of England maintained, as it at present is / and those scruples, which . . . we had in common when I last saw you, as to the effects & scriptural propriety of this (supposed) alliance of Church & State were wholly removed. – Perhaps, you will in some measure perceive the general nature of my opinions, when I say – the Church of France at present ought to be called – a *standing* church – in the same sense as we say a *standing* army.[64]

The description of a church establishment as a 'standing church' was not without precedent – the same term was used by the radical Joel Barlow in the second part of his *Advice to the Privileged Orders* – but Coleridge's use of the term in this context and the parallel drawn between a 'standing church' and 'standing army' connected his treatment of the Church of England with Country Party ideology.[65] Standing armies were seen as a threat to the Constitution because they provided the Crown with a coercive capacity which was independent of parliamentary control. Coleridge implied that the French Church would be dependent upon the corrupt, servile legislators whom he had already criticised in his articles on the new constitution. The effect of such dependence, as Coleridge noted in a slightly later contribution to the *Morning Post*, was to make religion an 'instrument of state policy'.[66] A national church such as the Church of England was, by contrast, an *established* rather than a standing church. It possessed an independent material basis which, like other forms of fixed property, insulated its possessors from the corrupt interference of the executive. Coleridge pointed out that 'a statute of Elizabeth's reign' referred to the clergy as 'the great venerable, third *Estate* of the Realm'. This meant that

> they & their property are an elementary part of our constitution, not created by any Legislature, but really & truly antecedent to any form of Government in England upon which any existing Laws can be built – .... The Church is not depend[en]t on the Government, nor can the Legislature constit[ution]ally alter it's property without consent of the Proprietor. ... Now this is indeed an Establishment ... it has it's own foundation / whereas the present church of France has no foundation of its own – it is a House of Convenience built on the sands of a transient Legislature – & no wise differs from a *standing Army*. The colonial Soldiers under the Roman Emperors were an *established* Army, in a certain sense – ... but the Church of France is a *standing* church, as its army is a *standing* army.[67]

Coleridge's remarks on the Church of England, and the critical comparison he drew with the French Church rested on precisely the same basis as his analysis of the French Constitution. Neither recognised that institutional forms should follow the distribution of property. The French Constitution was corrupt because it made property a consequence of political power and left public freedom to the none-too-tender mercies of avaricious, time-serving and dependent legislators. The Concordat extended this basic flaw into religious affairs: it made the practice of religion dependent on the whims of a set of corrupt legislators. The 1799 Constitution paved the way for the standing army of Napoleon Bonaparte to secure a standing legislature; the Concordat completed the infamous, corrupting, trinity by producing a 'standing church'.

IV CONCLUSION: THE CHURCH, CONSTITUTION AND COUNTRY PARTY ARGUMENT

Coleridge's *Morning Post* articles from the years 1799–1802 are usually discussed in terms of his break with the more radical stance adopted prior to 1799.[68] While such accounts are accurate enough in terms of Coleridge's political orientation, it has been the aim of the present chapter to show that his contributions to the *Morning*

Post are also important in identifying the theoretical apparatus which he used in order to embark upon a different political course. In particular, it has been shown that Coleridge's hostility towards France and his rejection of radical political reform were expressed in terms which depended, to a significant extent, on eighteenth-century discourses concerned with the role of independent property in achieving a constitutional balance which preserved both property and public freedom in unequal commonwealths. This line of argument was central to Coleridge's critique of the French Constitution, to his oblique but clear support for English constitutional and political practice, and to his acceptance of a church establishment on English lines. It also provides a useful and contextually coherent basis from which to consider some of the wider ramifications of this particular phase of Coleridge's political writings.

Coleridge's account of the Church of England as part of a political and social structure constituted by a balance of proprietorial interests occupied the middle ground between two opposing positions that were of contemporary importance. The first was that to which Coleridge himself had adhered in the 1790s.[69] Coleridge's acceptance of the Church of England in 1802 meant that he had rejected the literal interpretation of John 18:36 ('Jesus answered, "My kingdom is not of this world"'), but the available evidence does not provide any clues about how he now understood this text. However, his reference to the '(supposed) alliance of church and state' in the letter to George Coleridge indicated that his view of the Church was developed in opposition to that associated with William Warburton, an eighteenth-century Whig divine, author of an influential work entitled *The Alliance between Church and State* (1736). Warburton's book was a standard Whig defence of the political role of the Church of England, and, although the author and his school were vilified by Hume, who wrote of the 'illiberal petulance, arrogance, and scurrility' which distinguished them, it continued to find admirers up to the end of the century.[70] Warburton had argued that while Church and state were originally independent they had come together through a contractual arrangement which placed the Church under the 'guardianship' of the state. As the Church's guardian, the state must also be its superior. Once the alliance had been formed, the Church ceased to exist as a separate entity. Warburton described the clergy as a 'public order' maintained by the state, claimed that tithes were no different from other taxes, and explicitly denied that the Church constituted a separate estate of the realm. The Church was merely an ally of the state, not an essential part of it.[71]

Coleridge's treatment of the Church in 1802 differed from that of Warburton on two important issues: the material basis of the Church of England, and its location in the state. The Warburtonian Church was, in effect, a standing church similar to that created by the Concordat. As such, it was a vehicle of corruption and a threat to a constitution based on the balance of independent property interests. Furthermore, by insisting that the Church was an estate of the realm, Coleridge wished to stress that it was an essential part of the state. In 1802 the significance of this claim clearly lay in its implications for the Church's material independence, but it may also have been related to Coleridge's reasons for accepting the legitimacy of church establishments in general. One of the paradoxes of Warburton's position was that, although the Church was a political agency, the state was not dependent upon its alliance with a particular church for its survival as a state, and would survive if the alliance was abandoned.[72] Coleridge claimed, however that Church and state were indissolubly linked, because the Church was one of the independent components of the state. The implication of this was that, if the Church ceased to be a part of the state, then the state itself would be dissolved.

The choice of Country Party rhetoric was by no means an obvious one with which to confront the French Revolution and defend English institutions. J. A. W. Gunn has shown that arguments about the balanced constitution came under increasing pressure in the 1780s and 1790s from both radical and reactionary sources.[73] We have already noticed the absence of a concern for the idea of balance in Coleridge's radical phase, when he adopted Burgh's essentially unitary conception of the Constitution, and treated a balance between a popular and a despotic political system as a halfway house on the road to a form of full-blown popular government whose very popularity avoided the necessity for balancing differing and unequal forces. Coleridge's language in the years after 1799 reverted to the tradition of mixed-constitution discourse, but in defending the Constitution in these terms he was offering an alternative not only to radicalism, but also to High Church Toryism. Coleridge's position differed significantly from that of contemporary Tories, and was far more closely related to the ideas of Swift or Bolingbroke than to the reactionary, absolutist political theory of writers who were throwbacks to the non-jurors of the late seventeenth century and not averse to reviving the absolutism of Sir Robert Filmer. In stark contrast to such extremists, who stressed the need for an order maintained by a single orderer, and regarded the idea of a mixed and balanced constitution as a dangerous absurdity, Coleridge retained a concern with public and private freedom even when criticising radical political options.

Coleridge's abandonment of radicalism has been seen by Alfred Cobban as a movement towards a position very similar to Burke's. Cobban argued that Coleridge's criticisms of Jacobinism are reducible to a rejection of democracy, and that his hostility to democracy, like that of Burke, rested on a disbelief in human nature and distrust of the 'political capacity of the average man'.[74] It is hard to come to terms with Cobban's account, because it is based on statements drawn from a wide range of places within Coleridge's corpus, and ignores the possibility that what might be true of part of his work need not be true of the rest.[75] It is clear, however, that comparisons between Burke and Coleridge which depend on a shared antipathy to democracy are invalid.

In *Biographia Literaria* Coleridge claimed to have improved upon Burke's analysis of Jacobinism by 'distinguishing the jacobin from the republican, the democrat, and the mere demagogue'. He 'both rescued the word from remaining a mere term of abuse, and put on their guard many honest minds, who even in the heat of their zeal against jacobinism, admitted or supported principles from which the worse part of that system may be legitimately deduced'.[76] Coleridge first developed these distinctions in 1802 in an article that was critical of the Jacobinism of both the 'left' and the 'right'. Supporters of the *status quo* traded bare assertions off against the equally declamatory statements of the Jacobins, and seemed ready to resort to the repressive measures which had been a feature of Jacobin phases of the French Revolution.[77] These remarks served to distinguish Coleridge's position from that of reactionaries, while his discussion of Jacobinism showed that he cannot be identified as an opponent of democracy *per se*. Coleridge claimed that a person could favour democracy 'and yet be no Jacobin . . . , for instance, in the purely pastoral and agricultural districts of Switzerland, where there is no other property but that of land and cattle, and that property very nearly equalised'.[78] Bearing these remarks in mind, it is fruitless to regard Coleridge and Burke as sharing an abhorrence of democracy.

While Coleridge identified Jacobinism by reference to its disregard of property, he also claimed that it had social significance. It involved a rejection of 'hereditary rank ... and long prescription'.[79] In Burke's writings these phrases were part of a defence of English government by reference to the virtues of an ancient constitution legitimised by time and usage.[80] 'Ancient constitutionalism', as it is called, did not however play a role in Coleridge's defence of English institutions in the years 1799–1802, and was, indeed, incompatible with his remarks about the mutability of political forms as a result of changes in the distribution of property. Coleridge had no interest in the common law, or in the historico-legal scholarship upon which ancient constitutionalism depended. It is possible, however, that his growing interest in German biblical criticism provided an alternative basis for his perception of the value of inherited institutions and traditional social relationships.

German biblical scholarship provided a new way of thinking about tradition which stressed the importance of the historical experience of communities. When applied to theological beliefs and practices this meant, as E. S. Shaffer puts it, that, 'whatever the literal, documentable truth might be found to be, the historical experience of conviction within the Christian community was itself a form of validation'.[81] This interpretation of the significance of the past could apply to secular as well as to sacred beliefs and practices, and may perhaps account for Coleridge's increasingly apologetic attitude towards existing social and political institutions. If this was the case, it may also explain why he came to believe not only that political power should follow property, but that the resulting networks of relationships should accord with traditional patterns of social organisation, a central aspect of which was an aristocratic ethos based on hereditary rank and sanctified by 'long prescription'. Burke's ancient constitutionalism rested on the force of precedent, while the position being tentatively ascribed to Coleridge depended on a community's consciousness of the significance of its past, a consciousness embedded in what Coleridge was later to describe as 'culture', and to which he alluded in his comparison between France and Rome.[82]

There are thus important differences between Burke and Coleridge in the basis of their understanding and use of the idea of tradition, but at the same time there are, in the period under consideration, significant similarities in their views on the role played within society by at least some traditional forces. Burke's use of eighteenth-century discourses was eclectic. For the most part, he appealed to arguments about the civilising effects of commerce that were developed in opposition to Country Party ideology. However, these arguments were not used by Burke in an unalloyed form. He also claimed that, while commerce expanded the scope for civility, the behavioural norms upon which it depended were not themselves generated by commerce, but came from traditional institutions such as the Church and a hereditary peerage: 'commerce can flourish only under the protection of manners, and . . . manners require the pre-eminence of religion and nobility, the natural protectors of society'.[83] Burke's modification of commercial humanism to include a central role for aristocratic manners narrows the gap between his position and that of Coleridge, although, whereas Coleridge regarded the ethos of aristocracy as part of a balance of constitutional and social forces, Burke saw it as impinging directly on the whole social structure. Moreover, in Burke's analysis of the French Revolution, the feared outcome of commerce without manners was not a ministerial oligarchy, the bogy of the Country Party, but an alliance of financiers and footloose intellectuals cemented by the benefits to be reaped from socially dislocating confiscations of property. These actions both fed on and generated a form of revolutionary energy destructive of first traditional, and then modern, commercial, society. Burke's arguments were, of course, located in the early 1790s, when the surge of revolutionary energy was at its highest pitch, and when French society seemed to be undergoing a process of transformation unique in human experience. Traditional arguments were used to identify very non-traditional dangers. Writing a few years later, when the Revolution appeared to have been tamed by Napoleon, and when only the stupidity of the Allies could regenerate Jacobin enthusiasm,[84] Coleridge reverted to more consistent and far more traditional uses of elements drawn from one of the conflicting discourses upon which Burke had so catholically drawn.

Coleridge's and Burke's dissimilar use of apparently similar arguments can be seen in their treatment of the Church of England and its property. In the *Reflections* Burke provided a justification for independent Church property which was similar to that which Coleridge used in his critique of the French Concordat.

> The people of England, never have suffered and never will suffer the fixed estate of the church to be converted into a pension, to

depend on the treasury, and to be delayed, withheld, or perhaps to be extinguished by fiscal difficulties; which difficulties may sometimes be pretended for political purposes. . . . They tremble for the influence of a clergy dependent on the crown; they tremble for the public tranquility from the disorders of a factious clergy, if it were made to depend upon any other than the crown. They therefore made their church like their king and their nobility, independent.[85]

This sounds very like Coleridge's warning against the dangers of a 'standing church', but there are in fact significant differences between Burke's and Coleridge's defence of the Established Church.

Burke's argument did not depend upon the idea of the Church as an estate in a mixed and balanced constitution. It is true that he described the Church of England as 'the foundation of [the] whole constitution, with which, and with every part of which, it holds an indissoluble union',[86] but this claim referred to its role as a purveyor and protector of manners, not to its constitutional relationship with other forms of independent property. It played a central role in the state, but it did not do so because it was part of the state's constitutional basis. It was a 'foundation' of the Constitution, not part of it. Moreover, the context of Burke's remarks on the proprietorial independence of the Church suggests that political dependence in itself was at most a subsidiary concern. His discussion formed part of a critique of the confiscatory aspirations of the revolutionaries in France, and was directed against their attack upon what was, he claimed, private property. It left the legitimate proprietors dependent on those whose aim was not the control of religion but its annihilation. The state-supported clergy would become 'vile and of no estimation in the eyes of mankind'.[87] Burke, in other words, feared that clerical dependence would lead to the destruction of religion, and hence to the loss of its beneficial effect on manners. This was a unique and, for the time being at least, a short-lived problem generated by the peculiar circumstances existing in France in the early 1790s. By contrast, Coleridge treated the problem of Church autonomy in a far more traditional way. His concern for the independence of the Church related to eighteenth-century fears of ministerial oligarchy rather than to the temporary problem of rampant destructive atheism.

3
Principled Morality and Prudential Politics: *The Friend* (1809–10)

In the first decade of the nineteenth century, Coleridge continued to disengage himself from the radical position he had taken in the 1790s. By late 1802 or early 1803 he had abandoned an anti-war position and become a reluctant and tentative proponent of a renewal of the war (interrupted by the Peace of Amiens in March 1802), on the grounds that England must act to secure European stability in the face of the Napoleonic menace. Coleridge's break with Unitarianism was complete by late 1806, and his acceptance of the full doctrine of the Trinity allowed for a complete reconciliation with the orthodoxy of the Established Church.[1] From April 1804 until August 1806 he was absent from England. Employed part of the time as private secretary to Sir Alexander Ball, British High Commissioner in Malta, and then as Acting Public Secretary in the Maltese administration, he also travelled extensively in Sicily, Naples and central and northern Italy.[2] While in Malta Coleridge made notes for a projected work entitled 'Comforts and Consolations'. Some parts of this were included in *The Friend*, an ambitious serial venture, of which Coleridge had high financial hopes. The periodical ran for twenty-seven issues between 1 June 1809 and 15 March 1810, by which time its lack of financial viability and the disproportionate effort needed to produce material for it had been amply demonstrated.[3]

If Coleridge's financial hopes for *The Friend* were ambitious, his views on the function it was to perform were no less so. He wrote 'to found true PRINCIPLES, to oppose false PRINCIPLES, in Criticism, Legislation, Philosophy, Morals, and International Law'. The premature demise of the periodical, together with the fact, as Basil Willey says, that Coleridge spent much of the first fourteen numbers 'beating around the bush', meant that his programme was not completed.[4] However, although the treatment of moral and political principles in this work was disjointed and incomplete, it is of great importance since it represents Coleridge's first reasonably systematic statement of a political philosophy. *The Friend* provided an account of the relationship between politics and morals that was very different from that guiding his earlier views, a treatment of political obligation in relation to a moral conception of the state, and a consideration of the bearing of this on political practice, or the art of government. In dealing with the last of these issues, Coleridge stressed the crucial role of property in relation to political participation and offered an account of the political and social implications of various sorts of property that differed significantly from that which had appeared in his discussion of the French Constitution of 1799. While retaining his earlier belief in the political importance of landed property, Coleridge now acknowledged the value of commercial activity. In so doing, he used arguments that were usually advanced as defensive alternatives to the Country Party ideas that were prominent in his writings on the French Constitution.

I MORALS AND POLITICS

The Bristol lectures were based on the premise that moral precepts deduced from the Bible should have a direct, unmediated impact on the organisation and conduct of politics. Coleridge's early critique of the English Constitution and Established Church focused on their incompatibility with the requirements of Christian morality, and the pantisocratic scheme involved an attempt to create an environment where Christian morals and social interaction would correspond. The stress laid upon property in Coleridge's treatment of the French Constitution and Concordat suggested a shift away from the direct Christian moralism that had been a feature of his earliest political writings, but gave no indication of the rationale for this change of perspective. Coleridge's first full statement of his revised view of the relationship between politics and morals appeared in *The Friend*, where the problem provided the focal point of the political sections of that work. Coleridge's argument was structured around a critical consideration of two opposing views. The first, identified with William Paley, emptied both politics and morals of any identifiable moral element. The second depended upon a conflation of morality and politics that was very similar to the position Coleridge had taken in his earlier lectures. In *The Friend* the second of these positions was associated particularly with Rousseau, but was also attributed to contemporary English radical figures such as Major Cartwright and William Cobbett, whose attempt to ground political rights on 'mere personality' confused 'political with religious claims'.[5]

The moral theory presented in *The Friend* depended upon a series of statements about the conjuncture of good and evil in human nature, the existence of conscience, and the consequent necessity for free agency, or will, to enable men to act in ways that were consistent with their ideas about right and wrong.[6] These attributes explained the nature of morality, an aspect of life which Coleridge related to the religious basis of human personality. In contemporary notebook entries Christianity was described as a 'practical' rather than a 'speculative' doctrine. It appealed to the will, and was 'therefore all imperative'.[7] This position differed markedly from that underlying Coleridge's Unitarian conception of revealed religion.[8] This depended on 'proofs' and implied thereby a bargain between God and man by which the former was obliged to furnish evidence of his existence. Coleridge now thought that the demand for proofs put faith and conscience at the mercy of historical evidence and argumentative sophistry, and gave rise to a flawed conception of morality. It sought motives for action that were 'beyond & alien to Reason and Goodness' and thereby weakened and degraded 'the Souls of men by an unnatural [because external] Stimulus'.[9]

The results of such a system could be seen in Paley's dependence on rewards and punishments to provide motives for moral conduct, and in his portrayal of God as the ultimate source of these sanctions. In Paley's philosophy, virtue was reduced 'to a selfish prudence eked out by Superstition' in which a 'Ghost or a Constable' played a prominent role.[10] By ignoring the importance of will in a moral act, and by concentrating on outward behaviour, Paley confined divine judgements within the limits of human knowledge. 'Our Fellow-creatures can only judge what we *are* by what we *do*; but in the eye of our Maker what we *do* is of no worth, except as it flows from what we *are*.'[11] Coleridge's attack on Paley in *The Friend* struck at both the root and the branch of his system. The root was revealed religion; the branch was consequentialist utilitarianism, which, in the hands of the Edinburgh Reviewers yielded the 'fanatical Antinomian' doctrine that truth and falsehood were 'indifferent in their natures' and in their propensity for producing beneficial or injurious consequences.[12]

In place of the proofs of revealed religion, Coleridge insisted on the centrality of faith (which made miracles *results* rather than *proofs* of revelation) and on a purity of will that sought to regulate external conduct by reference to the demands of a conscience directed to the perfection of that will. Morality was inward, egalitarian and universal; it was not merely the utilitarian calculation of consequences, but examined the quality of the intention which produced it. 'Will, that is . . . the inward motives and impulses . . . constitute the Essence of *Morality*. . . .'[13] A moral person was a free agent, one whose conduct was determined by his own will, and by the recognition of the moral status of other human beings.[14] Coleridge specified the universal character of morality in language borrowed from Kant. Individuals should 'so act that [they may] be able without involving any contradiction to will that the Maxim of [their] Conduct should be the Law of all intelligent Beings'.[15] This principle, and the sort of intelligence which made individuals moral beings, depended upon the common possession of what Coleridge called 'reason'. Reason gave men access to the supersensuous, to the things of the spirit; it was 'the power by which we become possessed of principle . . . and of [such] Ideas . . . as [that of] . . . Justice, Holiness, Free Will, & c. in Morals'.[16] This definition has a close resemblance to Kant's practical reason, although Coleridge also seems to have regarded reason as an 'organ of faith', as 'the organ of inward sense and therefore the power of acquainting itself with invisible realities and spiritual objects'.[17] In other formulations, Coleridge gave an account of reason that was similar to what Kant called 'theoretical Reason', a faculty that enabled men to determine how far some of their ideas corresponded with others. Coleridge asserted that both forms of reason, the practical and the theoretical, were possessed equally by all humans and that all should be accorded the same moral status. All individuals possessed the idea of justice, and all had the capacity for determining whether their intentions corresponded with the idea, whether 'in doing such a thing, instead of leaving it undone, I did what I should think right if any other Person had done it'.[18] That capacity, and the idea upon which it was exercised, was independent of experience; it was due to God's creation of mankind in his own image, as eternal and infinite.

Coleridge regarded men's moral nature as a consequence of their unique possession of a religious nature which endowed them with reason.

The identification of morality as part of the province of reason provided the basis for Coleridge's rejection of Paley's system of morality. While acknowledging that a good action may be indicative of a good will, Coleridge argued that it was the quality of the will that determined the moral value of an action, not an assessment of the consequences of the action itself.[19] An irony of Paleyan philosophy was that, while it was often associated with freedom, it actually tended to serve as a bulwark of modern despotism. By ignoring the rational and moral character of mankind it treated virtue as something that depended upon '*talent*, a gift so unequally dispensed by Nature ... and the development and cultivation of which are effected by all the inequalities of fortune'.[20] It thus gave rise to conceptions of inequality that justified the usurpations of 'aristocracies of talent' which enthroned the 'understanding' and undermined moral freedom. However, the universal, inward and non-experientially conditioned character of reason meant that its sphere of operation had to be restricted. It could not be applied directly to the regulation of outward matters, since these were influenced by the vicissitudes of time and circumstance and fell within the province of the 'understanding', the discursive faculty which operated on the accumulations of experience and generalised from these in order to determine the best way of translating intentions into outward acts.

Coleridge used the distinction between reason and understanding to distinguish between the sphere of morals and that of politics. Morality related to the inward determinants of action, while politics was concerned with its outward side, and particularly with the regulation of human interaction. It is clear, however, that morals and politics were seen by Coleridge as being distinct rather than divorced. The way that they related and the factors which governed their interrelationship provided the focus for the political parts of the *The Friend*, where Coleridge dealt with the problem of political obligation.

II POLITICAL OBLIGATION

Coleridge's treatment of political obligation developed by reference to three approaches to the problem. The first explained it in terms of fear and was attributed to Hobbes; the second was based on expediency and was associated with Paley's moral theory; while the third view grounded obligation on a theory of morality which is very similar to that advanced by Coleridge in his critique of Paley. Coleridge attributed this last view to Rousseau, although Rousseau's ideas were presented in a Kantian guise. The discussion treated the problem of political obligation in general, but also included a consideration of the relationship between the grounds of obligation and the justification of particular regimes.

According to Coleridge, Hobbes explained the subject's obligation by reference to fear and power. Subjects obeyed out of fear, and sovereigns were able to compel obedience because they possessed the power to force their subjects to obey them. Since obligation was supposedly based on fear and the exercise of power, conceptions of 'right' and 'duty' were emptied of any moral content. Both obligation in general, and the rationale of particular forms of government, were explained in terms that were not related to moral discourse. Coleridge claimed that theories such as those of Hobbes were, quite literally, *'preposterous'*, contrary to nature, reason and human experience.[21] Because Hobbes attempted to explain obligation in non-moral terms, his theory assumed an essentially bestial view of human nature that implicitly denied, or at least ignored, the significance of those human characteristics that made mankind both religious and moral beings. A result of this was that Hobbes's theory was defective on its own terms. Coleridge claimed that, even in situations where coercion and fear played an important role in prompting obedience, they did so because they were brought to bear on creatures whose possession of reason endowed them with a conscience. Coercion may affect men's conduct, but, except where they were literally and perpetually in chains, obedience was largely dependent upon a sense of the rightness of that which the power of the law enforced. That sense was a product of reason acting on men's intentions: 'we can be subdued by that alone which is analogous in Kind to that which we subdue, namely, by the invisible powers of our Nature'. Law was not wholly external to the individual, and, if it were, it could not effectively regulate the conduct of moral creatures: *'for me* its power is the same with that of my own permanent Self . . . all the Choice, which is permitted to me, consists in having it for my Guardian Angel or my avenging Fiend!'[22]

In his consideration of Hobbes's theory, Coleridge responded to the claim that 'laws without the sword are but bits of paper' by retailing an abbreviated version of Harrington's rejoinder that 'without law the sword is but a piece of iron'. Harrington's quip appeared in 'The Preliminaries' of *Oceana*,[23] the argument of which had a significant bearing on the position developed by Coleridge in *The Friend*. Harrington had distinguished two sets of principles of government, one 'internal, or the goods of the mind . . . natural or acquired virtues', the other 'external, or the goods of fortune' or 'riches'.[24] The former of these principles related to 'authority', and was contrasted with the latter, which constituted 'power'. Authority came not from riches, but had to be sought 'nearer heaven, or to the image of God which is the soul of man'.[25]

Like Harrington, Coleridge rejected Hobbes's attempt to derive obedience from fear and from the exercise of power. Obedience related to authority rather than power, and depended on men's special status as creatures formed after the image of God. Hobbes's error was that he deprived political obligation of those attributes that made it a distinctly human phenomenon: 'Government is a thing which relates to Men, and what you say applies only to Beasts.'[26] While Coleridge's response to Hobbes utilised the language of Harrington, it also followed closely the critique of another seventeenth-century figure whose work Coleridge admired. This was the Cambridge Platonist Richard Cudworth. Cudworth accused Hobbes of '*Villanizing* . . . . Humane Nature' and of creating a conception of sovereignty that was 'nothing but an *Ignoble* and *Bastardly Brut of Fear*'.[27] Like Coleridge, Cudworth ascribed obligation to the natural bond between individuals and the recognition that sovereignty related to the good of the subject.[28]

Since obligation had a moral basis (it sprang from a sense of duty which reflected an acknowledgement of the appropriateness of particular arrangements) it could be said to be founded not indeed on the *fact* of contract, but on a recognition of reciprocity that Coleridge thought could be described in terms of the *idea* of a contract. That idea was a way of expressing the existence of a 'sense of Duty acting in a specific direction and determining our moral relations, as members of a body politic'.[29] Contracts were best described as 'perpetual' rather than 'original', a formulation that sounded like Burke's, but differed from it because Coleridge's produced a more flexible view of the possibility of modifying the ways in which the contract was institutionalised.[30] The idea of contract represented the basis of 'social union', but, since this was conditioned by what Harrington called 'goods of the mind', its form and terms could be altered to accommodate developments of the populace's sense of duty. In a contemporary notebook entry, Coleridge recorded a statement from Harrington which illustrated the mutability of a perpetual contract: 'Where the Spirit of the People is impatient of a Gov[ernment] by arms & desirous of a Gov[ernment] by Laws, there the Sp[irit] of a Peop[le] is not unfit to be trusted with Liberty.'[31]

Coleridge's critique of the Hobbesian theory of obligation was related closely to his earlier identification of the character of morality, and the role of reason in regulating those aspects of human conduct that fell within its province. Political obligation was essentially a form of moral obligation that reflected the distinctive nature of human beings. This had been recognised by Rousseau, and, although Coleridge was critical of many aspects of Rousseau's political philosophy, he regarded those parts of it which dealt with the moral basis of social and political life as being of great interest and significance:

> The System commences with an undeniable Truth, and an important deduction therefrom equally undeniable. All voluntary Actions . . . having for their Objects Good or Evil, are *moral* Actions. But all morality is grounded in the Reason. Every man is born with the faculty of Reason; and whatever is without . . . is not a Man or PERSON but a THING. Hence the sacred Principle, recognised by all Laws, human and divine, the Principle indeed, which is the *ground-work* of all Law and Justice, that a Person can never become a Thing, nor be treated as such without wrong. But the distinction between Person and Thing consists herein, that the latter may rightfully be used, altogether and merely, as a *Means*: but the former must always be included in the *End*, and form a part of the final Cause.[32]

In Rousseau's theory the derivation of personality from the common and uniform possession of reason served to delineate the limits of government action; obligation could not extend to laws that violated the moral personality of the subject. It thus provided a criterion by which the conduct of particular governments could be judged: 'whatever Law or System of Law compels' action which violates the personality of its members, 'disennobles our Nature, leagues itself with the Animal against the Godlike, kills in us the very Principle of joyous Well-doing, and fights against Humanity'.[33] Coleridge's insistence that the state should treat its subjects as moral beings reinforced the implications of his use of Harrington against Hobbes. In a notebook dating from the period when Coleridge was collecting material for *The Friend* he considered the character of the state in the context of a discussion of Harrington's *A System of Politics*: 'As the *Form* of a Man is the Image of God, so the Form of a Just Government is the Image of Man.'[34] Coleridge went on to explain that 'Forms' partake of the 'divine'; that is, they possessed ultimate qualities that could not be derived from the sum of their constituent parts, but were a function of the organic quality of the whole. That did not mean that the moral quality of the whole was unconnected to the moral quality of its members. The divine characteristics of government resulted from an 'infusion' of the moral qualities of individuals into the larger whole. The moral quality of the state was therefore dependent upon the virtue of those who comprised it – 'only the refin'd Spirit of a nation can be a good form of Government' – and that gave rise to the stress upon education and enlightenment which was a feature of Coleridge's political writings.[35]

In *The Friend*, Coleridge's account of the state was linked to that of Rousseau, and utilised the language of Kant. But the conception itself was essentially Platonic in character. Like much of Coleridge's philosophy, his political thought involved an attempt, as David Newsome puts it, to reveal the 'One behind the Many'.[36] Coleridge portrayed the state as a mystical, or 'divine', whole that lay behind, but at the same time constituted, the ultimate moral reality of the individuals who from time to time comprised it. It was divine because, to the extent that its authority was a 'good of the mind', it reflected the souls of its members, who were, of course, God's creation.

Coleridge's use of Harrington in developing his account of the nature of the state represented a continuation of the interaction between Christianity and aspects of civic humanism which appeared in the Bristol lectures.[37] In these lectures Coleridge's interpretation of Christianity had produced a radicalised version of a conception of property which he had derived from exponents of the Commonwealth ideology. In *The Friend*, however, the points at issue were the moral basis of the state, and the nature of the subject's obligation to it. Coleridge's treatment of these issues depended upon a Christianised Platonism that led him to portray the state as a moral entity fashioned in a form appropriate to men's status as creatures made by God in his own image.

The most important accounts of the transmission of the Harringtonian paradigm treat it as Aristotelian and secular,[38] but Coleridge's theory was both Platonic and religious. His conception of the state was diametrically opposed to the Aristotelian view that it contributed to the pursuit of the good life (rather than perfection), and that it achieved this by balancing different interests, rather than by encapsulating the divine characteristics of its members. That Coleridge could arrive at such a conception of the state with the help of Harrington suggests that the conventional picture of the Harringtonian paradigm may be in need of revision, and that the Platonic and Christian elements of it deserve more attention than they have been given hitherto. Accounts of Harrington have tended to concentrate on his treatment of the 'goods of fortune', but Coleridge's reference to 'goods of the mind' raises the possibility that some aspects of Harrington's political philosophy fit uneasily with the 'Harringtonian' paradigm. In any case, Coleridge was quite prepared to Platonise Harrington and to place him alongside other seventeenth-century Platonists whom he admired. This task was made easier than it might otherwise have been by the similarities between Cudworth's response to Hobbes and those of Harrington. However, Coleridge's sympathetic use of Harrington meant that he ignored the materialistic or mechanical aspects of his constitution-framing. Harrington believed that it was possible to construct constitutional systems that made men act well regardless of their intentions, but this was clearly not what Coleridge had in mind.[39] For him, the perfection of the state was dependent upon the moral qualities of its members.

Coleridge's theory of political obligation and his conception of the state were morally based, and depended upon his view of the role of reason in morality. To the extent that government could be said to be 'just', it would take account of the uniquely reasonable character of individuals who partook of divine reason. That did not mean, however, that a just law was the same as a moral precept: the province of law was the external activities of men, while morality related to the internal side, to intention. But Coleridge's moral conception of the state and of the subject's obligation to it meant that he thought that the individual's moral status as an end rather than a means should guide systems of legislation. Coleridge's account of the peculiar moral status of the exilic Jews in a contemporary notebook entry emphasised this point. He reversed his previous view of the childish nature of the Jews and now claimed that they were not children, because they had already learned bad habits which had to be unlearned. Being unable to act morally the Jews had to be 'led to the principle thro' the outward Deed, to morality thro' legality'.[40]

These remarks indicate that Coleridge's hostility to Paley's system was due to its tendency to dispense with morality and rely exclusively on expedience. But, in establishing the scope and character of morality in relation to politics, Coleridge also wished to identify its limitations – an aim that marked a significant departure from the fusion of morals and politics that had characterised the Bristol lectures. Coleridge's identification of the limitations of morals in politics rested upon his view of reason. Reason was not suitable for deciding the extent of political participation or dealing with other problems associated with the art of governing. These were matters for prudence, operating within the guidelines produced by reason.

III PRUDENCE IN POLITICS

Coleridge's account of the limitations of reason in politics and of the need to supplement it by prudence provided the basis for his consideration of Rousseau's theory. While accepting Rousseau's account of the nature of reason and of the role that it played with respect to the moral basis of the state, Coleridge rejected his attempt to make reason the sole arbiter in human affairs. In Rousseau's theory, and in the version of it that had guided the French revolutionaries, the equal and universal characteristics of reason were used to legitimise particular forms of government. Legislative arrangements that did not reflect men's moral equality, and failed to institutionalise reason in their operation, were denied legitimacy. Only those forms of government which were fully participatory, and whose deliberations represented expressions of a general will embodying the shared and common rationality of the community, could be described as just. Coleridge argued, however, that even in Rousseau's statement of his theory the primacy of reason was illusory, and showed that the forms and practice of politics were not a matter for reason alone.

In his critique of Rousseau, Coleridge concentrated on the claim that the general will would find expression even where some individuals pursued their particular interests and disregarded that of the community. By admitting the possibility of non-moral behaviour, and by depending on the self-cancelling negation of particular interests in the process through which the general will was expressed, Rousseau implied that reason did not act unalloyed in political processes, and covertly acknowledged that the triumph of reason was at best a probability dependent upon circumstantial considerations. The impact of circumstances was assessed by calculations based on experience; it depended, in other words, on the understanding, not on reason. Coleridge claimed that Rousseau and his followers attempted to ignore the problems presented by their own theory by reifying the general will ('that Sovereign Will, to which the right of universal legislation appertains, applies to no one Human Being, to no Society or Assemblage of Human Beings, and least of all to the mixed Multitude that makes up the PEOPLE: but entirely and exclusively to REASON itself'[41]), but this could not disguise the fact that the expression of the will in any given case was likely to be a matter of degree: 'thus we already find ourselves beyond the magic Circle of the pure Reason, and within the Sphere of the Understanding and the Prudence'.[42]

Rousseau's theory broke down because it sought to push reason beyond its proper limits, and confused the practice of morality with the practice of government. Morality regulated motives, while politics controlled 'the outward Actions of particular Bodies of Men, according to their particular Circumstances'.[43] Coleridge did not deny that morality was significant for the practice of government, for, as we have seen, both political obligation and the criterion of just government rested on a moral basis. But his view on the limitations of reason meant that law had to take account of circumstantial considerations that fell outside the scope of reason. The 'practical rules' formulated by statesmen were connected with morality but were not identical to it. They pointed out the means of administering the moral law in particular cases, and depended upon the extent to which prudential calculations matched 'measures to Circumstances'.[44] When Coleridge declared himself a proponent of expediency in politics he was not referring to 'mere' expediency, to the 'pretended prudence' of writers such as Paley, but to circumstantially based calculations that represented a practical attempt to apply the moral law to situations where something other than intention had to be taken into consideration. Morality was the 'abiding *spirit* of the Law' even though 'the *Letter* of the Law, that is, the application of it to particular instances and the mode of realizing it in actual practice, must be modified by the existing circumstances'.[45]

Coleridge's view of the limited and indirect role of reason in the practice of government led him to reject theories which withheld legitimacy from governments whose origins and structures were not directly deducible from the principles of pure reason. These theories presupposed that the universal and equal character of reason meant that there could be only *one* legitimate form of government. Reason generated political axioms that had the same status as ideas of space and extension in geometry: 'as there is but one System of Geometry, so according to this Theory there can be but one Constitution and one System of Legislation'.[46] Coleridge rejected this line of argument because it failed to distinguish politics from morality; politics was the art of establishing frameworks for action which took account of variations in the circumstances in which men found themselves. The wide variation of constitutional forms found in different times and in different places resulted from attempts to institutionalise those maxims of prudence which the understanding formulated in the process of making particular applications of general principles. The Jews, for example, needed the rigid legalism of the Decalogue to wean them from their bad habits. The revelation of Christ added a new dimension to human experience: the Gospels were not so much a new system of law, as a supplement and substitute for systems of law in general. They fulfilled the law of the Decalogue by 'vivifying it with the moral principle'.[47] Coleridge regarded political maxims as specific rather than general statements; they cast 'philosophic truth in the moulds of national laws, customs, and existing orders of society'.[48] They generated structures and attitudes which had moral value, but were not deducible from reason alone: 'Old customs, familiar sympathies, willing reverences, and habits of subordination almost naturalized into instincts' were 'the ordinary props and aidances of our infirm virtue'. Essential to virtue, they were, nevertheless, distinct from it.[49]

In his treatment of political obligation Coleridge argued that the state has a moral basis. His later account of the need to particularise the dictates of morality, and his statements about how this was done, provided a rationale for nation states. These institutions were the results of historically evolving patterns of particularisation; they provided the practical and emotional context for realising virtue under given sets of circumstances. The nation state facilitated the development of moral purpose and thus provided the necessary basis for the growth of wider senses of identity and interest, which were more effective because they started from an understanding of how the principles of morality should be applied in specific instances. Even figures of universal significance such as Plato, Luther and Newton owed their appeal to ideas that were first forged within a particular national context:

> Here and here only may we confidently expect these mighty minds to be reared and ripened, whose names are naturalized in foreign lands, the sure Fellow-travellers of Civilization! and yet render their own Country dearer and more proudly dear to their own Countrymen. This is indeed Cosmopolitanism, at once the Nursling and the Nurse of patriotic affection! This, and this alone, is genuine Philanthropy, which . . . fattens not exhausts the soil, from which it sprang, and in which it remains rooted.[50]

Coleridge contrasted true cosmopolitanism with the empty universality of the Napoleonic Empire; this impoverished both the French themselves and those to whom they claimed to be carrying universal reason. We must, Coleridge claimed, be patriots 'in order to be Men', and because humanity was universal the right to national independence must be recognised in others.[51]

Since Coleridge regarded the nation state as essential to the realisation of men's moral capabilities, it is not surprising that he described the force that sustained national entities in essentially religious terms, as 'Spirit'. In his 'Letters on the Spaniards', which are contemporary with *The Friend*, this spirit accounted for, and encapsulated, the particular characteristics of different nations. It complemented and moralised the operation of what were otherwise mechanical balances of property in the constitution, and, in cases where a 'high *national* sense and unusual virtues' existed, it could help compensate for the absence of institutionalised forces.[52]

If the universality of reason made it an inappropriate guide to political practice, so too did its egalitarianism. Men's equal possession of reason was used by writers such as Rousseau as a basis for claims about participation in legislative processes, but

Coleridge argued that the inconsistent way in which such claims were applied indicated a covert acknowledgement that participation in politics depended on something other than reason. The framers of the early constitutions of the revolutionary period in France had started by claiming that the universal possession of reason was the basis for universal political participation, but had then introduced exceptions – applying to women and children – that were inconsistent with their starting point. Coleridge regarded such inconsistencies as proof that the question of participatory rights could not be resolved by an appeal to reason alone. The framers of the French Constitution of 1791 were not acting on the basis of deductions from pure reason, but were actually formulating maxims of prudence, and these depended on the operation of the understanding. Their exclusion of women and children from the exercise of political rights was based upon an assessment of degrees of competence and independence, and such assessments were not the work of, or deducible from, reason:

> Nothing . . . which subsists wholly in degrees, the [changes] of which do not obey any necessary Law, can be Subjects of pure Science, or determinable by mere Reason. For these we must rely on our *Understandings*, enlightened by past experience and immediate Observation, and determining our choice by comparisons of Expediency.[53]

Once this was recognised, it was clear that the determination of political fitness really depended upon criteria that were formulated with reference to the lessons deduced from experience by the understanding, not from men's possession of reason.

In *The Friend*, Coleridge produced two sorts of criteria for involvement in politics. The first, and least significant, related to those who wished to practise the arts of government at a high level. The qualities required of these individuals were those of statesmanship: they needed the capacity to discern how general principles, especially those derived from the moral law, should be applied to particular cases. In a number of places in *The Friend*, Coleridge wrote in glowing terms about the character and conduct of Sir Alexander Ball, who was Acting Governor of Malta during his stay on the island. The warmth of Coleridge's remarks on Ball surprised De Quincey, who was unable to reconcile them with more sober assessments of Ball's character and abilities.[54] But this missed the real point of Coleridge's treatment of Ball, who appeared in *The Friend* as an archetype of intellectualised, principled statesmanship, not as a subject of biography. In his refutation of Hobbes's theory of obedience, Coleridge used an account of Ball's success in disciplining a mutinous and demoralised ship's company to illustrate the force of an appeal to men's reason; and, in a later, more general assessment of Ball's career, he stressed his successful integration of general principles and particular rules.[55] Throughout *The Friend* the sensitive generation of particular rules from general principles was contrasted with the combination of purely abstract reasoning and unprincipled opportunism and misrepresentation which Coleridge thought characterised both the radical and reactionary camps during the 1790s. Both groups 'justified the corruptions of the State in the same spirit of Sophistry, by the same vague arguments of general Reason, and the same disregard of ancient Ordinances and established Opinions'.[56] The failings of these groups were in the arts appropriate to actual, or aspiring, statesmen, but Coleridge did not regard such qualities as being necessary for political participation, for exercising a right to the franchise. Such rights were related to, and dependent upon, the possession of property. The state was based upon what Harrington had called the 'goods of the mind', but the exercise of political power depended upon the 'goods of fortune'.

IV   PROPERTY AND POLITICAL PARTICIPATION

Coleridge's treatment of the political significance of property in *The Friend* rested upon a distinction between the rationale of the state and the origins of government. As we have seen, the state's rationale was essentially moral: it could be explained by reference to the characteristics and incidence of reason; hence Coleridge's rejection of accounts of obligation which ignored reason and depended upon animalistic motives such as fear. However, in treating the origins of government, Coleridge denied a direct role for reason and argued that the 'form' of political structures could not be deduced from reason alone. The historical coincidence of government and property suggested to Coleridge that the former was created in order to protect the latter. 'The chief object, for which Men first formed themselves into a State was not the protection of their Lives but of their Property.'[57] If that were so, then reason could not be said to play a direct role in the formation of government, since property stood in an indirect and mixed relationship to reason. Reason was equal in all men, but property was, by its very nature, unequal. Its acquisition depended upon, or was significantly influenced by, environmental conditions, and by individual effort which relied upon the understanding. Since men were not equal in their understandings, they would not have opportunities for possessing similar amounts and kinds of property.

In *The Friend* Coleridge tentatively acknowledged that the 'form' (or 'idea') of property may be deducible from reason, a point that was more definitely stated in a contemporary notebook entry where the moral value of property was linked to the '*necessity* of individual action to moral agency, of an individual sphere to individual scheme[s] of action'.[58] But he insisted that the moral basis of property was restricted to its *form*; the '*matter*' of property rights and the extent of individual holdings were a consequence of chance and of the varying capacity's of men's understanding.[59] Since government and human laws related to property, and since property itself was not deducible from reason, it followed that it would be inappropriate to claim that universal rights should be binding in relation to matters and institutions that were not products of reason.

The dependence of government on property, and the relationship between the possession of property and the understanding, provided the basis for Coleridge's critique of attempts to generate claims to political rights on the basis of moral personality alone. That line of argument was associated in Coleridge's mind with the framers of the various French Constitutions of the 1790s, but his critique was directed more specifically at the arguments of the English reformer Major John Cartwright, author of *The People's Barrier*. One reason why Coleridge may have singled out Cartwright for special treatment was that *The People's Barrier* contained a clear challenge to the position he wished to advance. Cartwright invited 'the warmest and ablest advocates for all other principles' to 'criticise these with all freedom and scrutinise them to the very marrow'. He argued that, since government was directed to the pursuit of the '*common-weal*', laws must be made by the '*common consent*' of 'every Englishman'. Cartwright claimed that those who based political rights on the possession of property failed to appreciate the significance of Beccaria's dictum that 'Liberty' was 'the end of the social compact, *property* . . . only the means'.

> Although a man's property is a fit object of attention to his representative, it by no means constitutes his right to have that *being* embued with *free will*, capable of *happiness* and misery, answerable to his Creator and his fellow-creatures as a *moral* agent and therefore necessarily created free.[60]

In a telling phrase, Coleridge described Cartwright as a 'state-moralist',[61] one who sought to apply moral precepts directly to politics. Cartwright represented the moderate and restrained end of a continuum that embraced figures such as the Fifth Monarchy men of the seventeenth century, whose religious fanaticism was exceedingly dangerous because they did not acknowledge a distinction between religion and morals on the one hand, and politics on the other.[62] Cartwright's defence of universal suffrage was based on the relationship between reason, obligation and political rights that Coleridge had criticised in his consideration of Rousseau's theory, but he added to that a further argument concerning the relationship between individual happiness and the quality of government. He claimed that the only form of government that produced happiness for all individuals was one in which individuals governed themselves. However, Coleridge noted that Cartwright's 'right to happiness' was not consistently pursued in his theory of representation. Happiness was to some extent dependent upon the control of material resources, and a *right* to happiness would justify not only universal suffrage, but also universal or common possession. Cartwright's unwillingness to pursue the levelling logic of his line of argument undercut his specific claims about the basis of rights to the suffrage:

> Therefore, unless he carries his System to the whole length of common Labour and common Possession, a Right to universal Suffrage cannot exist; but if not to universal Suffrage, there can exit no *natural right* to Suffrage at all. In whatever way he would obviate this objection, he must admit *Expedience* founded on *Experience* and particular Circumstances, which will vary in every different Nation and in the same Nation at different times, as the Maxim of all Legislation and the Ground of all legislative Power. For his universal Principles . . . necessarily suppose

uniform and perfect Subjects, which are to be found in the *Ideas* of pure Geometry and (I trust) in the *Realities* of Heaven, but never, never, in Creatures of Flesh and Blood.[63]

Cartwright had thought that claims about the relationship between property and political power confused the means with the ends, but Coleridge's response undermined that criticism. Property was not the end of the state, although under certain circumstances a constitution that gave due weight to property helped to secure liberty. In a contemporary notebook entry Coleridge objected to accounts of the Constitution that reduced 'all to the influence of Property',[64] a position that was quite consistent with his belief that the franchise should relate to property-holding. Coleridge's views on the political significance of property did not depend on the 'influence of property' in any crude sense, but stressed that a properly ordered constitution could harness the 'goods of fortune' to the commonweal. If a constitution that allowed a direct relationship between property and political power served only the interests of large-scale property-holders, it would be oligarchic, but oligarchy was a corruption, not a true form, of government. True laws were practical applications of universal principles of morality, not instruments for protecting the rich at the expense of the rest of the populace.

Coleridge believed that Cartwright's use of the distinction between means and ends of government abstracted the pursuit of the end from the conditions necessary for its attainment. Against Cartwright's abstract rationalism Coleridge argued for a position that started from a similar premise – namely, that men were morally equal – but then took account of a fund of experience which suggested that the scope for moral action was likely to be most extensive if traditional constitutional practices that related the exercise of political power to the possession of property were followed.

Coleridge may also have had Cartwright in mind when considering what he called the 'antiquarian' justification of universal suffrage, a radical form of ancient constitutionalism which was used by some proponents of parliamentary reform.[65] According to this argument, the past was regarded as a source of just and wise practices whose recovery would correct the deficiencies of contemporary political institutions. Coleridge dealt with a version of this argument which focused on legislative and practical modifications that restricted the franchise to property-holders and thus undermined the ancient statutes that gave votes to freemen. Coleridge denied that the extension of the franchise could be justified by reference to the statutes. The antiquarian position ignored the fact that, when the original statutes had been framed, the terms 'freeman' and 'property-holder' were synonymous. Modifications in the way these statutes were applied had served to preserve the spirit of the originals in a situation where freemen did not necessarily possess politically significant amounts and forms of property.[66] The fact that these laws had not been repealed was a result of the political difficulties of doing so, but these had been avoided by changes in interpretation or application that reflected changes in property-holding patterns.[67]

Coleridge's rejection of attempts to justify the granting of political rights on the basis of human rights or outmoded legislation depended on the claim that these lines of argument failed to take account of the necessary connection between the exercise of political power and the possession of property. This failure was due to an extension of reason beyond its proper sphere and a disregard for the role that experience played in deducing particular rules from general principles. In Coleridge's view, the lessons of experience pointed to the need to maintain a close correspondence between the possession of property and the exercise of political rights. In *The Friend* Coleridge did not offer a detailed defence of the benefits of the correspondence between property and political rights found in the English Constitution. However, in that work, and in the contemporary series of 'Letters on the Spaniards' which appeared in *The Courier* in December 1809 and January 1810, he made it clear that his views on the constitutional significance of property were based on the perspective adopted in his earlier defence of the Constitution and Church of England.

In the fifth letter, Coleridge described representative assemblies as bulwarks against the establishment of the tyranny of single individuals, and claimed that tyrants always owed their possession of power to their control over armies, rather than parliaments. But, although assemblies could not be totally suborned, their balance could be destroyed through corruption. It 'is with a national assembly as it is with the common air of Heaven. If it be corrupted, it is the sorest visitation of offended Providence: if its equipoise be suddenly and violently destroyed, its tempers are terrifying, and every man has a tale of their fury.'⁶⁸ The idea of corruption also played an important role in Coleridge's critiques of the extreme opponents of the French Revolution and of radical activities in England. Coleridge accused the reactionaries of instigating a 'panic of property'.⁶⁹ They wilfully ignored the distinction between dependent and independent forms of property and defended the tools and fruits of corruption by arguments which only applied to independent property. 'The Wages of state-dependence were represented as sacred as the Property won by Industry or derived from a long line of Ancestors.'⁷⁰ At one point, Coleridge appeared to reject the view of the constitution as a mixture and balance. 'The supposed balance of the three constitutional Powers' was an idea from which he had 'never been able to elicit one ray of common sense'.⁷¹ This claim was not, however, inconsistent with the treatment of the French Constitution in the *Morning Post* articles of 1799–1800, since Coleridge's argument then had depended upon a view of the constitution as a balance of proprietorial interests institutionalised in the various parts of the constitution, not as a balance of powers residing in different and discrete elements.⁷²

In one important respect however, Coleridge's treatment of property in *The Friend* differed from that found in his earlier writings. While not abandoning his belief in the social and political significance of independent, landed property, Coleridge began to develop a more favourable perspective on non-landed forms of wealth. He thus sought to combine a mode of analysis derived from the Country Party tradition with a perspective on commerce that had previously been seen as an alternative to it.

V LAND, COMMERCE AND SOCIAL PROGRESS

In the twelfth number of *The Friend*, Coleridge published an essay – 'On the Vulgar Errors Respecting Taxes and Taxation' – which attacked the argument that money raised by taxation was a net loss to the nation, a loss that was directly due to the corrupt nature and bellicose policy of the administration. He denied that there was a negative relationship between the level of taxation and the freedom and prosperity of the nation. The present condition of Great Britain tended, if anything, to point to the opposite conclusion. Although the nation was, and had been, heavily taxed, personal freedom was more extensive and prosperity more widespread than when rates of taxation had been lower. Those who argued against current levels of taxation failed to see that what was important was not the amount of tax *paid*, but the amount of money *remaining* to individuals. In most cases, the disposable income of individuals had increased even while the rate of taxation increased.[73]

In his comparative remarks on the French and English Constitutions, Coleridge had expressed reservations about the constitutional implications of non-landed forms of property. His notebooks and later published writings show that he continued to have doubts about some features of commercial society, and about the moral effects of the commercial ethos.[74] But sections of *The Friend* indicated the development of a less critical perspective on some features of contemporary politics that had been condemned by Country Party ideologists. One sign of that was his less than complete rejection of some practices associated with 'corruption'. In his criticism of reactionary responses to the reform agitation of the 1790s Coleridge had, as we have seen, used the Country Party distinction between 'dependent' and 'independent' forms of wealth. Elsewhere, however, he suggested that a certain amount of corruption may be necessary, at least in the short term. The most honest response was to admit that some practices 'were Evils' but that they were 'necessary Evils; or, if they were *removable*, yet that the consequences of the *heroic* medicines . . . would be far more dreadful than the Disease'.[75] However, Coleridge's most interesting divergence from a Country Party position was manifest in his changed attitude to the social and political significance of commerce. He now acknowledged that commerce was a source of cohesive and civilising tendencies that beneficially modified the rude simplicity of an agrarian condition.

Coleridge's defence of taxation was based partly on the view that the revenue collected by the government did not disappear from the economy but was merely recirculated. The tax system and the governmental expenditure that it supported were ways of redirecting the wealth of the nation:

> The Gardens in the South of Europe supply . . . [an] apt illustration of a system of Finance judiciously conducted, where the Tanks or Reservoirs would represent the Capital of a Nation, and the hundred Rills hourly varying their channels and directions, under the Gardener's Spade, give a pleasing image of

the dispersion of that capital through the whole Population, by the joint effect of Taxation and Trade.[76]

In *The Friend* Coleridge criticised Napoleon's continental policy because it threatened to ruin the commerce not only of England, but also of Europe. Napoleon's policy had had the effect of reducing Europe 'to the wretched state in which it was before the wide diffusion of trade and Commerce'. It deprived the inhabitants of continental Europe of

> comforts and advantages to which they and their Fathers had been, for more than a Century, habituated, and thus destroys . . . a principal source of Civilization, the origin of a *middle Class* throughout Christendom, and with it the true Balance of Society, the parent of international Law, the foster-nurse of general Humanity, and (to sum up all in one) the main Principle of Attraction and Repulsion, by which the Nations were rapidly though insensibly drawing together into one system, and by which alone they could combine the manifold Blessings of distinct character and national independence, with the needful stimulation and general influences of Intercommunity, and be virtually united without being crushed together by Conquest. . . .[77]

The civilising and unifying functions of international trade were also at work within nations, and here it was not only trade, but also commerce, the bane of eighteenth-century proponents of the Country Party ideology, that played a positive role. The system of credit, with the national debt as its cornerstone, allowed for the fullest utilisation of individual and national resources, and also had a beneficial effect on national cohesion and on the growth of voluntary, reciprocally advantageous interaction. The National Debt was the 'cement' of the body politic:

> it . . . wedded in indissoluble union all the interests of the State, the landed with the commercial, and the man of independent fortune with the stirring Tradesman and reposing Annuitant. It is the National Debt, which by the rapid nominal rise in the value of Things, has made it impossible for any considerable number of Men to retain their former comforts without joining in common Industry, and adding to the Stock of national Produce.[78]

Coleridge's account of the benefits of debt-funding suggested that it could serve as a material reinforcement of the psychological cohesion generated by shared history, language and *mores*. His claim that the National Debt was the 'cement' of the body politic echoed the arguments of Sir James Steuart, the author of *An Inquiry into the Principles of Political Oeconomy* (1767).[79] Like Steuart, Coleridge thought that modern economies provided mechanisms that bound society together by 'multiplying reciprocal obligations, and creating a general dependence between its members'.[80]

If commerce provided a way of supporting what Coleridge later called the 'permanent' elements of the Constitution, it was also thought to advance freedom and the growth of civilisation. Coleridge maintained that the continental system waged war 'against mankind and the quiet growth of the world's improvement'. The destruction of commerce would cast Europe back into a state of 'barbarism'.[81] The process was already under way in France. Coleridge attributed Napoleon's successful bid for power to a prior weakening of the social, political and economic fabric of French society. The revolutionary period had undermined religious and moral principles, removed the monarchy, seriously weakened the landholding and commercial classes, and virtually destroyed the navy by abandoning its network of bases in the colonies. These developments were accompanied by the army's rise to power and prominence amidst the 'wrecks of all other Employments, save that of agriculture'. Napoleon was thus the creature rather than the creator of the conditions that facilitated his rise to power. When he came on the scene, 'France had already approximated to the formidable state so prophetically described by Sir James Stuart [sic] . . . in which the Population should consist chiefly of Soldiers and Peasantry'.[82]

Coleridge's reference to Steuart, and his description of a nation of soldiers and peasants as 'barbaric', marked a distinct and unmistakable break with the concern for agrarian simplicity that had been in evidence in his Bristol lectures. It also indicated a departure from at least one aspect of the Harringtonian ideal. Harrington's free commonwealth was peopled by peasants and soldiers, but Coleridge now regarded such a society as barbaric, or uncivilised.[83] In common with eighteenth-century political economists such as Steuart, Coleridge credited commerce with a central role in the progression from barbarism to civility. A civilised condition was marked by a growth of political and personal freedom, and a corresponding weakening of arbitrary power.

VI CONCLUSION: PROPERTY AND THE ENDS OF GOVERNMENT

Coleridge's account of the political and social significance of property illustrated his conception of the role of the understanding in the art of government. It supported his claim that the practice of government, and discussions about the institutional structures of political action, should be decided on the basis of expediency. However, Coleridge thought that his understanding of expediency differed from that of other contemporaries such as Paley, or the Edinburgh Reviewers, because it related prudence to a true account of men's reasonable, moral and religious natures. Coleridge's views on the relationship between prudence and morality played an important role in his consideration of the conditions of political change in light of the ends of the state.

He claimed that proposed changes to the institutional structure of the country should be assessed on the basis of three sets of criteria. The first dealt with the practicability of the proposed changes, the second with their suitability in light of existing circumstances, and the third with their contribution to government's more perfect fulfilment of its ends.[84] The first two of these criteria raised questions that were largely matters of expediency, but Coleridge's treatment of the third indicated that it was closely related to moral considerations. When discussing the ends of the state Coleridge cautioned that he spoke as a 'Christian Moralist, not as a Statesman'.[85] Presumably, the statesman's consideration of ends would be restricted to relatively short-run practical considerations. By contrast, a moral account of the ends of the state appeared to depend on the distinction between *form* and *matter* which Coleridge had introduced in his consideration of the relationship between property and reason.[86] The statesman considered how ends could be realised in existing circumstances, while the moralist identified the formal characteristics of ends which reflected men's reasonable, moral and religious nature.

The ends of government were considered under two different heads, the negative and the positive. Coleridge treated the former in a perfunctory manner. 'The negative ends of Government are the protection of Life, of personal Freedom, of Property, of Reputation, and of Religion, from foreign and from domestic attacks.'[87] He did not elaborate on the character of these ends, or the ways in which they should be pursued, but it is quite clear that the list was a more detailed statement of the negative requirements of the idea of free agency that Coleridge had developed in his moral theory. His treatment of the positive ends of government was far fuller than his brief statement of its negative ends.

It should be noticed at the outset that Coleridge's specification of positive ends implied that the pursuit of these ends was, or should be, a matter for government, and that forms of government which hindered, or failed to facilitate, their attainment were in some respects inadequate. In other words, they formed a criteria by which different forms of government could be judged.[88] Coleridge claimed that there were four positive ends of government:

> 1st to make the means of subsistence more easy to each individual: 2nd that in addition to the necessaries of life he should derive from the union and division of labour a share of the comforts and conveniences, which humanize and ennoble his nature; and at the same time the power of perfecting himself in his own branch of industry by having those things which he needs, provided for him by others among his fellow citizens . . . 3rdly the hope of bettering his own condition and that of his children. *The civilised man gives up those stimulants of hope and fear which constitute the chief charms of the savage life; and yet his Maker has distinguished him from the Brute that perishes, by making Hope an instinct of his nature and an indispensible condition of his moral and intellectual progression* . . . ; [and lastly] the development of those faculties which are essential to his human nature by the knowledge of his moral and religious duties, and the increase of his intellectual powers in as great a degree as is compatible with the other ends of social union and does not involve a contradiction.[89]

Coleridge believed that all but the fourth end were 'realized under our Government to a degree unexampled in any old and long peopled Country'.[90] John Colmer points out that the last phrase was meant to exclude countries such as the United States from Coleridge's assessment, but goes on to say that even this does not salvage the position. Coleridge offered no proof of a claim that does not stand up in light of the demonstrable failure of English government materially to assist in the realisation of any of the stated ends.[91] However, if Coleridge's position is considered in the context of the theory of property that appeared in his *Morning Post* articles, and was developed further in *The Friend*, Colmer's judgement needs to be qualified.

The point is that Coleridge's first three ends of government are related to the benefits he had previously associated with a society which maintained the conditions necessary for the pursuit of commercial activity. It was the mark of the English system of government that it had fostered such activity, and had not, as had been the case in France, destroyed the basis of it. Commercial activity could, in other words, be shown to be a means of facilitating the pursuit of the moral ends of the state. Government's protection of such activity, and its encouragement of it through its own use of credit and debit-funding, played an important role in maintaining an expanding economy which eased the provision of subsistence and opened up opportunities for all its subjects. Commerce was therefore essential to the pursuit of three of the positive moral ends that Coleridge had assigned to the state.

However, while commerce facilitated the pursuit of the positive ends of government, it did not exhaust them. Coleridge's moral conception of the state could not be accommodated to the purely mechanical and self-interested pursuit of universal goals that was a feature of the interdependence and general advancement produced by commercial activity. His Platonised Harringtonian conception of the state and his continued belief in the political and moral significance of landed property meant that anything more than a partial dependence on commerce was impossible. This point appeared very forcefully in his account of the Netherlands' sudden capitulation to Louis XIV in 1692 after holding off the Spaniards for three-quarters of a century. 'The national spirit, which inspired them, was gradually poisoned by their colonial tyranny and guilt, and by the genius of trade and commerce not duly poised by an agricultural interest, or rendered generous by a landed nobility.'[92]

Coleridge's doubts about the extent to which the fourth, educational and humanising, goal was advanced by the existing structure and practice of government provided the focal point of his critique of economic doctrines and practices in the 'Lay Sermons' of 1816 and 1817, and *On the Constitution of the Church and State* (1829). That critique was necessary because Coleridge came to believe that modern conceptions of property relationships could not be rejected out of hand but had to be integrated with more traditional ones.

4

Politics, Property and Political Economy, 1810–19

In *The Friend* Coleridge made property a central element in his political theory.[1] In one important respect, however, his treatment of property there differed from that in his earlier writings. Coleridge's positive remarks about the benefits of 'commerce' meant that he was now attempting to combine perspectives on the political and moral significance of property that were usually seen as alternatives. His critique of the French Constitution drew upon a tradition that gave a special role to landed property; this idea had formed the cornerstone of the ideology of Country Party groups opposed to the Whig administrations of the eighteenth century. When Coleridge highlighted the social and political benefits of commerce and disparaged the 'barbarity' of non-commercial societies, however, he recalled the language and arguments developed to *defend* Whig regimes and practices against the challenges of Country Party oppositions. *The Friend* thus combined two differing, and apparently incompatible, arguments about the social and political significance of property. Given Coleridge's attempt to portray the state as a moral entity justified by its special responsibility for ensuring and facilitating the treatment of its subjects as persons rather than things, the arguments about the benefits of commerce were particularly problematic.

Coleridge confronted these difficulties in his 'Lay Sermons' of 1816 and 1817, and in the published and unpublished writings that related to them.[2] These sermons appeared during the period of economic hardship and social and political dislocation that became acute after the conclusion of the war in 1815, but had begun to be felt in the last years of the war.[3] A collapse of agricultural and industrial prices was accompanied by a sharp contraction in the demand for labour in a market that was swollen by the influx of discharged servicemen. There was also a resurgence of working-class political activity and a marked increase in the incidence of civil disturbances. Within Parliament and 'out of doors', the crisis was attributed to both economic and political causes. The government was subject to demands to re-establish effective protective barriers against the import of foreign corn, to check inflation by a return to cash payments, and to embark upon a programme of retrenchment that would reduce the high level of taxation of the war years. These demands were advanced by people of widely differing political views. In addition, radical politicians and publicists also campaigned for a reform of the country's political institutions, especially the electoral system.[4]

Coleridge responded to the post-war crisis in a number of ways. He contributed many articles to *The Courier* on political, social and economic topics,[5] and he also wrote a long, involved and quixotic letter to the Prime Minister, Lord Liverpool. Liverpool claimed to have trouble understanding Coleridge's argument, but in the event managed to sum it up very succinctly:

> the object of his [Coleridge's] writings has been to rescue speculative philosophy from false principles of reasoning, and to place it on that basis, or give it that tendency, which would make it best suited to the interests of religion as well as of the State.[6]

The date of Coleridge's letter (28 July 1817) and the mention in it of accompanying copies of his works suggests that Liverpool was the recipient of the two 'Lay Sermons'. These pamphlets represented Coleridge's most elaborate contributions to the debate about the causes of, and cures for, the present crisis. They were addressed to the 'Higher' and 'Higher and Middle' classes respectively, and presented two different, although related, sets of arguments. The first, *The Statesmen's Manual*, was intended to encourage the upper classes to inform their actions by a 'philosophy of history' derived from reading the Bible in 'the spirit of prophecy'.[7] Coleridge claimed that this would provide a valuable corrective to the dangerous shallowness of much contemporary analysis and argument, but his detailed treatment of these was reserved for *A Lay Sermon*. In that work, he provided an account of the root of the present difficulties that hinged on the need to develop a perspective on property that reflected the requirement that individuals be treated as *persons* rather than *things*. Coleridge's position emerged from his critical treatment of three groups whose actions and ideas were thought to have contributed to the crisis. Specific targets were the proponents of the science of political economy, popular parliamentary reformers and agitators, and irresponsible members of the landholding classes.

I THE 'REPUTED MASTERS OF POLITICAL ECONOMY'[8]

In the late eighteenth and early nineteenth century, the term 'political economy' had two distinct, although related, meanings. First, it was used to refer to the emerging science associated with Scottish thinkers of the mid eighteenth century. Secondly, it described a perspective that stressed the general benefits that flowed from the increasing prominence of a commercial order in politics, and a commercial ethos in social relations. In this second sense, political economy was most commonly associated with the Whig regimes of the eighteenth century.[9] We have seen that, although Coleridge had originally been strongly opposed to commerce, he later adopted a far more sanguine perspective on its social and political benefits. This position was refined somewhat in the post-war period, but was not abandoned.

Coleridge did, however, adopt a most critical view of political economy as a discipline. His critical remarks about its character and implications were directed against a diverse and never clearly specified group, which embraced eighteenth-century Scotsmen such as Adam Smith and Sir James Steuart, French physiocrats, and English contemporaries such as Thomas Malthus. Coleridge regarded the *Edinburgh Review* as the public standard-bearer of both forms of political economy, a view that corresponded with the aspirations of the editor and promoters of that journal.[10] He argued that the discipline of political economy was intellectually flawed and morally pernicious. The first judgement focused on what Coleridge understood as the methodological basis of the new science, while the second dealt with its effect on contemporary political argument and activity, and particularly on the relationship between property and moral and political personality.

Coleridge's critique of the methodological presuppositions of political economy rested on an epistemological argument. He claimed that political economists never advanced beyond an abstract treatment of their subject. Political economy 'is a science which begins with *abstractions*, in order to exclude whatever is not subject to a technical calculation', but it then proceeds to assume these 'as the *whole* of human nature'.[11] In his 'Essays on the

Principles of Method' (1816), Coleridge stressed the importance of relational determinants of scientific knowledge. Law-like statements depended on the capacity of the thinking subject to consider a particular object in relation to other objects: 'in whatever science the relation of the parts to each other and to the whole is predetermined by a truth originating in the *mind*, and not abstracted or generalised from observation of the parts, there we affirm the presence of a *law*'.[12] The 'laws' of political economy failed to satisfy these conditions, since they abstracted and generalised from parts of human experience, and therefore political economy could not lay claim to the status of a science.

In *The Statesman's Manual*, Coleridge highlighted the methodological shortcomings of modern political economy by pointing to the fuller, more relationally informed ideas found in the Bible. In the Scriptures, political economy was generated by

> living *educts* of the Imagination; of that reconciling and mediatary power, which incorporating the Reason in Images of the Sense, and organizing (as it were) the flux of the Senses by the permanence and self-circling energies of the Reason, gives birth to a system of symbols, harmonious in themselves, and consubstantial with the truths, of which they are the *conductors*.

Modern political economy was, by contrast, merely the *'product* of an unenlivened generalizing Understanding.'[13] It started from an abstract conception of human relations, one that only took account of individuals in so far as they were driven by the need to produce and exchange goods. The Bible, however, gave men access to 'signs' or 'symbols' which represented revealed truths in forms that could be grasped and acted upon by human beings.[14] The ideas found there were relational in a double sense. In the first place, they represented the word of God, and thus partook of his complete capacity for seeing things in relation to all other objects. This capacity was, of course, only possessed completely by God, but the revealed word found in the Bible gave men easier and more complete access to it than could be hoped for from any other source. In addition, however, the Scriptures were part of an interpretative tradition that formed a complete historical entity and gave a meaning and significance to the present that extended far beyond the narrowly based abstractions that were the stock-in-trade of the political economists:

The truths and the symbols . . . move in conjunction and form the living chariot that bears up (for *us*) the throne of the Divine Humanity. Hence, by a derivative, indeed, but not a divided, influence . . . the Sacred Book is worthily intitled *the* WORD OF GOD. Hence too, its contents present to us the stream of time continuous as Life and a symbol of Eternity, inasmuch as the Past and Future are virtually contained in the Present.[15]

The methodological weaknesses of political economy seriously compromised its claims to be a science. They also, however, generated a one-sided and pernicious view of mankind and adversely effected its practical prescriptions. Political economy concerned itself with *'immediate utility'*; it focused on the analysis and 'gratification of the wants and appetites' of the animal parts of human nature.[16] One consequence of this was that political economists failed to understand an institution such as property that, while it had some obvious connection with physical wants, also had ethical significance. Rights in material objects were a requirement of men's ethical status, not merely a reflection of material necessity. Property rights recognised 'the spheres and necessary conditions of free agency. But free agency contains the idea of the free will; and in this . . . [man] intuitively knows the sublimity, and the infinite hopes, fears, and capabilities of his own nature.'[17]

It followed that the political significance of property could not be explained by reference to either physical necessity or mere power since these were not distinctively human attributes. 'High birth and property' were politically important because they were associated with 'moral discipline, the habits, attainments, and directing motives'.[18] These were moral qualities, and could not be reduced to material causes.

The political economists debased property by ignoring its connection with moral agency, and then compounded the error by using this abstract conception in ways that depreciated human, and hence moral, personality. The 'Lay Sermons' and Coleridge's other writings from the same period point to numerous examples of this tendency. One such appeared in a critique of Adam Smith's claim that economic forces tend to a state of equilibrium.[19] Coleridge argued that, although Smith's analysis could be applied to prices or to factors of production, it should not be used to disguise the effect of market movements on human beings:

Persons are not *Things*. . . . Man does not find his level. . . . After a hard and calamitous season . . . go, ask the overseer, and question the parish doctor, whether the workman's health or temperance with the staid and respectful Manners best taught by the inward dignity of self-conscious self-support, have found *their* level again!

Human worth was dependent upon men's moral status, and could not be reduced to a material value, or traded off against it.[20]

Coleridge's concern with the human values attached to activities and conditions that the political economists treated in purely material terms appeared most forcefully in his support for Sir Robert Peel's Bill of 1818 limiting the hours of juvenile labour in cotton factories. This Bill (finally passed into law early in 1819) had begun its long journey to the statute book in 1815. The issue had been the subject of an inquiry by a parliamentary committee in 1816, and Peel's Bill of 1818 was a less drastic version of the original proposal of 1815. It applied only to cotton mills and factories, set a twelve-and-a-half-hour maximum to the working day (while legislating for breaks that reduced the time of actual labour to eleven hours), and established limited inspection and enforcement machinery. Those who opposed the Bill rested their case on the effects of such legislation on Britain's competitive position, the danger of coming between parents and their children, the evils of state interference in free labour, and claims that the employment of children under prevailing conditions was beneficial, even pleasurable, for those involved.[21]

When Peel's modified Bill came before Parliament in April and May 1818, Coleridge became actively involved in a campaign to generate support for it. He claimed that the conditions of child labour in the manufacturing industries involved 'Soul-murder and Infanticide on the Part of the Rich, and Self-slaughter on that of the Poor'. The arguments of those who opposed Peel's Bill showed that political economy involved an 'utter contempt of all that distinguishes or rather forms the chasm, the *diversity* in *kind*, between man & beast'.[22] Coleridge was especially critical of opposition to the Bill that rested on the political economists' favourite shibboleth of 'free labour'. In an ironic letter published in *The Courier*, the benefits of free labour were identified with 'national prosperity' and constitutional stability, and were held to override claims for legislation based on 'cases of mere humanity'.[23]

In the same letter, Coleridge referred to an argument against the Bill which he privately regarded as quite strong – namely, that legislative action had a tendency to override ameliorative measures initiated by the voluntary actions of benevolent cotton masters. Coleridge's, point, however, as in his unfavourable response to animal-protection legislation,[24] was a moral one. People had to choose not between abstract freedom and legislative control, but between such control and the freely arrived-at, and voluntarily acted-upon, awareness of the moral claims of humanity.

Coleridge's longstanding antipathy to Malthus's theories highlighted his rejection of the moral implications of political economy. On a number of technical economic questions, Coleridge's views were not dissimilar to those of Malthus, but he considered that the general tendency of Malthus's work exemplified the abstract, dehumanising features of the discipline of political economy. For example, Coleridge claimed that Malthus's population theory assumed a bestial view of human nature: physical restraints on population were a necessary part of Malthus's theory only because he disregarded self-discipline and moral sensibility. Malthusianism tended to rob the ideas of 'vice' and 'virtue' of any distinct meaning, or turned moral argument on its head.[25] In *The Friend*, for example, Coleridge had claimed that Malthus taught that 'he who would prevent the Poor from rotting away in disease, misery, and wickedness, is an Enemy to his Country'.[26] This was a grossly unfair and inadequate interpretation of Malthus's theories,[27] but it was significant because it showed that Coleridge regarded Malthusianism as an economic manifestation of the 'fanatical antinomianism' which tainted the moral philosophy of Paley, and had become enshrined in the pages of the *Edinburgh Review*.[28]

It is important to bear in mind, however, that Coleridge's critique of political economy was restricted to an assault on the methodological premises of classical economics, and on some of the practical results of the new science. In criticising 'political economy' in this narrow and specific sense, he was not rejecting the more diffuse, but equally important, perspective to which the term had been applied before the rise of the discipline of classical economics. Nor was he unconditionally condemning the forms of commercial and financial activities that were central to 'political economy' in both the narrower and the wider senses. Although Coleridge criticised the 'reputed masters' of the dismal science, he reiterated his previously stated views on the real and positive benefits of commercial activity. He defended the speculative activities of traders on the grounds that rises in prices helped to conserve provisions in times of scarcity, described public credit as the 'vital air of national industry', and pointed to the real gains resulting from the increasing importance of commercial activity and the spirit which generated it: 'the largest proportion of our actual freedom . . . and at least as large a share of our virtues as our vices' were directly attributable to its influence.[29]

Coleridge's marginalia on Fichte underline the importance of distinguishing between his views of political economy in the narrower and broader senses. In comments on *Der geschlossne Handelsstaat* (1800), Coleridge objected to precisely those parts of Fichte's analysis which disregarded the benefits of commercial activity. He deplored Fichte's 'boorish inacquaintance with contemporary Statistics', was critical of his failure to discern the role that free acquisition played in encouraging production, and ridiculed his attempt to distinguish use rights from exclusive possession. Fichte's 'dream' that states could develop in isolation from their neighbours – a response to the view that international trade and intercourse assisted both domestic development and international co-operation – was likely to produce tyranny rather than freedom. 'Of all the silly Dreams . . . this is the silliest – as repulsive to the Imagination as it is absurd to the Reason.' Fichte would have made a 'more pernicious & despicable Tyrant than Caligula or Eliogabalus'.[30]

While Coleridge's criticised the discipline of political economy, he appreciated the benefits of commercial activity, with respect both to its material improvements and to its contribution to the development of social and political freedom. His critique of the science of political economy was not part of a general rejection of market relationships as such, or of the sort of social and political structures they made possible. Indeed, Coleridge's acceptance of commercialism distinguished his position from that taken by many popular proponents of political and social reform, and provided an important element in his critique of contemporary radicalism.

II RADICAL REFORM: NEW JACOBINS AND OLD DEMAGOGUES

Coleridge's remarks on the forces of radical reform in the post-war period and just before assumed a distinction between subterranean lower-class discontent on the one hand, and a more open agitation for economic and political reform (led by politicians and journalists such as Sir Francis Burdett and William Cobbett) on the other. He portrayed lower-class activity as a manifestation of a new form of Jacobinism that was even more dangerous than that of the 1790s. Then, 'the heat, enthusiasm, and temerity of visionary youth; and even the audacious cowardice of mobs . . . were but the infant noises of Jacobinism'.[31] Now, it existed in the less visible but more threatening guise of working-class combinations, secret societies and other groups held together by secret oaths and fears of retaliation. These groups constituted what Coleridge called an *'unnatural* State' of society, unnatural because they created social bonds that rested on the tyranny of the group over the individual:

> Shut up in a labyrinthine prison of forms and bye-laws, of engagements by oath and contributions by compulsion, they move in slavish files beneath a jealous and ever-neighbouring control, which despotises in detail; in which every man is made his brother's keeper; and which arming the hand and fixing the eye of all against each, merges the free-will of the individual in the merciless tyranny of the confederation.[32]

This chilling picture of conspiratorial politics represented working-class organisations as false forms of particularisation. They isolated individuals from wider and less intrusive networks of social control and deferential relationships, and restricted rather than enlarged the scope for moral action. Working-class activism exhibited the 'bestial passions, with brute force and terrorism' that was one of the distinguishing marks of 'Jacobinism'.[33] Like Hamlet's ghost, the members of extreme working-class organisations moved and mined 'in the underground chambers with an activity the more dangerous because the less noisy'.[34] However, the more overt manifestations of the Jacobin spirit were found in the utterances of radical publicists and politicians who attempted to harness popular distress to their causes.

Coleridge's treatment of the proponents of radical reform was liberally spiced with allusions to their unlearned, profligate characters and the unsavoury nature of their personal and financial affairs.[35] These remarks were intended to undermine the credibility of the radical leaders, and were indistinguishable from the muck-raking journalism that Coleridge elsewhere condemned.[36]

However, his critical references to the reformers' characters reflected his belief that the state was a moral entity dependent upon the moral qualities of its members.[37] This placed a premium on the moral character of individuals and made the personal failings of the reformers of some importance since they would inflict their moral shortcomings on the state.[38]

In a *Courier* article, Coleridge portrayed the radicals' *modus operandi* in a burlesque on Rousseau's general will. The reformers made no attempt to put forward a definite programme, but pretended that this would be generated by mass meetings of the populace: 'let them only be close packed together, like hay in a rick, and a little *wetted*, and they will be sure to *illuminate* the whole country'.[39] Unable or unwilling to advance positive proposals, the radicals grasped at any opportunity which seemed to provide scope for inflaming the passions of the lower classes. They traded on prevalent distress and discontent, and sought to heighten the degradation of the poor in order to use popular misery for their own ends. In so doing, they threatened to fatally weaken the social fabric of the country:

> every principle, every feeling, that binds the citizen to his country, the spirit to its Creator, is in danger of being undermined. – Not by reasoning, for from that there is no danger; but – by the mere habit of hearing them reviled and scoffed at with impunity.[40]

The agitators' manipulative attitude towards the lower classes suggested a degree of indifference to their moral well-being that matched the gloomy fatalism of such political economists as Malthus – 'the Cobbetts & Hunts address . . . the lower Ranks . . . as Beasts who have no future Selves – as if by natural necessity you must *all* for ever remain poor & slaving'[41] – but there was a crucial difference between them. The political economists used a shallow, inadequate methodological apparatus, and a corrupt moral standpoint to encourage a perspective on popular distress that was marked by rigid, insensitive and complacent support for commercialism. The radicals, on the other hand, propagated ideas about the causes of popular distress which were based on 'vindictive and discontented fancies'[42] which were hostile to the very existence of commercial society. In attacking the leaders of the movement for popular reform, Coleridge was particularly concerned to discredit economic doctrines that attributed hardship to features of modern life that were essential to the existence of a viable, beneficial commercial economy.

The focal points of radical argument were the rate and incidence of taxation, and the size of government revenues. It was argued that taxation placed an excessive burden on the nation and significantly diminished the amount of capital available for productive investment. The capacity of the government to raise large sums of money was also politically and constitutionally dangerous. William Cobbett, for example, using a line of argument that had been the stock-in-trade of Country Party opposition politicians in the eighteenth century, argued that high levels of taxation gave governments the capacity to corrupt representative institutions, weakened the political influence of landed property, and raised the spectre of executives dominated by pensioners, stock-jobbers and government contractors.[43] These were old arguments, but in the post-war years claims about the harmful economic and political effects of high levels of taxation were sometimes combined with a broadly based critique of both the disciplinary and generic notions of political economy. Cobbett is a case in point. He identified the idea that 'taxes do no harm in the end; that if they be taken out of the pocket of one man they are put in the pocket of another' with that 'race of political economists, bred at Edinburgh and at Oxford'.[44] A corollary of the radical view of the economic and political effects of taxation was that both economic hardship and political corruption could be eliminated, or at least curtailed, by a policy of retrenchment.

In *A Lay Sermon*, Coleridge dealt with the argument that taxation reduced the sum total of wealth by restating arguments that had appeared in the first version of *The Friend*.[45] He argued that, so long as taxes did not outstrip the level of productivity, and provided that the receipts of government were dispersed throughout the community, the prosperity of the nation was not adversely affected by taxation. Indeed, it may benefit from the stimulating effect

> given to the circulation itself by the reproductive action of all larger capitals, and through the check which taxation, in its own nature, gives to the indolence of the wealthy in its continual transfer of property to the industrious and enterprizing.[46]

Coleridge claimed that retrenchment would only aggravate problems that were primarily due to the contraction of demand, and to the expansion of the labour force resulting from the cessation of hostilities and the revival of the economies of the European countries.[47]

This defence of taxation was only one of Coleridge's responses to the radicals' analysis of factors contributing to post-war distress. He also argued that tithes did not detract from the total of agricultural production or necessarily hinder the process of redistribution. They divided the product in a particular way at one stage of the distributive process, but it still remained available for recirculation in much the same way as revenue from taxation.[48] Coleridge was equally dismissive of radical attacks on the system of credit, on the use of machinery in manufacturing industries, and on the self-interested, but socially beneficial, activities of trading capitalists whose forestalling provided a mechanism for regulating the supply of good in times of scarcity.[49]

Much of the rhetorical force of Coleridge's case against the radicals rested on his imputation of sinister motives,[50] but the basis of his critique was the alleged weaknesses of their economic analysis of the causes of post-war distress. In arguing this part of his case, Coleridge mounted a defence of policies and practices – taxation, pensions and public credit – that were key elements in a social and political structure that looked beyond the nostalgic agrarianism represented by writers such as Cobbett. When attacking the radicals, Coleridge played the role of a defender of commercial society and of its political ramifications. However, unlike the *Edinburgh* reviewers, he did not wish to see traditional and commercial elites integrated with one another, nor did he think that traditional values should disappear.[51] On the contrary, he argued that the 'true seat' of existing distress lay in the failure to modify commercialism by practices and perceptions that had a close social and ideological affinity with the traditional social structure.[52] That failure was in large part due to the behaviour and outlook of traditional elites. An important share of responsibility for the present crisis had therefore to be borne by the upper classes, since they had helped to create an environment in which radical agitation could flourish.

III   JACOBINISM'S 'QUALITY COUSIN'

In the years after 1811, Coleridge's attitude towards the landed classes became increasingly hostile. This did not mean that he had any doubts about the social and political importance of the gentry, but resulted from his assessment of their willingness to fulfil their proper social and political functions. A clear sign of Coleridge's critical view of the behaviour of the landed classes appeared in a letter to Daniel Stuart written early in 1817. In this letter, Coleridge explained to Stuart that a Jacobin mentality was not restricted to the lower classes or to radical agitators:

> as far . . . as the mersion of derivative, official and representative Duties, Powers, and Privileges in *personal* rights is one of the principle ingredients in Jacobinism, the unconscious *Jacobinism* of our Gentry is the other Half. As Jacobinism properly so called is a mule-monster . . . composed of 1. abstract reason and 2. bestial passions, with brute force and terrorism; so is this *Quality Cousin* of Jacobinism made up of sickly fastidious refinement . . . and of the self-degrading application to themselves of the Jew Principle – Mayn't I do what I like with my own?[53]

In the past Coleridge had often voiced doubts about the upper classes' commitment to the role prescribed for them by their possession of landed property and political power.[54] However, his remarks to Stuart were directly related to what he saw as a marked tendency for members of the upper classes to use their political influence in order to secure the passage of legislation that passed on the cost of adjusting to economic changes to other, less powerful members of the community. The gentry's conduct was particularly transparent in the bullion controversy of 1811, and in the debates over the Corn Law at the end of the war.

Serious doubts about the depreciation of paper money issued by the Bank of England had first begun to emerge in 1809. By 1811 a growing lobby of 'bullionists' wished to deflate the economy through a return to cash payments, even if that seriously affected the government's capacity to continue the war. One particular stage of the controversy came to an end on 15 May 1811 when the bullionists were defeated in the Commons, but the issue continued to be hotly debated until cash payments were finally renewed in early 1820.[55]

Coleridge wrote a number of *Courier* articles bearing on the bullion controversy, the main point of which was to expose the inadequate basis upon which both sides rested their cases.[56] Many of his comments were of a technical nature, but one incident in the crisis led him to make some general observations on the upper classes' abuse of their political position. In June, Lord King, a leading bullionist, had stipulated that his tenants should pay their rent either in gold or in paper money at a discounted rate. In an article published in support of a government Bill that made banknotes legal tender (and thus stopped King's stratagem from being widely copied), Coleridge not only attacked King's arguments about the depreciation of paper money, but also criticised his attempt to place his own interest and that of his family above that of the nation. King's action was based on the quite erroneous idea that individuals had unlimited rights over their property. It showed that while King 'may be a good father . . . he is . . . a bad subject' and an irresponsible legislator.[57]

Coleridge thought that King's conduct over the bullion issue indicated that the gentry were willing to use their legislative position to further their own interests, but he regarded the Corn Law crisis as a more far-reaching and significant example of the same tendency. The Corn Law of 1815 was designed to protect domestic producers by prohibiting the importation of corn when the domestic price fell below 80 shillings per quarter; it replaced an act of 1804 that had been inoperative for long periods because of the effects of the wartime blockade and inflation. The 1804 Act had, however, come into operation after the bumper harvest of 1813, when producers began to suffer as a result of overproduction. The new Act came at the end of an agitation that had started in 1813, and gathered momentum as the return to peace opened up British markets to foreign (largely Baltic) producers.[58] Although the government's willingness to bow to protectionist demands was actually based on the view that the Corn Law was a temporary expedient that would facilitate a transition to an economic environment where farmers could reap the benefits of extensive sales and not have to depend on high prices, the Law was widely considered as a triumph for the landed classes.[59] One historian has described it as one of 'the most naked pieces of class legislation in English history',[60] a view that would most certainly have been endorsed by Coleridge.

On 23 May 1814, Coleridge described the gentry's representatives in Parliament as 'mad or ideotic' and the Corn Law debates as 'more disgraceful than even the Bullion',[61] and in March 1815 he spoke against the Bill at a public meeting in Calne in Wiltshire. Coleridge's warm reception by the crowd – 'Loud were the

Huzzas! – and if it depended on the Inhabitants at large, I believe they would send me up to Parliament'[62] – was probably due to strongly worded criticism of the landed classes. As he told a correspondent,

> the more I examine the measure, the more indignant do I become at its Injustice & Cruelty, the more astonished at the absurdity and self-contradiction of the arguments advanced in it's behalf . . . in my conscience I hold the new Bill . . . [no] more or less than the Commutation of the War & Property Taxes for a Poll-Tax . . . not proportioned, as the Property Tax in some measure was, to the ability of the Payer, but pressing heavier, the lower it descend – so that the poorest pay the most. . . .[63]

He speculated that, because the landed gentry had shown themselves to be 'Calculating Legislators' making laws in their own interest parliamentary reform was inevitable.

These criticisms depended on the assumption that, while property gave political power to its possessors, it also laid duties upon them which should govern the way their power was used. The Corn Law debates showed that the landed gentry were quite prepared to abuse their position and neglect their duties. Three years later, during a debate over the regulation of juvenile labour, Coleridge castigated the landed classes for devoting themselves to the pursuit of their own interests. In what was probably a reference to the Earl of Lauderdale ('that *Scotch* Coxcomb, the plebeian Earl of Lauderdale'[64]), who had been a prominent supporter of protectionism in 1815 but was an equally staunch opponent of factory legislation in 1818–19,[65] Coleridge accused the upper classes of mixing doctrines drawn from political economy with arguments of a more traditional kind:

> Whenever it suits the interests of the Rich, i.e. their imaginary Interests, not as men, but as Rich, they can then discover that . . . [political economy] is, like Geometry, an abstract science, from which in practice all sorts of deviations must be allowed . . . , thus they find it most easy to justify a commercial *Minimum* in the products of their own Estates; but when Morals, Health, Humanity, plead – O they are then inviolable Truths – Free Labour must not be interfered with &c.[66]

However, while Coleridge clearly disliked the hypocrisy and self-seeking that lay behind the grossly inconsistent arguments of those who supported both the Corn law and a free market in labour, his opposition to the former was not part of a general rejection of a social structure based upon a strong landed interest. On the contrary, he attacked the Corn Law because of the damage it did to the cause of landed property. He therefore took a quite different view to that of both *Edinburgh* reviewers and radicals who wished to weaken aristocratic and landed influence and saw protectionism as a way of shoring it up and artificially strengthening its position *vis-à-vis* the commercial and manufacturing interests.[67] But, unlike many supporters of the landed interest, who argued that the Corn Law was necessary to preserve the material basis of paternalistic, deferentially structured rural communities, Coleridge seems to have thought at this time that protectionism was neither economically necessary nor morally justifiable.[68] The debate on the 1815 Corn Law was not really about the economics of farming, but about the upper classes' use of their political position in ways that were incompatible with the basis of the social structure and the rationale of their position in it.

IV LANDED PROPERTY AND THE 'COMMERCIAL SPIRIT'

In *A Lay Sermon* Coleridge argued that the landowners' selfish conduct over the Corn Law could be traced to a general cause that undermined the basis of the society upon which their position depended. The landed classes were increasingly being influenced by 'the spirit of commerce'; this tendency was the most significant factor exacerbating the difficulties generated by the post-war downturn in trade. The 'true seat and sources' of the 'existing distresses' were 'resolvable into the OVERBALANCE OF THE COMMERCIAL SPIRIT IN CONSEQUENCE OF THE ABSENCE OR WEAKNESS OF THE COUNTER-WEIGHTS'.[69] Coleridge thought that an 'overbalance' was displayed to some degree in the commercial world itself, especially in its marked propensity for reckless speculation based on unsound credit, and the socially dislocating cycles of booms and busts that resulted from it. However, those practices, and the instrumental view of humanity that characterised commercial activity, were unavoidable features of a system that produced many benefits. What Coleridge objected to were the generalised effects of commerce on people's perceptions of one another, and of the true value of economic activity.[70]

Coleridge's critical remarks on the moral effects of commerce prefaced his consideration of the basis and the language of the political economists, and he obviously considered that the two issues were closely related. Although he was aware of the advantages of a commercial society, Coleridge had reservations about its moral implications. In particular, he strongly resisted the argument that commerce was capable of generating satisfactory moral and cultural discipline and advancement. In the 'Lay Sermons' Coleridge argued that commercial society overlooked important moral values, but he insisted that the real issue was not the strength of the commercial interest as such, but its strength in relation to counteracting tendencies. In the past, the growth of commerce had not produced an overbearing intrusion of the commercial spirit into non-commercial relationships, because a satisfactory balance had been struck with other social and moral forces. For example, the 1688 Revolution had produced a 'providential counterpoise' between the commercial and the landed interests. It was

> not more propelled by the spirit of enterprize and hazard in our commercial towns, than held in check by the characteristic VIS INERTIAE of the peasantry and landholders; both parties cooled and lessened by the equal failure of the destruction, and restoration, of monarchy.[71]

The growth of the commercial interest since the Glorious Revolution need not have upset the balance, and, indeed, Coleridge did not claim that the landed interest had been swamped by the superior weight of numbers and resources of the commercial interest. The real danger (well represented by the 'Quality cousins of Jacobinism') was that the landed interest would be undermined internally – that is, by its members' adoption of the ethos of commerce.

Coleridge's remarks on the Corn Law and on factory legislation included accusations that the landed classes resorted to commercial arguments when dealing with issues that were of great significance for the welfare of the lower classes. He thought that the same attitude was apparent in the gentry's management of their estates, and particularly in their relationships with their tenants and labourers. When discussing the 'natural counterforces' to commerce, Coleridge reiterated earlier statements about the role played by ideas of nobility as a 'counterpoise to the grosser superstition for wealth', and complained that 'ancient feelings of rank and ancestry' were revered less than in former times.[72] He argued that these ideas were being undermined by the landed classes' adoption of an ethos to which their social position, their upbringing, their *mores* and their possessions were supposed to provide an effective counterweight. This development was directly relevant to the present crisis because the growing commercialisation of agriculture was undercutting the deference networks upon which the landed classes' social pre-eminence and social usefulness depended.

The treatment of agriculture in *A Lay Sermon* involved a partial return to the agrarian ideal that Coleridge had seemed to reject in *The Friend*.[73] This was particularly apparent in his remarks on the impact of the Highland Clearances, which had greatly increased pastoral farming at the cost of crofting. Coleridge thought that the conduct of Scottish landowners showed them pursuing commercial gain in disregard of their moral responsibilities. By giving their sheep precedence over their tenants, the lairds had destroyed the bonds between themselves and their social inferiors. To illustrate this claim, Coleridge recounted a conversation with a Highlander about the decay of the Highlands as military centres. In the past, lairds had no difficulty in raising troops from among their peasantry. They were able, in effect, to maintain a military force that, quite literally, lived off their estates. But, by destroying the peasant basis of the traditional social structure, 'improving' landlords had undercut their standing as military leaders able to contribute to the defence of the commonwealth. 'Once', Coleridge reported a Highlander as saying, 'a Laird needed but have whistled, and a hundred brave lads would have made a wall of flame around him with the flash of their broad-swords! Now . . . let him whistle to his sheep and see if *they* will fight for him!'[74]

Since connections between military capacity and certain socio-economic structures were common themes in eighteenth-century social and political thought, Coleridge's use of a military example of the implications of commercialisation was probably not accidental. Adam Ferguson, to whom Coleridge referred in a contemporary notebook entry, had argued that commercialism weakened social affections and had drawn a contrast between commercial societies and the 'rude' 'unpolished', but socially cohesive and militarily effective communities found in such places as the

Scottish Highlands.[75] In any case, Coleridge's anecdote underlined his ambivalent attitude to some of the implications of commerce, particularly those that encouraged the landed classes to manage their estates in ways that unbalanced one of the crucial counterweights of the commercial spirit. He maintained that both the privileges and responsibilities of landholders were related to agriculture's special status in the state, and claimed that the purposes of agricultural activity were essentially the same as those of the state because they were necessary to its 'continuance and independence'.[76] The links between the ends of state and the landed interest were historical, logical and experiential.

The historical connection was reflected in the differing patterns of tenure for fixed, as opposed to moveable, property, and in the maxims of 'ancient prudence'.[77] Furthermore, the special character of agricultural activity was a logical requirement of social order within an unequal society. If agriculture was required to balance trade, then its ends must be the same as those to which the perfection of the balance was a means – namely the material, religious and moral well-being of the entire community.[78] Finally, the experience of late republican Rome and Napoleonic France proved that an independent landed interest played an important role in fostering the traditional, deferential relationships which were a requirement for orderly freedom in an unequal commonwealth.[79]

Coleridge's identification of the ends of agriculture with the ends of the state meant that landed property existed for, and had its justification in, the moral purposes which the state helped to realise. Property rights had originally only been recognised in moveable objects, and had been the more perfect the more mobile the object;[80] even now, the moral basis of property rights in land meant that they were conditional, not absolute. Property was a trust, 'with duties to be performed, in the sight of God and . . . Country',[81] and these duties related primarily to the fulfilment of the ends of the state. Coleridge's statement of these ends was similar to that which had appeared in *The Friend*. The state existed

> 1 To make the means of subsistence more easy to each individual. 2 To secure to each of its members THE HOPE of bettering his own condition or that of his children. 3 The development of those faculties which are essential to his Humanity, i.e. to his rational and moral Being.[82]

Since the ends of the state were moral, they embraced individuals as ends not means, as persons not things, and this applied also to that property which existed for the sake of the state's ends. The special character of landed property meant that it possessed a moral dimension that differed from the maxims that governed commerce:

> The personal worth of those, whom I benefit . . . or whether the persons are really benefited or no, is of no concern of mine. . . . To introduce any other principle in Trade, but that of obtaining the highest price with adequate security for Articles fairly described, would be tantamount to the position, that Trade ought not to exist.[83]

Coleridge's account of the ends of the state had important implications for his view of the way that land should be used. He argued that landowners were not to treat their estates in the same way as they would commercial property. On the contrary, they should regard the economic exploitation of their land as a 'subordinate consideration to the living and moral growth that is to remain on the land. I mean, a healthful, callous-handed but high- and warm-hearted Tenantry, twice the number of the present landless, parish-paid Laborers.'[84]

A practical reflection of Coleridge's concern with the moral responsibilities of landholders was his favourable response to the suggestion that smallholdings should be provided for farm labourers. This suggestion had been made by the Earl of Winchelsea in a communication to the Board of Agriculture,[85] and Coleridge endorsed it because it provided a way of realising moral goals in a direct fashion, not, as was the case with commerce, as an accidental result of individuals' pursuit of their self-interest. Coleridge may also have thought that Winchelsea's scheme had the additional advantage of weakening one of the gentry's incentives for commercialising their estates.[86] Winchelsea's steward claimed that labourers who possessed their own land lived at a higher standard than their landless counterparts, and lowered the cost of labour by their improved productivity. This made it possible for the gentry to retain the outward trappings of their social pre-eminence without undermining its moral basis. A further benefit was that labourers with their own plots of land were less dependent on Poor Law authorities than the landless, and that, in parishes where there were a significant number of peasant labourers, poor rates tended to be significantly lower than elsewhere. Coleridge was alarmed at the pauperisation of the lower classes and looked to the gentry to satisfy their claims to be able to maintain themselves, not to turn them into 'Neopolitan Lazzaroni'.[87] In general, then, Winchelsea's scheme made the moral and material interests of the landed classes coincide. While fulfilling their moral duty by supporting those 'rounds in the social ladder'[88] which were important to the continued existence of deference networks, members of the landed classes could also maintain the material basis of their position. In other words, a resort to commercialism was both harmful and unnecessary.

Although most of what Coleridge wrote in *A Lay Sermon* about counterbalances to the spirit of commerce focused on forces external to it, he also complained that the 'overbalance' occurred within the commercial world itself.[89] However, given his conception of commerce as an activity which necessarily ignored the distinction between things and persons,[90] it is difficult to conceive of counterbalancing forces within the sphere of commerce that would not undercut its rationale and reduce its beneficial effects. The fact that Coleridge never came to grips with this problem meant that his theory was only applicable to a society which retained a significant body of landholders and was not wholly or largely commercial. Indeed, he virtually admitted this when he claimed that a tempering of the commercial spirit would only be possible within a society that possessed a complex network of countervailing forces, some of which would be brought to bear on those engaged in commerce. Presumably these forces would moderate commercial behaviour without adversely affecting its beneficial tendencies. At any given time, an assessment of whether the spirit of commerce was assuming alarming proportions necessitated a fine, comparative judgement. It was a matter of

> relative, rather than positive determination; . . . it depends on the degree in which it is aided or resisted by all the other tendencies that co-exist with it; and that in the best of times this spirit may be said to live on a narrow isthmus between a sterile desert and a stormy sea, still threatened and encroached on either side by the Too Much or the Too Little.[91]

Although Coleridge regarded the counterbalancing of the commercial spirit as necessary to the pursuit of the moral ends of the state, he did not support the direct use of coercive state powers in order to achieve this. He objected to attempts to use legislation to force landlords to perform their duty, and, except where those affected were not free agents, he does not appear to have favoured the uninvited involvement of the state in the commercial and manufacturing sectors. While he thus supported the regulation of juvenile labour, he claimed that, in general, manufacturers 'must *consent* to regulations'.[92] In a letter written in the year in which Peel's Bill became law, Coleridge described the spirit of '*Volunteership*' as one condition of the 'practicability' of our *wonderous* Constitution',[93] but it is clear that the stress upon a voluntary acceptance of responsibility in *A Lay Sermon* was an issue as much of principle as of practicality. The principle involved was not that of *laissez-faire*, but derived from Coleridge's conception of the moral basis of property.

If landlords were subject to close supervision and interference they would tend to become stewards of the public rather than trustees. Coleridge associated the former conception with views being propagated by the Spencean socialists,[94] and objected to it because it was incompatible with the requirements of morality, and contrary to the justification of property as necessary to free and, hence, moral agency:

> All Reform or Innovation, not won from the free Agent by the presentation of juster Views and nobler Interests, and that does not leave the merit of having effected it sacred to the individual proprietor, it were folly to propose, and worse than folly to attempt. Madmen only would dream of digging or blowing up the foundation of a House in order to employ the materials in repairing the walls.[95]

Because he was opposed to counterbalancing the commercial spirit by forces supplied directly by the state, Coleridge was left with the problem of identifying counterweights that were compatible with free agency. He argued that these could be provided by education and religion.

V THE SPIRITUALISED INTELLECT AND THE SPIRIT OF COMMERCE: EDUCATION AND RELIGION IN THE 'LAY SERMONS'

In the 'Lay Sermons' Coleridge's remarks on education dealt largely with upper-class enlightenment, although it was understood that one of the consequences of that would be a willingness to take responsibility for the education of the lower classes. The first 'Lay Sermon', *The Statesman's Manual*, appealed to the upper classes to use the Scriptures as a basic source of the enlightened principles and examples which made Christianity not merely a speculative, but also a practical, religion. The Bible particularised the universal and thus allowed its readers to recognise the universal in particulars and to see how principles applied to given circumstances. It therefore fulfilled the same function as secular works that sought to generate behavioural maxims from general principles. However, the Scriptures were divinely inspired, direct statements of universals, and they combined with this advantage the capacity to strike a chord in the heart which galvanised humans into action; they thereby integrated knowledge and motivation. The

> great PRINCIPLES of our religion, the sublime IDEAS spoken out everywhere in the Old and New Testament, resemble the fixed stars, which appear of the same size to the naked as to the armed eye. . . . At the annunciation of *principles*, of *ideas*, the soul of man awakes, and starts up, as an exile in a far distant land at the unexpected sounds of his native language. . . .[96]

To understand the Bible in this way, and to reap the benefit of those non-biblical, and in some cases non-Christian, writers who generated maxims from universal truths – those 'red letter names even in the almanacks of wordly wisdom': Thucydides, Tacitus, Machiavelli, Bacon and Harrington[97] – required a form of education that Coleridge thought was in serious decline, even among the upper classes.

Coleridge addressed his first 'Lay Sermon' to those from whose 'station and opportunities I may dare anticipate a respectable portion of that *'sound book learnedness'*, into which our old public schools still continue to initiate their pupils',[98] but he seems privately to have thought that such a group was small, shrinking, and by no means corresponded with the upper classes as a whole. In July 1812 he called for a reform of ideas about upper-class education, and three years later he blamed the poor standard of parliamentary debate on 'such Educations as our Gentlemen receive!'[99] The famous and extraordinary letter to Lord Liverpool in July 1817 argued for a connection between political and social dislocation and Lockean philosophy, and made it quite clear that both the lay and clerical members of the upper class would continue to be seduced by it until their education was reformed on the basis of Platonic philosophy. 'As long', Coleridge warned Liverpool,

> as the principles of our Gentry and Clergy are grounded in a false Philosophy, which retains but the name of *Logic*, and has succeeded in rendering Metaphysics a name of opprobrium, all the Sunday and National schools in the world will not preclude Schism in the lower & middle classes.[100]

A craving for novelty,[101] coupled with the belief that the Bible was already familiar, discouraged the study of the Scriptures and the works of the 'red letter names' whom Coleridge regarded as exponents of true, Platonic philosophy, which located the conscious subject at every step in the cognitive process. In *The Friend* Coleridge upheld a Platonic conception of the state and of the relationship between the moral value of individuals and that of the state. In the 'Lay Sermons' he argued that a Platonised Christianity which transcended the realm of sense impression and gave men access to the infinite provided the only escape from a system that was intellectually shallow, theologically barren and politically and socially disastrous. In the preceding century this philosophy and its 'red letter' exponents had been pushed aside by writers such as Hume and Paley whose historical and philosophical works were based on, and addressed to, the understanding and could not enlighten the reason or enliven the soul.[102] To counteract this, Coleridge argued for a revival of 'the austerer studies', principally philosophy and theology. These would put men back in touch with a tradition from which they had been too long divorced, and one result of that would be the development of a more balanced perception of the value of commerce. Such demanding and intellectually absorbing activities would distract attention from the pursuit of wealth. He advanced a similar rationale for intellectualised religions. These served as a 'counter-charm to the sorcery of wealth'.[103] Religion would only serve that function, however, if it had a significant intellectual content; religions of 'feelings and motives' such as Evangelicalism would not do. Despite the piety and sincerity of its adherents and the admirable effects of Evangelical discipline, this religion tended to foster rather than hinder the spirit of commerce. The fact that Evangelicals took 'all truths of spiritual import' for granted, leaving 'the understanding vacant and at leisure for a thorough insight into present and temporal interests' explained their commercial success. But it also showed why Evangelicalism 'neither does or can check or circumscribe the Spirit of Barter'.[104]

The capacity of intellectualised religion and intellectual activity to provide a demanding distraction was, however, only one of the means by which they could counterbalance the commercial spirit. The intellect also opened up spheres of experience that were not dependent upon the senses, and were beyond and above the sort of concerns that dominated the thoughts of those who did depend wholly upon sense impressions: 'in order to tame mankind and introduce a sense of virtue, *the best human means is to exercise their understanding*, to give them a glimpse of a world superior to the sensible; and while they take pains to cherish the animal life, to teach them not to neglect the intellectual'.[105] In Coleridge's usual terminology, the faculty in question here was the reason rather than the understanding; the exercise of rationality gave human beings access to a world that was peculiarly theirs, and allowed them to see that the fruits of the understanding were subordinate to other, distinctly human, values. When the motives and feelings of religion were infused with the power of the intellect, religion moved towards what Coleridge called a 'total act of the soul';[106] this precluded the combination of unquestioning acceptance and mentally vigorous worldliness that was the hallmark of Evangelicalism and other deliberately non-intellectualised religious faiths.

Coleridge therefore coupled the view of philosophy and religion as distractions with a belief in positive potentialities that were integral to these activities. These, he argued, would encourage members of the upper classes to recognise and give full weight to considerations that were not part of the spirit of commerce. In concrete terms, that meant that other human beings should be recognised as religious and moral equals, and treated as ends rather than means. Coleridge clearly hoped that, if such considerations were taken into account, property would be utilised in ways that recognised the humanity of non-property-holders. The moral rationale of property necessarily limited the role of the state in regulating it, but that did not alter the fact that, so far as landed property was concerned, property rights were morally, if not legally, dependent upon the fulfilment of obligations that were directly related to the underlying moral character and justification of the state.

VI CONCLUSION: MORALISM AND INSTITUTIONALISATION

In the 'Lay Sermons' Coleridge argued that the apparent incompatibilities between the moral characteristics of the state and the implications of commerce could be resolved by ensuring that the landed class fulfilled the duties attached to their social position. If this were done, society would be able to reap the benefits of commerce without abandoning the pursuit of those human values which lay at the heart of the state. This required that the upper classes adopt an intellectualised, Platonic form of Christianity in place of Lockean materialism, but it also meant, as the conclusion of *A Lay Sermon* made clear, that they should purify their own characters. This requirement was seen as a necessary preliminary to social amelioration: 'Let us become a better people, and the reform of all the public (real or supposed) grievances, which we use as pegs whereon to hang our own errors and defects, will follow of itself.'[107]

This exhortation, and the more concrete remedies that Coleridge proposed – voluntary regulation of manufactures, popular education, and landholders' fulfilment of their responsibilities – placed the onus upon individual, moral reform. However, while such an assessment corresponds with important themes in the 'Lay Sermons', it would be misleading to regard it as a complete account of the arguments of these works, or as a guide to the position taken by Coleridge in his final work on political theory, *On the Constitution of the Church and State* (1829).[108] The central theme of this work was that moral enlightenment was of such importance that it could not be left to individuals. Of course, given Coleridge's view of the nature of morality, the role of the individual was crucial, and, in any case, the moral quality of the state depended upon that of its members. But individuals needed to be supported and guided by agencies that had a clearly defined role in establishing the basis of the moral perspective that encouraged individuals to recognise, and act in accordance with, the moral potentialities of their fellow humans.

5

Property, Politics and Cultivation: *On the Constitution of the Church and State* (1829)

Late in 1829, Coleridge published his last major work in political philosophy, a small octavo volume bearing the title *On the Constitution of the Church and State, according to the Idea of Each*. A revised version of the book appeared in 1830 together with a piece entitled 'Aids toward a Right Judgement of the Late Catholic Bill'. Coleridge later remarked on the 'deep sense I have of the truth, urgency, and importance of the Principles set out' in the work, and a contemporary reviewer described its author as 'perhaps the most comprehensive thinker of the age'.[1] This work contained Coleridge's fullest statement of a political philosophy, albeit one that was closely related to positions already formulated in *The Friend* and the 'Lay Sermons'. *Church and State* focused on the institutionalisation of social, economic and intellectual forces discussed in the 'Lay Sermons', and utilised arguments about the character and role of the state that had already been sketched in *The Friend*. In discussing these matters, Coleridge offered an account of a constitutional structure that necessarily included not only the organs of government (the executive and the legislature), but also a national church, incorporating the 'accredited, learned, and philosophic Public' he had mentioned in the 'Lay Sermons'.[2] Coleridge's interest in national churches (a term clearly reminiscent of seventeenth-century discussions of church establishments) is apparent at a number of points in his writing, the first positive discussion appearing in the turn-of-the-century correspondence discussed in Chapter 2. But, while the subject matter of *Church and State* had long been of interest to Coleridge, the immediate context of the work, the debate over Catholic Emancipation, is of central importance in understanding both the form of his argument and its significance.

I THE CONTEXT OF *CHURCH AND STATE*: CATHOLIC EMANCIPATION AND THE CHURCH OF ENGLAND

Catholic Emancipation necessitated the repeal of the Test Acts of 1673 and 1678 which required office-holders and members of both Houses of Parliament to take an oath against transubstantiation. When the issue of emancipation was first raised in the 1780s, it had concerned a relatively small number of politically non-threatening English Catholics, but the union with Ireland in 1800, and the abolition of the Irish Parliament, transformed the issue into an aspect of the Irish question.[3] It thus became more contentious, and, as Coleridge himself commented, more intractable.[4] The emancipation issue led to Pitt's departure from office in 1801, and to the fall of the 'Ministry of all Talents' in 1807. The sticking point on both occasions was George III's interpretation of his Coronation oath to uphold 'to the utmost of [his] power the laws of God, the true profession of the Gospel, and the Protestant reformed religion established by law'.[5] In the years that followed, and especially in the 1820s, emancipation became one of the most pressing problems in British politics.[6] A crucial question for those who were not utterly and unconditionally opposed to emancipation was that of 'securities', or the terms attached to any measure of relief for Roman Catholics. For example, a Relief Bill of 1825 was hedged round with conditions, the most important being the stipulations that the priesthood be paid out of state funds, and that the property qualification be increased so that a significant number of Irish Catholic freeholders would be excluded from voting.[7] That Bill failed to reach the statue book, and the issue was only finally settled in 1829.

Coleridge began work on *Church and State* during the crisis produced by the 1825 Bill, and finally completed it after the passage of the 1829 Act.[8] Although this measure incorporated a number of securities, Coleridge claimed that he would be satisfied by a single safeguard obliging Catholics to promise never to seek to obtain a share of the national property set aside for the National Church.[9] This stipulation, and Coleridge's insistence that the parts of the Coronation Oath relating to the Church of England dealt with the constitutional position of the Church rather than its doctrines,[10] meant that his approach to Catholic Emancipation was political and eschewed theological dogmatism. As Coleridge wrote to a correspondent in 1822, 'you will not, I trust, suspect me of any *religious* bigotry in the matter, or that I should exclude any man from a seat in the Cabinet for worshipping a Wafer, more than for worshipping the [Mother of the Lord?] & even higher up'. Unlike his old friend Robert Southey, who raised opposition to emancipation to the status of a fundamental principle, Coleridge was prepared to deal with the various proposals on their merits.[11] His position depended on a constitutional principle about the necessity for a national church, and he was prepared to accept the recognition of political rights for otherwise qualified Roman Catholics, provided that this did not threaten the status and property of the Church of England.

Appeals to 'the constitution in Church and State' were common among contemporary defenders of the Church of England.[12] For example, many of those who opposed emancipation did so by reference to the Revolutionary Settlement of 1688–9 which excluded both Catholics and Dissenters from political office, and made the state distinctly and exclusively Anglican. This claim had a strong emotional appeal since the settlement was seen as the culmination of a 'long, painful struggle with Popery'.[13] The legally established Church of England was held to be central to the Anglican constitutional edifice, and it was argued that emancipation would place it at the mercy of a Parliament that would include members of a different and essentially antagonistic faith.

A belief in the existence of an alliance between Church and state was central to this line of argument. Henry Drummond, for example, claimed that the 'nation and the church are one' and that consequently, the 'total and unqualified repeal . . . of all tests of Christianity in the office-bearers of the state implies, and does effect, the separation of the church from the state'.[14] Drummond was an extreme Tory, however, an ultra, and went on to relate the alliance to 'the indefeasible union of divine and human law'; it was a buttress against popular government, and a barrier to resistance against God-ordained Christian monarchy.[15] But Drummond's was only one of the more extreme statements of a widespread belief in the necessity for a close connection between a Protestant church and a Protestant state. By treating the Catholic Emancipation question in relation to the principles underlying the Constitution, Coleridge was thus responding to an important strand of contemporary argument.

However, the debate over emancipation produced a further, less direct, but no less important context for *Church and State*. Although

Coleridge had begun the work in 1825, it did not appear until December 1829, when the issue of Catholic relief had already been settled. In this case, however, his customary tardiness did not really matter. This was partly because his discussion of the emancipation issue appealed to fundamental principles, but also because controversy over the Catholic question had produced a sub-context which outlived the resolution of the particular set of problems that had sparked it off, and was, in fact, to become more rather than less important in the years that followed.

The debate over Catholic Emancipation provoked discussion about the nature, role and justification of the Established Church. These arguments were part of a widespread re-examination and/or defence of the Anglican establishment by both sympathetic and unsympathetic critics, and were prompted as much by fears of Dissenters and atheists as they were by fears of Roman Catholics.[16] It was claimed that the removal of doctrinal tests threatened the position of the Church by modifying a political structure that protected its special political, social, legal and proprietorial position. These fears were exacerbated by the hostility of popularist and philosophic radicals. The radical press of the period portrayed the Church in most unflattering terms: illiberal in its politics, indifferent to the spiritual and material needs of the common people, and loaded with abuses, it compared most unfavourably with the pre-Reformation Church described in William Cobbett's *History of the Reformation*. A less extremely stated, but nevertheless obvious, air of hostility pervaded the pages of the *Edinburgh Review*,[17] and helped to create an environment in which the Church and its supporters felt themselves to be under siege.

A common response to these threats was to restate Protestant ascendancy ideas, but more reasoned, conciliatory and constructive attempts to justify the Church's favoured position also appeared. Some of these depended upon arguments about the theological soundness of the Church's doctrine and the government's duty to uphold it. Bishop Blomfield, for example, saw the issue of Catholic Emancipation in terms of 'the duty of a Protestant government to distinguish between truth and error'.[18] Others stressed the role of the Church and its clergy in fostering social harmony; a belief in God was the cement in a harmonious society made up of very many different and unequal elements. The Church was also portrayed as an essential agency of social control, offering leadership and a regime of ideological and vocational education.[19] These sorts of considerations were meant to explain the utility of a Church-state alliance, and to provide a rationale for the privileges enjoyed by the Established Church and rightfully withheld from its non-established rivals. Foremost among these privileges was the control of large amounts of property.

An alternative to these arguments about the virtues of establishment appeared in Richard Whately's *Letters on the Church* of 1826. He argued that the Church was hindered by its established status and would do well to rid itself of the obnoxious alliance with the state.[20] Whately's lack of interest in the Protestant Constitution attracted the favourable attention of the *Edinburgh Review*,[21] but the real importance of a comparison between his sympathetic disestablishmentarianism, the moderate views outlined above and the intransigence of High Tories such as Drummond is that it points to the variety of opinions about the nature and role of the Church, and of the propriety of its integration within the constitutional structure of the state. The wide-ranging character of these debates, and the confused picture of the Church that emerged from them, provided an important context for Coleridge's *Church and State*. This work was located within the debate over Catholic Emancipation, but that was part of a more extensive and inconclusive discussion about the nature, role and justification of the Church.

II THE CONSTITUTION OF THE CHURCH AND STATE AS 'IDEAS'

Church and State was based upon the widely accepted view that the Church and state were inseparable, but it differed from the received wisdoms in its understanding of these institutions and the ways in which they were related. Coleridge's treatment of these issues depended upon a conceptual framework which isolated the crucial characteristic of such institutions and dealt with them as 'ideas'. This approach was important because it drew attention to the fundamental rationale of both Church and state, and provided criteria for evaluating the ways in which these ideas were realised.

When Coleridge referred to the Constitution as an 'idea', he made it clear that he did not regard it primarily as a body of laws either coalescing, or hinging on, one critical law such as the Bill of Rights, or the anti-Catholic provisions of the existing system of representation. An 'idea' was that conception of a thing, which is not abstracted from any particular state, form or mode, in which the thing may happen to exist at this or at that time; nor yet generalized from any number or succession of such forms or modes; but which is given by the knowledge of *its ultimate aim*.[22]

This meant that any particular constitution was a more or less adequately realised example of a structure which facilitated the attainment of the ultimate end in question. 'An idea is a POWER . . . that constitutes its own Reality – and is, in order of Thought, necessarily antecedent to the Things, in which it is, more or less adequately, realized. . . .'[23] Coleridge claimed that the reality of an idea depended upon its effects upon the minds whose conduct it influenced, not upon its representation in the world of objects. For most individuals, the motivational influences of ideas were unconscious – 'it is the privilege of the few to possess an idea: of the generality of men, it might be more truly affirmed, that they are possessed by it'[24] – but actions were nevertheless manifestations of the ideas. A particular idea embodied 'a *principle*, existing in the only way in which a principle can exist – in the minds and consciences of the persons, whose duties it prescribes, and whose rights it determines'.[25]

Principles made up criteria against which manifestations of the idea could be judged. In Coleridge's view, therefore, ideas were inherently critical. For example, the principles making up the idea of a system of representation could be used to assess whether existing institutions were essential, benign or malign 'excrescences' of the idea.[26] Although Coleridge concluded the first chapter of *Church and State* with a quotation from Sir John Davies' *Irish Reports*,[27] he was interested in Davies' views on the independent development of the English Constitution rather than in the static conception of the Constitution implied by Davies' ancient constitutionalism. An important implication of Coleridge's conception of the constitution as idea was that actual constitutions ought to change in order to realise the idea more adequately in the institutions of the country. As J. D. Coates points out in his discussion of *Zapolya*, the image of the river which Coleridge used to describe the state conveys ideas of movement and development:

> By wholesale laws to embank the Sovereign power
> To deepen by restraint and by prevention

Of lawless will, to amass and guide the flood
In its majestic channel.[28]

The state both directs and is shaped by the forces it directs.

Although *Church and State* contains a great deal of historical material, Coleridge did not intend to produce a historical account of the Constitution or a description of its present form. The constitution as idea was an essentially normative concept.

> this Essay [concentrates] not on the history nor on the *actual form* of the British Legislature: but on the *Ultimate* Aims implied in the Constitution of the Same, by which [alone] as the regulative Idea, it can be rendered intelligible, and by reference to which as its true Criterion, it must be judged.[29]

An important consequence of this approach was that questions about the propriety of Catholic Emancipation could not be resolved by an appeal to the historical development of the Constitution. In particular, the demands made by, and on behalf of, Catholics could not be discredited merely by showing that they would introduce a change into the constitutional structure established in 1688–9. The real question was whether, and under what conditions, the emancipation of Catholics was compatible with the fulfilment of the ultimate end that the Constitution existed to serve.[30]

Coleridge claimed that this end had to be understood in relation to the ends of the state: 'a Constitution is an idea arising out of the idea of a state'.[31] This idea incorporated the concern for moral development that had provided the basis of Coleridge's position in *The Friend*. Although he held to an organic conception of the state, he continued to value it because it contributed to the fulfilment of individual human beings. This was made quite clear in a marginal comment on Lessing's *Ernst und Falk*. Coleridge wrote that men were 'made for . . . the State, *rather* than the state for *the* Men', but pointed out that the words 'made for' meant 'have their final cause in', a position that was identical to the one he had advanced in the first version of *The Friend*.[32] This view accorded with conceptions of human interaction that were represented in the 'idea' of social contract, but was not to be found in most social-contract theories. An 'ever-originating' (rather than an 'original') social contract embodied the distinction between 'a subject' and 'a serf'. Although the former may be under the control of others, his personality was recognised (the 'higher idea of *person*, in contra-distinction from *thing*'), and the subject was treated as an end, and not therefore merely as a means. The 'idea' of a social contract expressed the principles that lay at the heart of the state and distinguished a commonwealth from a slave plantation.[33] In fact, Coleridge's treatment of the ends of the state in *Church and State* was slight, and did not differ significantly from the theory sketched in *The Friend*. He concentrated instead on the institutional form of the state in the narrow sense of 'government' (executive and legislature), and in the broader sense where it was taken to include the national church. Property played a crucial role in shaping the character of all the major institutions that made up the state.

III PROPERTY AND GOVERNMENT IN THE CONSTITUTION

Coleridge treated 'government' as a political expression of the social forces he had identified in the 'Lay Sermons' and elsewhere. These forces were based upon differing kinds of property, and the Constitution was viewed, therefore, as a reflection of social forces, not as a set of institutions which could reshape society.[34] The notion of balance – '*lex equilibrii*'[35] – which had appeared as a social ideal in the *Lay Sermon* was now transformed into an instrument of constitutional analysis. It described the internal unity of a system which did not concentrate all social power in one focal point (as in an absolute monarchy), but maintained a variety of independent social forces. Unity was generated by a process of 'equipoise and interdependency'.[36] Coleridge claimed that it was the principle of balance itself, rather than the existence and arrangement of any particular set of institutions or social forces, that constituted the state: 'the *lex equilibrii*, the principle prescribing the means and conditions by and under which this balance is to be established and preserved' was 'the constitution of the state'.[37] His theory of the state showed how the principle of balance was realised in the organisation of powers within the Constitution.

In *Church and State* the Constitution was analysed in relation to three sets of interconnected factors. The first of these – the interests of 'permanence' and those of 'progression' – explained the main structural features of the English system of legislation; the second and third – the 'free and permeative life and energy of the Nation' and 'organised powers', and 'actual and potential' powers –

identified conditions that had to be satisfied if the balance of social forces was to be socially and politically efficacious. Such a balance was a necessary condition for the existence of a constitution, but was not alone sufficient for the beneficial operation of the constitutional structure.

The language of balance was commonplace in discussions of the English Constitution, and was often used to describe the relationship between elements that represented aristocratic and democratic qualities.[38] For Coleridge, however, the Constitution focused interests based on property rather than qualities. The distinction between permanence and progression identified what Coleridge had earlier described as

> the two great moving Principles of Social Humanity – religious adherence to the Past and the Ancient, the Desire & the admiration of Permanence, on the one hand; and the Passion for increase of Knowledge, for Truth as the offspring of Reason, in short, the mighty Instincts of *Progression* and *Free-Agency*, on the other.[39]

In *Church and State* these principles were identified with proprietorial interests, and these were treated in a way that took Coleridge's previous statements about the relationship between property and political power for granted. At the beginning of chapter 10, Coleridge reproduced a version of the statement from *The Friend* about the close causal connection between the existence of government and people's desire to protect their property. 'The chief object, for which men . . . first formed themselves into a *State* . . . was not the protection of their lives but of their property.'[40] The forces of permanence were associated with landed property, and those of progression with mercantile, manufacturing and professional wealth. Coleridge stressed that these interests were *opposites*, not *contraries*. Their interaction generated a fitting, beneficial unity similar to that produced by the negative and positive poles of a magnet. The contending forces did not cancel one another out: they produced a condition that differed from each of them, but depended on the presence of both.[41]

When discussing the permanent interest as a factor in the Constitution, Coleridge focused on its psychological, legal and historical dimensions. It embraced past, present and future generations, and embodied a concern for patterns of interrelationship that were immune from fluctuations produced by the passage of time. Among the more exalted, this world view was expressed in primogeniture, hereditary titles and entails; among the humble, it found utterance in 'the proverbial obduracy of prejudices characteristic of the humbler tillers of the soil, and their aversion even to benefits that are offered in the form of innovations'.[42] This account of landed property was not incompatible with Coleridge's earlier views about the moral dimensions of landownership, (indeed, he continued to stress the necessary connection between property rights in land and the fulfilment of social duties[43]), but it focused on those features which marked it out as a distinct *interest* which contributed a fixed and stable element to the social structure and to the balance of political forces in the Constitution. Similarly, Coleridge's remarks on commercialism drew attention to dynamic features that enabled it to interact productively with the solid mass of the landed classes. Commerce was associated with 'advances in civilisation', the growth of the 'rights and privileges of citizens', and the development of the arts, practical knowledge and public information.[44]

Although Coleridge's account of the interests of permanence and progression depended upon the conception of different sorts of property that he had developed in *The Friend* and *A Lay Sermon*, he now discussed them in relation to the structure of government. In a presentation copy of *Church and State* Coleridge noted that the legislature represented 'interests' rather than the wishes or opinions of 'the People',[45] a claim that added an additional dimension to his frequently stated view that politics and the law were directly concerned with the non-personal rather than the personal. The distinction between law and morality was one of the major themes of *The Friend*, but in a notebook entry which was roughly contemporary with *Church and State* Coleridge related this to the state's constitutional structure. He described the state in terms that made the existence, maintenance and balance of differing interests an essential feature of it, one which was the distinguishing characteristic of political activity:

> The proper object of a State is *Things*, the permanent *interests* that continue in the flux of its component Citizens, hence a distinction & if I might say so, a polarisation of ranks and orders is the very condition of its existence. . . . The aim . . . of a State is to preserve and defend the . . . difference between the integral

parts of its total Body, by establishing and watching over the differential grounds, & causes, and exponents of the difference. . . .[46]

This view of the state had important implications for Coleridge's response to proposals for reforming the system of representation. He claimed that if reform were directed towards the more effective representation of interests it could be beneficial. However, if it were based on 'delegation of men . . . you can never, in reason, stop short of universal suffrage; and in that case, I am sure that women have as good a right to vote as men'.[47] The tendency to ignore the importance of interests was apparent in the desire mechanically to relate parliamentary representation to territorial divisions, and Coleridge's reservations about this made him reluctant to condemn 'accommodations' which provided for the representation of new interests which were not connected with any distinct geographical area.[48] The arrangements he had in mind were probably those whereby rising members of the commercial interest bought control of parliamentary seats. Such 'borough mongering' was widely condemned both by reformers and by members of the landed classes who felt that their position was being undermined by the intrusion of *nouveaux riches* into electoral politics. Coleridge, however, chose to see it as a means of ensuring that those with property would have the opportunity for converting it into quite legitimate political influence.

In general, Coleridge was critical of contemporary reform proposals because they were not based on a consistent set of principles.[49] Whatever its shortcomings, and Coleridge seemed prepared to admit that it was far from perfect, the unreformed electoral system at least reflected the principle that the legislative organs should represent the interests of the nation as expressed in the two major forms of property. The political power of the permanent interest was focused in the House of Lords, and in those seats in the Commons that were occupied by knights of the shires. Coleridge described members of the Lords as 'Major Barons' who directly represented their own proprietorial interests. In the Commons, the less influential members of the permanent interest, the 'Minor Barons', sat as representatives of those whose possessions were not extensive enough to entitle them to direct and personal access to legislative power. The minor barons were in a minority in the House of Commons and so the influence of the permanent interest in that House was counterpoised by a greater number of representatives of the progressive interest who sat for boroughs, seaports and cities. Each interest therefore controlled one of the legislative chambers, and, as a result, neither could act without some support from the other.[50]

The role that Coleridge ascribed to the forces of permanence and progression depended upon the fact that they were separate estates of the realm representing distinct proprietorial interests. The connection between estates, interests and representation meant that the Crown's role in the constitutional structure was largely symbolic, although, as we shall see, the royal veto gave the monarch a crucial, if limited, constitutional function. However, because the Crown was not a separate estate, it could not represent interests. It functioned as the 'beam' of the balance and expressed the unity produced by the interaction of the permanent and progressive interests.[51] It embodied 'the majesty, or symbolic unity of the whole nation, both of the state and of the persons . . . the cohesion by interdependence' of its constituent parts.[52] This account of the role of the Crown resembled that of the extreme Tory Francis Leckie, who had described it as 'the soul which animates the body, and which constitutes its unity'.[53] However, despite these linguistic similarities, Coleridge's position differed markedly from that of Leckie. Coleridge's view of English government was essentially aristocratic and republican, in the sense in which these terms had been used by seventeenth-century Commonwealthsmen. 'The idea of a state', Coleridge said, 'is undoubtedly a government [of the best] – an aristocracy.'[54] While he thought that the Crown was necessary to express the unity of the state, it need not be associated with one royal line and could conceivably be non-hereditary. For example, although he was very critical of Oliver Cromwell's usurpation and his contempt for Parliament, Coleridge thought that if he had been offered the throne 'under a solemn national Contract' England might 'have been a republican Kingdom – a glorious Commonwealth with a King as the symbol of its Majesty, and Key-stone of its Unity'.[55] Coleridge regarded the Crown as a constitutional necessity, but he reduced its direct role in politics, and did not adhere to the exaggerated conceptions of kingship that appeared in some contemporary writings. Not did he subscribe to the Tory sentiments about the history of monarchy in England.[56] Coleridge regarded the idea of Charles I as royal martyr as sacrilegious, and was exceedingly contemptuous of him and his son. If Charles was a martyr, it was to the vice of lying, while his son's reign had been a 'foul blotch' on the history of the Church of England and on much else besides.[57]

The Crown played a part in balancing the forces of progression and permanence, but its constitutional role was related to the existence of these interests and was not independent of them. In any case, the maintenance of a balance between these two interests was a necessary rather than a sufficient condition for the healthy operation of the Constitution and the state. It was also necessary to maintain a correctly balanced relationship between these institutionalised forces and free powers that were not integrated in the constitutional structure, and between actual and potential powers within all parts of society. This had important implications for the conditions of entry to legislative positions, but it also meant that the power connected with property was only one element within the constitution of the state.

The interests of permanence and progression were organised powers within the Constitution, confined within 'determinate vessels'.[58] Coleridge was adamant that those without the requisite qualifications should be excluded from these vessels. Whatever the virtues of particular individuals, there should be no 'direct political power without cognizable possession', no direct access to the central points in the organised powers of the state without those 'fastening and radical fibres of a collective and registrable property, by which the Citizen inheres in and belongs to the Commonwealth'.[59] However, when individuals did possess property, they should not be capriciously refused entry to the organised forces of society. There was no justification for legislation (such as the Test and Corporation Acts) that excluded otherwise qualified individuals from direct participation in the political life of the nation. The first of these cases upset the relationship between free and organised powers because it transformed one into the other without going through the medium of property; the second failed to acknowledge the due claims of those whose free energy was incorporated in property and who were part of an interest that had a legitimate place within the formal structure of the Constitution. However, the relationship between free and organised powers could also be upset if part of the political structure was dominated by one section of a relevant interest group – when, for example, 'the Imposing name of the Interest of the whole – the landed

Interest' was given to but a few representatives of that interest.[60] In that case, a set of organised powers was in danger of being usurped by a very partial representation of the relevant interest.

All these cases concerned the maintenance of organised powers and the need to ensure that the free energies of the state did not undermine its institutional structure. Coleridge claimed that the republics of ancient Greece had suffered from such a fate – they had fallen into dissolution from the excess of free energy which shattered 'the organic structures, they should have enlivened' – but it was equally important to ensure that the state did not fall victim to the excess of organised power that had destroyed the Venetian Republic: 'All political power was confined to the determinate vessels, and these becoming more and more rigid, even to an ossification of the arteries, the State, in which the people were nothing, lost all power of resistance ad extra.'[61] In *Church and State* Coleridge did not indicate how the free, permeative life of the state was actually expressed, but earlier remarks about the spirit of 'volunteership' in the operation of the English system of government, and his view on the importance of deference networks in social life, may indicate what he had in mind.[62] In addition, there is an interesting marginal comment on *Lives of British Statesmen* which provides a further, more significant clue. In the note in question, Coleridge identified a range of civic duties and claimed that most members of the population would qualify for an active role in at least one of the spheres of 'judicial (*i.e.* as a jury man), municipal and elective' activity.[63] Only the last of these involved the exercise of what Coleridge called 'direct political power' which depended on property; the others represented avenues for the exercise of the indirect power which, as the Venetian example showed, fostered national identity and patriotism and supported, strengthened and 'enlivened' the formal organised structures of the state.

Coleridge's aristocratic and republican conception of government was one expression of his empathy with the Commonwealthsmen of the seventeenth century, 'the stars of that narrow interspace of blue sky between the black clouds of the first and second Charles's reigns'.[64] However, his ideas on the constitutional significance of free and organised powers led him to insist on the importance of sub-parliamentary forms of activity which embraced the energy of the democracy of the nation. 'Democracy is the healthful life-blood which circulates through the veins and arteries, which supports the system, but which ought never to appear externally, and as the mere blood itself.'[65] In the English context, the energy of democracy was 'in the corporations, the vestries, the joint-stock companies, &c.'[66] It gave to the body politic a character that departed from the model aspired to by some of the English republicans of the seventeenth century:

> It was the error of Milton, Sidney, and others of that age, to think it possible to construct a purely aristocratical government, defecated of all passion, and ignorance, and sordid motive. The truth is, such a government would be weak from its utter want of sympathy with the people to be governed by it.[67]

Republican aristocracy was an important part of the Constitution, but in its pure and austere form it was not an acceptable model of government, because it ignored both the free energy of democracy and the psychological ramifications of it.

In addition to maintaining a correct balance between free and organised energies, the Constitution also had to bring the 'actual' and 'potential' powers into 'due proportion'.[68] This condition was directed particularly at parliamentary claims to omnipotence, a point that was made quite clear by Coleridge's quotation of a passage from Charles Dallison's *Royalist's Defence* (1648) upholding the power of the judiciary – 'the Judges of the Realm by the *fundamental* Law of *England* have power to determine which Acts of Parliament are binding and which void'; by his reference to the injustice of the suppression of Convocation;[69] and by the use of a variant of George Wither's *Vox Pacifica* that identified forces in the body politic that were not realised fully in the institutions of government:

> Let not your King and Parliament in *One*,
> Much less apart, mistake themselves for that
> Which is most worthy to be thought upon:
> Nor think they are, essentially, the STATE.
> Let them not fancy, that th' Authority
> And Priviledges upon them bestown,
> Conferr'd are to set up a MAJESTY,
> A POWER, or a GLORY of their own!
> But let them know, 'twas for a deeper life,
> Which they but *represent* –
> That there's on earth a yet auguster Thing,
> Veil'd tho' it be, than Parliament and King.[70]

John Colmer has pointed out that Coleridge's very qualified acceptance of parliamentary omnipotence reflected a feeling of unease about those who filled such institutions, and about the way they actually functioned.[71] However, it was also significant in relation to his views on the need to distinguish between politics and morals. Contemporary commentators on the English Constitution often assumed an uncritical or despairing attitude to parliamentary omnipotence, but Coleridge's distinction between 'actual' and 'potential' power mitigated the effects of this by separating politics from morals. The 'auguster Thing' of Wither's verse may have been understood by Coleridge as the moral imperative that provided the ultimate rationale for any form of political authority, and the grounds of obligation to it.[72] Coleridge's treatment of this indicated that he thought that Parliament's power should be limited to political matters and implied that it would undermine its legitimacy if it attempted to encroach beyond its proper sphere. In *Church and State*, this caution was meant to apply particularly to parliamentary interference with the Established Church.[73]

In common with some other defenders of the Established Church, Coleridge regarded an omnipotent Parliament as a potential threat to its existence, one that would become acute if Catholics and Dissenters sat in the House of Commons. As Bishop Phillpotts wrote, 'That there are "fundamental laws", if not above the power, yet beyond the moral competence, of the whole legislature to rescind them, what Englishman will hesitate to affirm?'[74] One safeguard against those who were tempted to exceed their 'moral competence' was the royal veto. Coleridge claimed that in the present case the veto could properly be applied to matters which were subject to the Coronation Oath:

> However unconstitutional therefore the royal veto on a Bill presented by the Lords and Commons may be deemed in all ordinary cases, this is clearly an exception. For it is no additional power conferred on the king; but a limit imposed on him by the constitution itself for its own safety.[75]

Coleridge's distinction between potential and actual power provided the basis for questioning Parliament's right to pass legislation that adversely effected the position of the National Church. The royal veto was an example of a fund of potential power within the structure of the Constitution, and its use was justified because of the constitutional importance of the Established Church. The defence of the Church was no ordinary case, because the 'constitution of the state' was not independent or self-supporting. It was part of a larger whole – the 'constitution of the *Nation*'[76] – which necessarily included the National Church. This institution balanced the state in much the same way as the interests of permanence and progression balanced one another within the state. The state and the National Church were 'two poles of the same magnet; the magnet itself, which is constituted by them, is the CONSTITUTION of the nation'.[77]

IV THE NATIONAL CHURCH AND THE CONSTITUTION OF THE NATION

As we have seen, Coleridge subscribed to the widely held view that there should be a special relationship between the Church and the state. However, the debate over Catholic Emancipation showed that there were a wide variety of views about the meaning of this. The various, and in some cases, inconsistent, arguments produced by the Church's supporters meant that its friends were not defending a generally agreed-upon, monolithic conception. Attempts to gauge the effects of opening up the highest offices of state to those who were not members of the Church of England produced defences of the Church which were, at the same time, definitions of what it was or ought to be. These statements purported to show what might be lost either by the mere fact of enlarging the political nation to include non-Anglicans, or as a result of the presence of such people in the executive and legislative branches of government. The diversity of views about the effects of emancipation was due in part to the wide range of conceptions about the nature of the establishment and the justification for it. Thus, while there was some measure of general agreement among defenders of the Church about the necessity for a Church–state alliance[78] (Whately's 'sympathetic' case for disestablishment being an exception to this), the argumentative force of this was greatly reduced by the variety of interpretations of what the alliance meant.

By contemporary standards, Coleridge's statements on the implications of Catholic Emancipation were distinctly cool and non-alarmist. Although he disliked Roman Catholicism and distrusted the pretensions of the Papacy to universal temporal authority, he was not dissatisfied with the terms of the 1829 Relief

Act, and thought that any threat posed by emancipated Roman Catholics could be met by a declaration affirming the sanctity of the property of the Church of England. Coleridge's concern for church property was integral to his defence of the establishment. He claimed that the Church was an essential element in the constitutional balance and argued that its place within this structure depended upon its status as a property-holder.

Although much of what Coleridge said about the National Church was based upon his understanding of the history of the Church of England, he treated that institution, as he treated the constitution of the state, by reference to its idea: 'something deeper and better than priestcraft and priest-ridden ignorance was at the bottom of the phrase, Church and State, and intitled it to be the form in which so many thousands of the men of England clothed the wish for their country's weal.'[79]

Property was as crucial to Coleridge's view of the National Church as it has been to his treatment of the other elements of the Constitution. The National Church, like the interests of permanence and progression, was based on a distinctive form of property, but its property was reserved for the direct fulfilment of *national* rather than *personal* purposes. Coleridge underlined this difference by a terminological distinction; the property of the Church made up the '*Nationalty*', while personal property, whether in fixed or movable objects, comprised the '*Propriety*'. The relationship between these two forms of property was governed by the principle of balance.

> These, the *Propriety* and the *Nationalty*, were the two constituent factors, the opposite, but correspondent and reciprocally supporting counter-weights, of the *commonwealth*; the existence of the one being the condition, and the perfecting, of the rightfulness of the other.[80]

Coleridge insisted that a national church based on its own property was an essential feature of the state. It was not, as Paley argued, merely a matter of expediency, nor was it, as the *Edinburgh Review* claimed, a corporate body created by, and under the control of law.[81] Since the Church was not the creation of the state, the property that supported its existence must also be independent of it. It was, Coleridge claimed, 'co-original' with both Church and state.[82]

Coleridge's view of Church property differed from that of many contemporary defenders of the Church because he sought to place it beyond the bounds of parliamentary control or alteration. The idea that Church property was a trust meant that trustees could be empowered to ensure that the purposes for which the trust was established were being carried out. In the hands of more conservative Churchmen that might merely mean some modifications to the distribution of income among the clergy, the introduction of new regulations, or the proper enforcement of the old. But, as Geoffrey Best points out, this line of argument was potentially dangerous since it could serve to justify extensive restructuring, and even the appropriation of, Church property. In each case, the 'principle was the same: it was redistribution . . . justified by the same appeal to public policy and national need'.[83] Although Coleridge regarded Church property as a trust, he wished to undercut the implications that were usually drawn from this. He did so by showing that the Church was essential to the state, and that the Church's independent control of its property was a necessary part of this.

In *Church and State* Coleridge reiterated his earlier claim that the Church formed a '*third* great venerable estate of the realm', comparable in kind with the other estates, made up of holders of landed and of non-landed property.[84] This estate was intended to balance or counteract both of the other two. Although the Propriety had important beneficial social implications – directly in the case of land, indirectly in the case of commercial wealth – it was necessarily under the personal control of its owners. Moreover, as Coleridge had shown in *A Lay Sermon*, the connection between free, moral agency and personal property made the misuse of property rights, and the neglect of the duties attached to property, a constant possibility.[85] In *A Lay Sermon* Coleridge had written of the need for a 'learned and philosophic Public' to counteract the influence of the commercial spirit.[86] In *Church and State*, he assigned that role to the National Church and justified its control of the Nationalty by reference to the need for a body able to provide an effective counterweight to the spirit of commerce. When Coleridge criticised the French Church in 1802 he had been concerned with the dangers of political control of the Church, and had linked the status of the Church of England as a 'third estate of the realm' with its material independence of the state.[87] The argument of *Church and State* ran along the same lines, although the focus had now shifted from a fear of the executive (a feature of

Country Party ideology) to a fear of the interests of personal property which were capable of dominating both the executive and legislative organs of the state.

The National Church provided a counterweight to the quite legitimate concentration of proprietorial interests in both Houses of Parliament. It did so by using its property to establish and maintain an educational elite, or 'clerisy'.[88] In *The Friend*, Coleridge had identified the enlightenment of the population as one of the ultimate ends of the state, and he later described this task as one of the most effective ways of checking the spirit of commerce. The fact that he now assigned this role to a specific institution that was endowed with a portion of the nation's wealth showed why the National Church was to be considered as part of the constitution of the nation and essential to the state. Coleridge made it clear that the clerisy was to provide education for all members of society, although he was especially concerned with its impact on social and political elites. The clerisy were not merely to instruct the population. The goal was not 'civilisation' but civilisation 'grounded in *cultivation*, in the harmonious development of those qualities and faculties that characterise our *humanity*. We must be men in order to be citizens'.[89] Education that elicited human qualities would, of itself, provide an antidote to the dehumanising materialism that lay at the heart of political economy and generated views of human interaction that were bereft of any recognition of the men's shared, God-ordained, humanity.

Coleridge argued that the endowment of the clergy was essential if they were to fulfil their constitutional role. In the absence of an establishment, members of the clergy would either be distracted, self-absorbed, working farmers like Fielding's Parson Trulliber, or, what was perhaps worse, salaried placemen unable to take an independent and critical view of the conduct of all social classes.[90] A clergyman who was dependent either on his parishioners or on his own exertions would lack the standing he needed within the community in order to serve as a bridge between different classes.[91] On the other hand, a clergyman who was dependent on the government would be admitted to the houses of the rich as a client of those whose property gave them a predominant voice in the political arena. Coleridge insisted that members of the Church must be in a position to make all classes aware of their rights and duties. At a time when significant sections of the parochial clergy were successfully exploiting their glebelands, enforcing their rights and becoming closely identified with the upper classes of the laity,[92] Coleridge argued that the Church of England had been weakened by its close identification with the rich and its neglect of the poor:

> The fatal error into which the peculiar character of the English Reformation threw our church, has borne bitter fruit ever since, – I mean that of its clinging to court and state, instead of cultivating the people. The church ought to be a mediator between the people and the government, between the poor and the rich. As it is, I fear the church has let the hearts of the common people be stolen from it.[93]

These remarks on the failings of the post-Reformation Church exemplified the critical potentialities of Coleridge's conception of an 'idea' as a criterion against which institutional forms and behaviour could be judged. Although Coleridge was a staunch defender of the National Church, he identified a role for it that differed significantly from other contemporary accounts. The Church was something other than an agency of social control, and its educational functions were not restricted to civilisation, far less to vocational training. More important than that, however, was the fact that Coleridge's account of the constitutional and social significance of Church property implied a rejection of commonly held views about the existence of a Church–state alliance. Unlike those who understood the Church as part of what J. C. D. Clark has called the 'Anglican church-state', Coleridge insisted on abandoning the notion of alliance. In its Warburtonian formulations it suffered from the fatal defect of treating the Church as a useful but non-essential aspect of the state. It could also imply that the Church was materially, and hence also politically, dependent on the legislative and executive branches.[94] Coleridge argued that the Church of England was a National Church and therefore an essential part of the constitution of the nation. It was able to contribute to the commonweal because it was institutionally distinct and psychologically removed from the state conceived in a narrow sense as a set of politically organised energies focused in the two Houses of Parliament. Coleridge defended the favoured position of the Church by reference to its constitutional role as a counterpoise to the other proprietorial interests, which rightfully dominated both Lords and Commons. This role necessitated its material independence, and Coleridge's treatment of Church property was specifically designed to insulate it from future depredations by a legislature that contained a significant number of indifferent or hostile 'Liberalists', Dissenters and Roman Catholics.[95]

Coleridge's nostalgic and quixotic remarks about Convocation reflected the importance he attached to the Church's independence. He described the King, who was head of both Church and state, as the 'Protector and Supreme Trustee of the NATIONALTY', but stipulated that he should always act with the two 'Houses of Convocation'. The clergy had traditionally assembled as an estate in Convocation, but this body had been prorogued in 1717. Coleridge described the 'practical suppression' of Convocation as an indication that 'no great principle was ever invaded or trampled on, that did not sooner or later avenge itself on the country'. An earlier notebook entry suggested that the 'great principle' embodied a concern for the position of the clergy as an independent estate with its own unchallengeable property rights. 'I am inclined . . . to hold that in good policy not to say common Justice, the Clergy, as a Property *sui generis*, ought either to have their Convocation restored or to elect a [Parliamentary] representative in each diocese. . . .'[96] These remarks about Convocation and the related claim that the clergy formed an 'estate', suggest that J. S. Mill's attempt to portray Coleridge as a supporter of the view that 'the State is at liberty to withdraw the endowment from its existing possessors, whenever any body of persons can be found . . . by whom the ends of the establishment . . . are likely to be more perfectly fulfilled'[97] was based on wishful thinking. In fact, Coleridge wished to insulate the Church from the interference of a legislative body which might contain an increasing number of enemies of the Church of England.

One peculiar feature of the Warburtonian position was that the connection between any particular state and any particular church was accidental; the state merely allied itself with the church which had the broadest basis.[98] Coleridge, however, shared with many other defenders of the Church an interest in supporting an establishment that was undeniably, and indeed providentially, Protestant and Anglican. He associated Protestantism with intellectual freedom,[99] with rules of living that allowed its clergy to be part of the community they served – 'he is neither in the cloistered cell, nor in the wilderness, but a neighbour and family-man'[100] –

and with the abandonment of the universalistic pretensions of the Papacy that made a *national* church an impossibility. In a lengthy note to *Aids to Reflection*, Coleridge quoted a passage from *Reliquiae Baxterianae* that highlighted the dangers of a church possessed by a 'spirit of Particularism counterfeiting Catholicity'. The 'great and irreconcilable' differences between the Roman and Reformed churches were due not to 'doctrines of faith', but to the Papacy's 'Church Tyranny . . . the usurpations of their Hierarchy, and Priesthood, under the name of spiritual authority exercising a temporal Lordship'.[101] Coleridge's stipulations about those who were unfit for membership of the National Church were essentially Protestant conditions: neither those who acknowledged obedience to someone other than their legal sovereign, nor those who swore not to enter into those conjugal ties that bound a man to his country, were to be members of the National Church. In a sense, the Anglican character of the establishment needed no special defence, since the Church of England was the historically derived National Church, growing up in, and ministering to the needs of, a specific community. Unlike the Catholic Church, which claimed to be universal, or the churches of the Protestant Dissenters, which were particular, the Church of England was, and had been, part of the fabric of the nation.[102]

On many important practical issues the major threat of the Church of England came from Protestant Dissenters rather than from the Roman Catholics. For example, Coleridge was dismissive of all non-Anglican educational initiatives because they were tainted by the 'mechanic philosophy' that it was the Church's role to counteract. They were 'marked with the same asterisk of spuriousness, . . . the same distemper – spot' and were merely 'empirical specifics for morbid *symptoms* that help to feed and continue the disease'.[103] The intemperance of Coleridge's response was due to the fact that he regarded such alternatives as covert attempts to displace the Church of England and to seize its property; it was not based on a belief that the existence of an established church required doctrinal uniformity. On the contrary, Coleridge believed that one of the special virtues of the Church was its 'mild and liberal' theological spirit.[104] This permitted the coexistence of a diversity of religious views with those of the Anglican establishment. Such toleration was of crucial importance to the very idea of a church established by law. As a legally recognised institution, the Church of England was a political, social and educational body, not a religious one. It was, in short, a *national*, rather than a *Christian*, church. The distinction between these types of church was crucial to Coleridge's argument in *Church and State* and to his attempt to defend the Church from all its enemies.

V THE NATIONAL CHURCH AND THE CHURCH OF CHRIST

An important aspect of Coleridge's defence of the Church of England as an established church was his willingness to treat it in a purely legal, constitutional frame of reference. The Church was an essential element in the constitution of the nation, but its position as a national church was independent of what Coleridge called 'theological dogmata'. National churches were the 'Offspring of Human Law' and did not owe their position to the character of their doctrine.[105] Indeed, they predated Christianity: both the Druidical and Levitical churches were truly national churches. The importance of this characterisation was that it meant that the Church of England was immune from theological critiques that undermined its national character and tried to reduce it to the status of a sect that had no special, exclusive claim to the property set aside for national purposes. In a separate section of *Church and State* Coleridge offered a brief treatment of the Church of Christ which showed that the Church of England owed its position as National Church to human rather than divine legislation. This explained its special character and helped to justify its established position.[106]

Coleridge claimed that the Church of Christ was distinguished by four, largely negative, characteristics. It had no legal form; it was 'visible and public' not 'mystic or subjective';[107] it was not the opposite of any particular state or worldly institution; and it was not necessarily associated with any national, local or particular institution. It was, in other words, catholic or universal, rather than national or particular.[108] The Church of Christ was not a 'KINGDOM, REALM . . . or STATE . . . of the WORLD'. It stood as a 'compensating counterforce' of states in general ('the *sustaining, correcting, befriending* Opposite of the world! the compensating counterforce to the inherent and inevitable evils and defects of the STATE, *as* a State, and without reference to its better or worse construction as a particular state'), modifying the evil *results* of political and social interaction, but not seeking to correct or change the particular structures of states.[109] The Church of Christ was not part of the institutional structure of any state, and was based on quite different principles from those which were served by, and dictated, the distribution of political power within a body politic. It 'disregards all external accidents, and looks at men as individual persons, allowing no gradation of ranks, but such as greater or less wisdom, learning, and holiness ought to confer. A church is, therefore, in idea, the only pure democracy.'[110] A national church was, by contrast, part of a nation and had a material basis like the other elements of the Constitution.

Coleridge emphasised the difference between the two kinds of church by a terminological innovation. It was common to use the word *ecclesia* in connection with the Church; taken from Greek, where it referred to an assembly of citizens, its Christian meaning was, Coleridge noted, 'the communion of such as are called out of the world'. This, however, was the Church of Christ, not the National Church. Coleridge described this as an *enclesia*, 'an order of men, chosen in and of the realm' – a coinage that not only underlined the difference between the two forms of church, but it also made it clear that the popularist and democratic connotations attached to the Greek meaning of the word *ecclesia* applied only to the Church of Christ and not, as a writer in the *Edinburgh Review* suggested, to the National Church.[111]

Although the Church of Christ could not be exclusively associated with any particular state or national church, that did not mean that it was invisible and purely spiritual. The Church of Christ was not 'the kingdom of God which is *within*'; it was 'objective in its nature and purpose, not mystic and subjective'.[112] This characterisation enabled Coleridge to argue that the established character of the Church of England did not divorce it from the Church of Christ. The National Church was something in addition to a Christian church, and could claim no monopoly of that status, but, since the Church of Christ was visible and objective, a national church such as the Church of England could, as Coleridge commented, '*include* a Christian Church'.[113] Although 'Christ's Kingdom was not of this world', that did not entail, as Coleridge had argued in his Bristol lectures,[114] that those who were of this world, excluded themselves from that Kingdom.

Many of Coleridge's comments on the National Church indicated that its dual character could produce practical difficulties. A frequent source of tension was the tendency for the visible head of the National Church to interfere in issues that concerned only the Church of Christ. In marginal comments on Blomfield's *Charge*, Coleridge discussed a famous example of such unwarranted interference, arising when Queen Elizabeth I suspended Archbishop Grindal from his office for refusing to suppress 'exercises', or private meetings of the clergy to study the Scriptures. Coleridge described Elizabeth's action as 'jealous semi-romanish' and thought it represented an encroachment upon those activities of the Church of England that concerned its Christian rather than its national status.[115]

Coleridge's concern to distinguish the religious and legal dimensions of the National Church was particularly apparent in his commentaries on the lives and works of seventeenth-century divines. His major point of disagreement with otherwise admired writers was their apparent willingness to use state power for religious purposes and their tacit acceptance of what amounted to religious persecution. In response to Richard Baxter's puzzlement that '*Cromwell* . . . and such others, commonly gave out that they could not understand what the Magistrate had to do in Matters of Religion; and that they thought that all Men should be left to their own Consciences', Coleridge wrote that this was 'one among a thousand proofs of Cromwell's attachment to the best interests of human nature!'[116] Coleridge greatly admired Baxter, but was consistently critical of his willingness to use the power of the civil magistrate to maintain Church discipline, and enforce adherence to particular articles of faith. 'On what ground of Right could a Magistrate inflict a penalty thereby to compel a man to *hear* what he might believe dangerous to his soul, on which the Right of burning the refractory individual might not be defended?'[117] In a comment on the writings of Jeremy Taylor, Coleridge was exceedingly critical of Churchmen who sought to bolster their position by acquiring civil power over their flocks:

> it is really shocking to hear Christian Divines talk in the same way, that a Jewish High-Priest might have done unblameably . . . the lust of sacerdotal Power is at the bottom of all this – In all but a *mundane* Religion, *not of this world* – i.e. in all but true [Christianity] Priests are Magistrates, Powers, Agents – in [Christianity] only Teachers, Persuaders, Comforters.[118]

He claimed that the willingness of good men such as Baxter to use the sword of civil magistracy against those who were not of their own religious professions ruined the Commonwealth and pushed Cromwell towards a dictatorship.[119]

The failure to appreciate that civil power had no role in the affairs of the Church of Christ, even for that portion of it that was included within the National Church, was, Coleridge claimed, a feature of the seventeenth century. When taken as the starting point for the practice of a national church and the policy of a government (as it had been during Archbishop Laud's period of supremacy), it gave the Church of England a character that was indistinguishable from that of Rome. Laud was not a theological 'Romanist', but he was rightly suspected of being attached to the 'pomp, pride, vanity, and temporal tyranny of the Roman Church . . . and these, not mistakes in faith, are the poison-bag on which the papal fang rests'.[120] In a marginal comment on Hooker's *Works*, Coleridge claimed that an understanding of the distinction between the Church of Christ and the National Church would have avoided many of the difficulties that had beset religion in England since the Reformation:

> How readily would . . . all the disputes respecting the powers and constitutions of Church-government have been settled, or perhaps prevented, had there been a insight into the distinct nature & origin of the National Church and the Church under Christ! To the ignorance of this, all the fierce contentions between the Puritans and Episcopalians under Eliz. and the Stuarts; all the errors and exorbitant pretensions of the Church of Scotland; and the Heats and Antipathies of our present Dissenters, may be demonstrably traced.[121]

The distinction between the two forms of Church meant that both national and Christian churches could co-exist peacefully without confusing law and religion. National Churches were not necessarily Christian, but the advent of Christianity had provided them with a 'providential boon, a grace of God, a mighty and faithful friend'. Coleridge likened the National Church to a vine whose fruit was improved by the proximity of the olive tree of Christianity.[122] The relationship between the two churches was symbiotic: the olive allowed the vine to grow to perfection, but at the same time members of the Church of Christ needed to receive intellectual enlightenment from the clerisy if they were to develop a perception of religion which would enable them to counter the ill effects of political interaction. The clergy's function was to 'infuse into the minds of their flocks juster & more spiritual conceptions of the Christian *Church*'.[123] Furthermore, a national church could serve to prevent the intrusion of temporal power into the Church of Christ, and act as a bulwark against religious intolerance. In the absence of a national church there was a danger that an institution masquerading as *the* Church of Christ would seek to assume an unregulated secular power on the basis of claims to spiritual universality. Like Richard Baxter, Coleridge believed that the National Church was a rock against which the universalistic pretensions of the Papacy could be broken. 'The Papacy was and still is essentially extra-national; – it affects, *temporally*, to do that which the spiritual Church of Christ can alone do – to break down the natural distinction of nations.' If national churches did not exist, 'the mere spiritual Church would become, like the Papacy, a dreadful tyranny over mind and body'. A further possibility was that the Church of Christ would exist as a multitude of sects, but that would pose a threat to liberty of conscience, as it had done in the English Revolution. A national church provided a bulwark behind which all other Christian churches could enjoy toleration because it was a 'political establishment connected with, but distinct from, the Spiritual Church'.[124]

The distinction between the Christian Church and national churches helped to justify the position of the latter. By stressing the universal character of the Church of Christ, Coleridge was able to reinforce the association between national churches and particular polities, but he did so in a way that made the relationship mutually beneficial. A national church was an essential part of the state, but it functioned better if it included a Church of Christ within it. However, since a national church and a Christian church were different from one another, their interrelationship had to take account of their differing natures and bases, and avoid the temptation to fuse religion and law, or use law as a support for religion.

By distinguishing church establishments from the Church of Christ, Coleridge was able to respond to critiques of the Church of England that held that the very existence of a church establishment involved an unwarranted, un-Christian intrusion of politics into religion.[125] He offered an account of the basis of the Church of

England that confined it within the limits of legal determination, but in so doing he strengthened it against claims that were theological rather than political. The Church was essential to the existence of the nation, but it would not serve that purpose unless it was distinguished from the Church of Christ. A failure to realise the nature of the distinction weakened the position of the Church, even in the hands of its would-be defenders. A comment made by Coleridge in February 1832 made that point quite clear, and also showed that the problem of defining and defending the Church outlasted the discussion of Catholic Emancipation itself:

> Would to God that the bishops or the Clergy in general could once fully understand that the Christian church and the national church are as little to be confounded as divided! I think the fate of the Reform Bill, in itself, of comparatively minor importance; the fate of the national church occupies my mind with greater intensity.[126]

VI CONCLUSION: COLERIDGE AND STATE THEORY

Church and State was Coleridge's last published statement of his political philosophy, and formed an appropriate resting place. In this work, he took up incomplete statements from his earlier writings and welded them into a coherent theory of the state. *Church and State* contained a generalised description of the state which related to the rationale for obedience to it, and a consideration of the role that particular institutions played in strengthening the state by facilitating the attainment of the goals from which it derived its moral status. As we have seen, Coleridge regarded the National Church as an essential part of the state, and this connected his work with the Anglican state theory which flourished in the eighteenth century and continued to have a strong grip on the English mind in the early decades of the nineteenth century.

However, Coleridge did not merely retail conventional notions of the Anglican Church–state. On the contrary, his theory marked a significant departure from prevailing patterns of Anglican political theory. This was due to his conception of morality and its relationship with politics, and also to his understanding of the political significance of different sorts of property. Despite the fact that government derived its ultimate rationale from its capacity to facilitate the realisation of moral goals, it could only have an indirect influence on morality. Because of this, a moralising institution such as the National Church was an essential part of the structure of the state, but, because its job was to balance the outcome of the interaction of political forces, it could not be integrated with government or with governing elites. As a result, Coleridge produced a variety of Anglican political theory which resisted the commonly held notion that Church and state should be institutionally and psychologically fused. This had important implications for the institutional relationship between Church and state, and, as we shall see in the Conclusion of this study, the role that Coleridge assigned to the Church also involved a transformation of the basis of the traditional structure of social and political relationships.

Conclusion: Land, Commerce and the Limits of Tradition

Property was important in Coleridge's political theory because he regarded it as a crucial factor accounting for the existence of power, for the ways in which it was distributed, and the manner in which its exercise should be institutionalised and structured. Over the course of his lifetime, however, Coleridge's understanding of the political and moral implications of property underwent significant changes. Having initially believed that the relationship between property and political power made both property and the state morally problematic, he nevertheless argued in favour of the equalisation of power and influence by means of the erosion of property differentials and the diffusion of property throughout society. These aspirations were closely related to the participatory ideals associated with classical republican theory, but by 1800 Coleridge had reverted to a more conservative use of these discourses, one that made political participation dependent upon existing patterns of ownership. He now regarded a divorce between property and political power as a major threat to the stability and to the moral usefulness of European polities. Regimes that were not grounded on property generated political systems based on *personal* power, not on the institutionalisation of social forces connected with proprietorship.

In arguing these points, Coleridge constantly had in mind the experience of the French Revolution. The establishment of corrupt personal power in the Consulate was merely the outcome of the Jacobin ascription of *personal* political rights. In developing this argument, Coleridge drew heavily upon assumptions about the political and social significance of landed property that had played a prominent role in the ideology of eighteenth-century Country Party opposition groups, and in this respect his theory was closely related to eighteenth-century concerns rather than involving a revolt against them. Country Party language retained a lasting place in Coleridge's political theory, and a concern with the virtues associated with landed property became a feature of it. However, in his major mature contributions to political theory (*The Friend*, the 'Lay Sermons' and *Church and State*) Coleridge combined Country Party arguments with those developed by defenders of commercial society. This move was of considerable ideological importance because it involved an attempt to integrate two perspectives on the political significance of property that had originally developed as rivals.

Coleridge's political theory thus fused the language of tradition with that of modernity. Landed property was valued because it was identified with virtues and patterns of social interaction that related closely to the moral character of the state and the pursuit of its moral goals. By contrast, commercial activity was not directly related to the moral ends of the state, but could assist their fulfilment. Commercial societies integrated governments into systems of relationships that, because they depended upon trust and reciprocity, weakened the position of absolute rulers and thereby contributed to the growth of public freedom. They also expanded private freedom by enlarging the range of economic activity and the possibilities of proprietorship, and thereby contributed to the fulfilment of moral objectives. In the *Biographia Literaria* Coleridge noted with satisfaction that his journalistic essays had contributed to the consideration of contemporary events from 'a moral point of view';[1] this aspiration also informed his treatment of economic issues. In his mature political theory this concern led him to add to traditional arguments about land and commerce a new and distinctive dimension which called for a reconsideration of political institutions and the way people related to them.

In the 'Lay Sermons', and more fully in *Church and State*, Coleridge argued that without assistance aristocracy and commerciality would not produce the moral benefits of which they were capable. The reason for this was that there was an inevitable tendency for the 'spirit' of commercialism to infiltrate and erode the paternalistic and aristocratic ethos associated with landed property. Coleridge was impressed mainly with the political benefits of commerce; he did not accept claims about its wider moral significance. While prepared to acknowledge that commerce enlarged the scope for a certain sort of intellectual progress and even for the advancement of civilisation, he was sceptical about its contribution to 'cultivation', or to understanding the moral basis of humanity that was integral to it. As we have seen, Coleridge's response to the shortcomings of commerce was to argue that the moral and intellectual fibre of the landed classes needed to be reinforced by an educational regime which inculcated values that counteracted the pervasive influence of the spirit of commerce. He identified the Church of England as an agency whose history, institutional structure, material basis and true rationale made it an ideal vehicle for this.

It was a central element of Coleridge's argument that the aristocracy, commerciality and clerisy were not, and ought not to become, part of the same unified establishment. The clerisy were to ensure that the landed classes did not become integrated with the commercial interest, and this meant that members of the National Church had to remain ideologically and materially divorced from both the aristocracy and the commerciality. In insisting on the material independence of the National Church, Coleridge was concerned to ensure that its members could exist as pure elements immune from the need to popularise, or compromise, the philosophical antidote to the commercial spirit. Such independence was necessary if the clerisy were to resist the spirit of commerce and the philosophy of sense impression that was its intellectual manifestation. The clerisy's institutionalisation within a separate estate of the realm based on its own property guaranteed material independence, while their ideological independence was ensured by their attachment to a value system derived from Platonised Christianity. This philosophy provided a bulwark against the materialistic, mechanical, rationalism of prevailing popular philosophy, and directed attention away from the world of sense impression and towards those aspects of human existence which were emanations of spiritual forces.

Coleridge identified Lockean materialism as the most important philosophical rival of Christian Platonism, and thought that the seventeenth century provided powerful weapons in the struggle against it. He claimed to have found there the distinction between 'reason' and 'understanding' that lay at the heart of his delineation of the relationship between ethics and politics, and it seems likely that one of the attractions of Kantianism was its capacity to restate important elements of a philosophical perspective that had been driven from the field by Locke and his followers.[2] Coleridge's marginalia show that his reading of seventeenth-century authors was important in sharpening his conception of the progressive nature of the state, and in helping him to isolate the essential features of a national church. One of his major finds in the seventeenth century was a group of Platonic statesmen – Harrington, Milton, Neville and Sidney – whose special merit was to have resisted the early stages of materialism in politics. In particular, the English republicans adopted political goals that embraced the more complete fulfilment of the ends of the state. They thus provided a source of moral and intellectual inspiration for those who wished to confront the political implications of Lockean materialism, and it was this that distinguished them from their opponents and gave their efforts permanent value.[3]

Coleridge's use of the seventeenth century was itself Platonic in character, since it treated history as a struggle to holdfast to values and conceptions which were in danger of being eroded. Change was possible (even desirable) in the realm of phenomena, but the forms to which these approximated were not subject to mutation.[4] An important implication of this was that criticism of existing values required a reference point in the past that, if not identified with perfection itself, at least represented values that were more nearly perfect. The moral and political philosopher was thus engaged in a process of *recovery*, but this was not necessarily reactionary because what was being recovered were moral and intellectual standards, not institutions or practices.

While Coleridge's understanding of the history of philosophy was Platonic in form, his answer to the question 'Who should rule?' displayed an important deviation from the model advanced in Plato's *Republic*. As David Newsome has noted, Coleridge's clerisy were to act as 'monitors' rather than as Platonic Guardians.[5] They did not rule, but ensured that those who did so operated on the basis of Platonic values. The claims made by Coleridge on behalf of the clerisy were far more modest than those Plato made on behalf of the Guardians, because he dissociated the capacity to *know* good from the power to *do* good. The clerisys' role was crucial to the pursuit of human values in a political context, but it was restricted to influencing the attitude and conduct of those whose possession of property gave them direct access to the institutional structure of political authority.

The monitorial role that Coleridge ascribed to the clerisy was a direct result of his conception of the relationship between personal property and political power and of his views on the effects of the spirit of commerce on the possessors of landed property. In a marginal comment made in the late 1820s, Coleridge noted that the expansion and diffusion of property had concentrated political power in the House of Commons, and weakened other institutions such as Convocation and the judiciary.[6] The belief that there had developed a single locus of power in the state explains why Coleridge was keen to identify sources of influence that were not part of the organised powers of the Constitution. In any case, the development of an omnipotent Parliament made an active and conscientious clerisy a pressing necessity, but one that could not, by virtue of the problems it was meant to alleviate, be equated with Platonic conceptions of philosophic statesmanship. Coleridge's political thought involved an attempt to relocate the role of philosophical knowledge within the *body politic*.

Coleridge's understanding of the political significance of property thus led him to modify one of the central features of Platonic political theory. It also gave his theory a degree of sociological realism that distinguished it from the views of some later proponents of the clerisy idea. In the hands of Thomas Arnold, for example, the relationship which Coleridge had identified between Church and state was transmuted into the idea of a 'Christian commonwealth'. Arnold wrote that members of the National Church were 'directly called upon to Christianize the nation', and commented that, if 'the true moral character' of both Church and State were upheld, these institutions were 'perfectly identical'.[7] While these comments are not necessarily incompatible with Coleridge's general views, they produce an excessively abstract conception of the state. From Coleridge's point of view, the attainment of the 'true moral end of the state' would make both it and the National Church unnecessary. In Arnold's hands, the discussion of Church and state slipped into a utopian mode. For example, he looked forward to the time when the knowledge of the Church would be 'blended' with power of the state to produce a condition in which 'the Church is become sovereign, and the State has become Christian'.[8] This formulation ignored the distinctly political thrust of Coleridge's analysis of the implications of property, and led Arnold to confuse political and religious claims, a procedure for which Coleridge had castigated Cobbett and Cartwright.[9]

Conclusion

The fact that Coleridge sought to counteract the spirit of commerce by elevating Platonism to a central place in the educational experience of the upper classes is of crucial significance for understanding the general character of his political philosophy. His insistence on the need for a clerisy implied a lack of faith in the gentry's capacity to fulfil the duties attached to their station, and this meant that Coleridge cannot be seen as a supporter of a traditional aristocracy. The growth of commerce and the pervasive influence of its intellectual and moral corollaries had made the basis of the traditional aristocratic order outmoded and inadequate, and Coleridge's mature political theory attempted to provide a substitute for it. The significance of this feature of Coleridge's theory can be illustrated by comparing his position with that of Edmund Burke.

There are, of course, marked similarities between Coleridge's political philosophy and that of Burke. Both writers responded to events in France, and both developed conceptions of the historical basis of human life that focused on the nation state and rejected the natural-rights doctrines and the cosmopolitanism which they identified with the French revolutionaries. In addition, as we have seen, Coleridge at times offered an account of the basis of aristocratic order that was similar in some important respects to that found in Burke's *Reflections*. Like Burke, he thought that the traditional social role of the landed classes was largely unconscious and unreflective. It had its origins in what was customary, and gave rise to patterns of behaviour and thought that were so much matters of habit that they seemed, in Burke's phrase, to form part of men's 'second nature'.[10] In Coleridge's analysis, the *mores* of the gentry and their social standing were the product of 'ancient feelings of rank and ancestry', and the 'superstition of birth'. His early discussion of these feelings suggested they were inherited; they formed the basis of an aristocratic culture that was self-sustaining. This culture was traditional because it maintained itself through processes that were neither literate nor the products of intellectual endeavour.

In his turn-of-the-century discussions of the French Constitution and in his articles on France and Rome, Coleridge identified threats to the aristocratic order resulting from coercive influences brought to bear by outside forces. Thus the French revolutionaries had made the aristocracy the subject of a 'hostile oath' and had stripped them of their land; Napoleon had further weakened aristocracy in French politics by perverting the relationship between property and political power.[11] However, the argument of both the 'Lay Sermons' and *Church and State* pointed to a new threat to traditional aristocracy, one that was the result not of force, but of voluntary capitulation before the imagined material and intellectual attractions of commercial society. One symptom of the pervasive effects of philosophical materialism was modern print culture. This point was made in both *The Friend* and in the 'Lay Sermons', but it was expressed with particular force and clarity in *Biographia Literaria*.[12] In an early chapter of this work, Coleridge argued that literature had descended from the status of a 'religious oracle' to one which, (in the words of one of his seventeenth-century favourites, Jeremy Taylor) catered to 'him that reads in malice, or him that reads after dinner'.[13] Coleridge argued that there was a direct relationship between the quality of the audience who received these productions, and the intellectuals whose judgements in the reviews tended to elevate the unworthy and to condemn the worthy to oblivion. The result was that 'Bacon, Harrington, Machiavel, and Spinosa, are *not* read, because Hume, Condillac and Voltaire *are*'.[14] Coleridge clearly believed that the root of this problem was identical with that which had led to the neglect of 'principles' in political discourse – there was a lack of 'fixed canons . . . previously established and deduced from the nature of man'[15] – and this could be traced to the erosion of the contemporary intellect. It was now especially receptive to philosophical materialism, and becoming increasingly impervious to both the theoretical and practical virtues of more profound, because more appropriately human, conceptions.

These intellectual failings were particularly marked among traditional elites. The apparent material attractions of commerce were so tempting to the landed classes precisely because of their intellectual malaise, and the effect of this was to sap the behavourial norms associated with traditional aristocracy and to encourage the prostitution of traditional rationales for the gratification of non-traditional aspirations. Coleridge's response to this problem implied that the growth of commerce had a profound and permanent effect on the structure of social relationships and on their intellectual and moral supports. In these circumstances, no reliance could be placed on traditional mechanisms. Burke's 'coat of prejudice'[16] was now too threadbare to keep out the chill winds of Lockean materialism and the ethics of commerce.

In its place Coleridge wished to enshrine a highly intellectualised Platonic conception of religion. The clerisy would induce the gentry to adhere to the roles that were appropriate to their station and necessary for the continued existence of a moral state. This was to be achieved by instituting forms of upper-class education that would provide a more intellectually and spiritually satisfying diet than Lockean materialism or Humean scepticism. Coleridge believed that the commercial spirit could only be checked by displacing the philosophical system with which it had become identified, and this stipulation had important implications for his understanding of the character of aristocracy in modern society. Because its members had now to be helped to re-create appropriate attitudes and behaviours through intellectual efforts stimulated by a literate elite, it ceased to be traditional. Coleridge hoped that its behaviour would correspond with that expected of the holders of landed property, but this was to spring from their attachment to Christian Platonism and would no longer be merely habitual and unreflective.

Coleridge's views on the impact of commerce and of the clerisy's role in counteracting its harmful effects led him to a solution that placed a premium on the role of the intellect. This paralleled his concern to uphold speculative philosophy against claims that it was pedantic, obscurantist and related to modes of Enlightenment thinking that were destructive of traditional social and political relationships. These charges were made by William Wordsworth in *The Prelude* and rejected by Coleridge in *Biographia Literaria*.[17] In the 'Lay Sermons' and in *Church and State* he traced out the political ramifications of his rejection of the unalloyed traditionalism that Wordsworth shared with Burke. The rediscovery of Platonism and the inculcation of its philosophy and moral values by the clerisy was to form the intellectual basis of an aristocratic order in politics whose role was defined by philosophy rather than by unreflective tradition. As in the past, landed property lay at the heart of the state, but, because it now coalesced with commercially derived wealth, it needed something more than tradition to sustain it.

In conclusion, it is worth making the point that a number of Coleridge's contemporaries were struck by the non-traditional features of his political philosophy. Although the argument of *Church and State* was sometimes forced into the mould of belligerant, partisan Tory Anglicanism, this was by no means the only response that Coleridge elicited.[18] In the closing years of his life, he was virtually adopted by the British Association for the Advancement of Science, a body that was overtly non-dogmatic and non-partisan on political and religious matters.[19] After his death, Coleridge's philosophy played an important (and well-documented) role in the development of the 'Liberal Anglicanism' associated with writers such as Thomas Arnold and F. D. Maurice.[20] However, J. S. Mill's response to Coleridge's political thought provides the most telling support for the interpretation offered in this study. While Mill rejected Coleridge's metaphysics and dismissed his economic thought as 'arrant drivel',[21] he held his political philosophy in high regard, largely because he recognised that its tendency was incompatible with both traditional Toryism and with the overwhelming and uncritical bias towards the landed interest found among Whig grandees. Mill commented that, if Coleridge's principles were adopted by the Tories, then 'we should not wait long for further reform, even in our organic institutions'.[22] Given this view, it is perhaps not surprising to find a revival of interest in Coleridge among mid- and late-nineteenth-century liberal thinkers who shared many of Mill's political aspirations, but who attempted to weld these to a philosophy that exhibited a Coleridgean blending of Platonism and German Idealism. These writers included T. H. Green, the founder of British political idealism, and his follower J. H. Muirhead, one of the first British scholars to take Coleridge's philosophy seriously.[23]

List of Abbreviations

Aids to Reflection	Samuel Taylor Coleridge, *Aids to Reflection and Confessions of an Inquiring Spirit*, new edn (1884)
Biographia Literaria	Samuel Taylor Coleridge, *Biographia Literaria*, ed. James Engell and W. Jackson Bate, 2 vols, CC, VII (Princeton, NJ, 1983)
CC	*Collected Works of Samuel Taylor Coleridge*, gen. ed. Kathleen Coburn, 16 vols (Princeton, NJ, 1969–)
Church & State	Samuel Taylor Coleridge, *On the Constitution of the Church and State According to the Idea of Each*, ed. John Colmer, CC, X (Princeton, NJ, 1976)
CL	*Collected Letters of Samuel Taylor Coleridge*, ed. Earl Leslie Griggs, 6 vols (Oxford, 1956–71)
CM	Samuel Taylor Coleridge, *Marginalia*, ed. George Whalley, 2 vols so far published, CC, XII (Princeton, 1980–)
DNB	*Dictionary of National Biography* (1885–)
EOT	Samuel Taylor Coleridge, *Essays on his Times in 'The Morning Post' and 'The Courier'*, ed. David V. Erdman, 3 vols, CC, III (Princeton, NJ, 1978)
Friend	Samuel Taylor Coleridge, *The Friend*, ed. Barbara E. Rooke, 2 vols, CC, IV (Princeton, NJ, 1969)
HJ	*Historical Journal*
JHI	*Journal of the History of Ideas*
Lay Sermons	Samuel Taylor Coleridge, *Lay Sermons*, ed. R. J. White, CC, VI (Princeton, NJ, 1972)

Lectures 1795	Samuel Taylor Coleridge, *Lectures 1795: On Politics and Religion*, ed. Lewis Patton and Peter Mann, CC, I (Princeton, NJ, 1971)
Notebooks	*Notebooks of Samuel Taylor Coleridge*, ed. Kathleen Coburn, 3 vols so far published (New York and Princeton, NJ, 1957–)
NTP	Samuel Taylor Coleridge, *Notes, Theological, Political and Miscellaneous*, ed. Derwent Coleridge (1853)
PW	*The Complete Poetical Works of Samuel Taylor Coleridge*, ed. E. H. Coleridge, 2 vols (Oxford, 1912)
Table Talk	*Specimens of the Table Talk of Samuel Taylor Coleridge*, ed. H. N. Coleridge, 2nd edn (1870)
Watchman	Samuel Taylor Coleridge, *The Watchman*, ed. Lewis Patton, CC, II (Princeton, NJ, 1970)

Unless otherwise indicated, the place of publication of all books referred to in this study is London.

Notes

INTRODUCTION

1. John Colmer's *Coleridge, Critic of Society* (Oxford, 1959) is the best book-length study of the full range of Coleridge's political thought; David Calleo's *Coleridge and the Modern State* (New Haven, Conn., 1966) is useful on Coleridge's mature thought, although the historical focus of this study is rather fuzzy. More recent discussions of aspects of Coleridge's political theory can be found in Marilyn Butler, *Romantics, Rebels and Reactionaries: English Literature and its Background 1760–1830* (Oxford, 1981); Deirdre Coleman, *Coleridge and 'The Friend' (1809–10)* (Oxford, 1988); Anthony John Harding, *Coleridge and the Idea of Love* (Cambridge, 1974); Nigel Leask, *The Politics of Imagination in Coleridge's Critical Thought* (1988); Nicholas Roe, *Wordsworth and Coleridge: The Radical Years* (Oxford, 1988); and William Stafford, *Radicalism, Socialism and Nostalgia* (Cambridge, 1987). The extensive article literature is referred to in the Notes and Bibliography.
2. The major recent interpretative works relating to the context of Coleridge's political thought include J. C. D. Clark, *English Society 1688–1832* (Cambridge, 1985); J. A. W. Gunn, *Beyond Liberty and Property: The Process of Self-Recognition in Eighteenth-Century Political Thought* (Kingston, Ont., and Montreal, 1983); J. G. A. Pocock, *The Machiavellian Moment: Florentine Political Thought and the Atlantic Republican Tradition* (Princeton, NJ, 1977), and *Virtue, Commerce, and History* (Cambridge, 1985).
3. See Biancamaria Fontana, *Rethinking the Politics of Commercial Society* (Cambridge, 1985); Albert O. Hirschman, *The Passions and the Interests: Political Arguments for Capitalism before its Triumph* (Princeton, NJ, 1977); and Pocock, *The Machiavellian Moment* and *Virtue, Commerce, and History*. The quotation is from *Virtue, Commerce, and History*, p. 291.
4. Butler, *Romantics, Rebels and Reactionaries*, pp. 4–5.
5. C. V. La Grice, 'College Reminiscences of Mr Coleridge', *Gentleman's Magazine*, n. s., II (1834) 605–7; James Gillman, *The Life of Samuel Taylor Coleridge* (1838), I, 49–50. For another contemporary view of Coleridge's political position in the early 1790s see Burton R. Pollin and R. Burke, 'John Thelwall's Marginalia in a Copy of Coleridge's *Biographia Literaria*', *Bulletin of the New York Public Library*, LXXIV (Feb 1970) 73–94. This material is discussed in George Watson, 'The Revolutionary Youth of Wordsworth and Coleridge', *Critical Quar-*

terly, 18, iii (1976) 49–54; and John Beer, 'The "Revolutionary Youth" of Wordsworth and Coleridge: Another View', *Critical Quarterly*, 19, ii (1977) 79–87.

6. In the winter of 1792 there were a number of riots directed against the property of Dissenters in Cambridge. After one crowd had been dispersed by magistrates, a Fellow of St John's told his students that the riot was a 'laudable ebullition of justifiable zeal'. See H. Gunning, *Reminiscences of Cambridge* (1854) pp. 251–2.

7. See Frida Knight, *University Rebel: The Life of William Frend 1751–1841* (1971) p. 144. For Coleridge's connections with Frend and his conduct at Frend's trial see ibid., pp. 118–19, 140–1. Coleridge was associated with two other radicals with Cambridge connections. One was George Dyer (1755–1841), whom he met in late August 1794 (*CL*, I, 97). Dyer was a poet, and was also the author of *Complaints of the Poor People of England* (1793), which argued for the cultivation of wastelands and universal suffrage as means of improving the material and moral condition of the lower orders. Coleridge also knew Benjamin Flower (1755–1829), a Cambridge bookseller and editor of the radical *Cambridge Intelligencer*. Flower published Coleridge and Southey's *The Fall of Robespierre* in 1794. His *The French Constitution; with Remarks on Some of its Principle Articles* (1792) was highly critical of church establishments. For a recent account of Coleridge's connections with radicals and Unitarians at Cambridge, see Roe, *Wordsworth and Coleridge*, pp. 18–19, 85, 111–12.

8. *CL*, I, 280 (17 Dec 1796). On Coleridge's Unitarian views see J. Robert Barth, *Coleridge and Christian Doctrine* (Cambridge, Mass., 1969) ch. 1; and Basil Willey, *Samuel Taylor Coleridge* (1972) chs 2 and 3.

9. For the critical implications of radical Dissent see Isaac Kramnick, 'Religion and Radicalism in England: Political Theory in the Age of Revolution', *Political Theory*, 5 (1977) 505–34; the *religious* starting point of 1790s radicalism has been investigated in Clark, *English Society*, 335ff. On Coleridge's relationship with radical Dissent, see Leonard W. Deen, 'Coleridge and the Radicalism of Religious Dissent', *Journal of English and Germanic Philology*, 61 (1962) 496–510.

10. *Table Talk*, p. 327 (23 June 1834); *Religious Musings*, 387.

11. Clark, *English Society*, p. 334, citing Joseph Priestley's *An Essay on the First Principles of Government, and on the Nature of Political, Civil and Religious Liberty* (1768).

12. On the significance of Burke's attack on Price see Clark, *English Society*, pp. 247–58; and on Horsley's contrasting attitude to English Protestant Dissenters and French Catholics see [Samuel Horsley], *A Review of the Case of the Protestant Dissenters; with Reference to the Test and Corporation Acts* (1790), esp. pp. 18 and 29, and *The Welsh Freeholder's Farewell . . . the Case of the Emigrant French Clerisy . . .* (1794). For an account of Price's views on the positive significance of the French Revolution see D. O. Thomas, *The Honest Mind: The Thought and Work of Richard Price* (Oxford, 1977) pp. 294ff.

13. See Jack Fruchtman, Jr, *The Apocalyptic Politics of Richard Price and*

Joseph Priestley (Philadelphia, 1983) *passim;* Clarke Garrett, *Respectable Folly: Millenarians and the French Revolution in France and England* (Baltimore and London, 1975) ch. 6; and W. H. Oliver, *Prophets and Millennialists* (Auckland and Oxford, 1978) chs 1–3.
14. Cited in Garrett, *Respectable Folly*, p. 134.
15. Knight, *University Rebel*, p. 126.
16. See below, pp. 11–35.
17. *CL*, I, 48 (5 Feb 1793).
18. *CL*, I, 83 (6 July 1794); see also pp. 85–89 (13 July 1794).
19. *The Life and Correspondence of Robert Southey*, ed. C. C. Southey, 6 vols (1849–50) I, 221. See the Introduction to *Lectures 1795*, pp. xxiii–xxiv; and J. R. MacGillivray, 'The Pantisocracy Scheme and Its Immediate Background', in M. W. Wallace (ed.), *Studies in English* (Toronto, 1931) pp. 131–69.
20. M. E. Sandford, *Thomas Poole and his Friends*, 2 vols (London, 1888) I, 96–9.
21. See *CL*, I, 113–14 (21 Oct 1794), 119–20 (23 Oct 1794), 121–2 [3 Nov 1794].
22. See the discussion of John Thelwall's *Rights to Nature*, below, pp. 35ff. Other contemporary examples include William Ogilvie's *The Rights of Property in Land* (1781), Tom Paine's *Agrarian Justice* (1795– 6), and Thomas Spence's *The Real Rights of Man* (1775, 1793, 1796). These pamphlets have been collected in M. Beer, *The Pioneers of Land Reform* (1920). The Manuels have pointed out that the communistic features of pantisocracy were unusual for this period; see Frank E. and Fritzie P. Manuel, *Utopian Thought in the Western World* (Cambridge., Mass., 1979) p. 736.
23. Sandford, *Thomas Poole and his Friends*, I, 98.
24. See *CL*, I, 99 [1 Sept 1794], 114 (21 Oct 1794). Southey's view of life under pantisocracy was exceptionally bucolic: 'When Coleridge and I are sawing down a tree we shall discuss metaphysics; criticise poetry when hunting a buffalo, and write sonnets whilst following the plough' – *New Letters of Robert Southey*, ed. Kenneth Curry, 2 vols (New York, 1965) I, 72.
25. See below, pp. 21–7.
26. See Deen, 'Coleridge and the Radicalism of Religious Dissent', p. 500. Coleridge came to suspect that Southey's interest in the scheme was conditioned largely by personal considerations; see *CL*, I, 164–6 (13 Nov 1795), but note that this was written after the original project had been abandoned and when relations between Coleridge and Southey were somewhat strained. Southey's letters suggest that his interest in pantisocracy was predated by an independent interest in emigration. See *The Life and Correspondence of Robert Southey*, I, 211. Disillusionment with the French Revolution, escapism and a regard for opportunities in the new world are mentioned in Southey's remarks on the benefits of pantisocracy; see ibid., I, 189, 193, 211, and *New Letters of Robert Southey*, I, 61, 65, 73, 81, 91.
27. Joseph Priestley, *Memoirs of Dr Joseph Priestley Written by Himself* (1809) pp. 85–6.

28. See *CL*, I, 86 (6 July 1794), 96 (2 Aug 1794), 121 (24 Oct 1794), 167–8 (13 Nov 1795).
29. See Oliver, *Prophets and Millennialists*, p. 40.
30. *Religious Musings*, ll. 303–7.

CHAPTER 1   COLERIDGE AND CONTEMPORARY RADICALISM: THE BRISTOL LECTURES (1795) AND *THE WATCHMAN* (1796)

1. *Lectures 1795*, p. 3. The motto is taken from Mark Akenside's *To the Right Honourable Frances Earl of Huntington*, v. 2.
2. *Lectures 1795*, p. 5.
3. Ibid.
4. Ibid.
5. Ibid., p. 6.
6. Edmund Burke, *Reflections on the Revolution in France* (1790), cited in *Lectures 1795*, p. 5, n. 3.
7. *Lectures 1795*, p. 6.
8. Ibid., p. 8.
9. Ibid., p. 10.
10. Ibid., pp. 11–12.
11. Ibid., pp. 12–13.
12. On English Jacobinism see Carl B. Cone, *The English Jacobins* (New York, 1968); Gary Kelly, *The English Jacobin Novel 1780–1805* (Oxford, 1976); Olivia Smith, *The Politics of Language 1791–1819* (Oxford, 1984); E. P. Thompson, *The Making of the English Working Class* (Harmondsworth, 1972). According to Richard Dinmore, a radical from Norwich, Jacobinism entailed 'the right of every man to the profits of his own industry; to be subjected to equal laws; and to have an equal share (either personally or by representation) in the enacting of these laws' – R. Dinmore, Jr., *An Exposition of the Principles of the English Jacobins* (Norwich, 1796) p. 10. Using Dinmore's criterion, Coleridge's position in 1795 looked like Jacobinism, and when Coleridge was described as a Jacobin he did not deny it – see *CL*, I, 152 [late Feb 1795]. Scholarly views on the character of Coleridge's early views are divided, although there is a marked tendency to stress the religious and moralistic content of the Bristol lectures. In fact, as J. C. D. Clark has shown, religion played a central role in political radicalism in the 1790s precisely because of the connection between the state and religious orthodoxy; see J. C. D. Clark, *English Society, 1688–1832* (Cambridge, 1985) ch. 5. A recent account of Coleridge in the 1790s – Nicholas Roe, *Wordsworth and Coleridge: The Radical Years* (Oxford, 1988) – argues most convincingly that Coleridge was a radical up to about 1798 and had close ties with other radical figures, foremost among whom was John Thelwall; see particularly pp. 3–4, 18–19, 85, 93, 111–12, 117, 154. Aspects of Coleridge's position in the 1790s are also discussed in Nigel Leask, *The Politics of Imagination in Coleridge's Critical Thought* (1988) chs 2–3.

13. Samuel Horsley, *A Sermon Preached . . . on Wednesday, January 30, 1793: Being the Anniversary of the Martyrdom of King Charles the First* (1793); [John Reeves], *Thoughts on English Government Addressed to the Quiet Good Sense of the People of England* (1795). Horsley and Reeves were part of a High Tory reaction to the Revolution which was essentially absolutist in character; see J. A. W. Gunn, *Beyond Property and Liberty: The Process of Self-Recognition in Eighteenth-Century Political Thought* (Kingston, Ont., and Montreal, 1983) pp. 164ff.
14. See William Godwin, *An Enquiry Concerning Political Justice* (1793), 3rd edn (1798), ed. F. E. L. Priestley, 3 vols (Toronto, 1946) I, bk IV, ch. 3. Very similar arguments can be found in the following works by radical activists: [James Thompson Callender], *The Political Progress of Britain* . . . (1795), pp. 119–20; Daniel Eaton, *The Philanthropist*, no. 1 (16 March 1795) pp. 3–7, no. 5 (27 April 1795) p. 5; Joseph Gerrald, *A Convention the Only Means of Saving Us All from Ruin* (1793) p. 4; Robert Hall, *An Apology for the Freedom of the Press and for General Liberty* (1793) *passim*; Thomas Holcroft, *A Narrative of Facts Relating to a Prosecution for High Treason* (1795) pp. 58–9; Thomas Paine, *Letter Addressed to the Addressers on the Late Proclamation* (1792) p. 14.
15. John Thelwall, *The Tribune: A Periodical Publication Consisting Chiefly of the Political Lectures of J. Thelwall*, 3 vols (1795), I, iii, 62.
16. *Lectures 1795*, pp. 14, 17. Roe (*Wordsworth and Coleridge*, p. 96) comments that mob violence was often directed against reformers, the most famous example being the sacking of Joseph Priestley's house in Birmingham in 1791.
17. *Lectures 1795*, p. 35. See Roe, *Wordsworth and Coleridge*, ch. 6, for a detailed discussion of Coleridge's views of Robespierre.
18. *Lectures 1795*, pp. 37, 43, 44.
19. See Jack Fruchtman, Jr., *The Apocalyptic Politics of Richard Price and Joseph Priestley* (Philadelphia, 1983) p. 49, for Priestley's and Price's combination of religious and political concerns.
20. *Lectures 1795*, p. 45.
21. See below, pp. 74–88.
22. Thelwall, *The Tribune*, II, xxiv, 194; II, xvi, 16; I, vii, 157–8.
23. Peter Mann, Introduction to *Lectures 1795*, pp. xxviii, lxxvii; John Colmer, *Coleridge, Critic of Society* (Oxford 1959) p. 23ff.
24. *Lectures 1795*, p. 83.
25. See also *CL*, I, 153 [late Feb 1795], where Coleridge quotes a comment that 'in these days . . . the advocate for Liberty and Deist are almost synonymous'. A little earlier Coleridge had complained that Thomas Holcroft 'absolutely infests you with *Atheism*' – *CL*, I, 139 (17 Dec 1794).
26. *Lectures 1795*, p. 91.
27. Ibid., pp. 67–8n.
28. Ibid., pp. 209, 210.
29. Ibid., p. 68n.
30. Ibid., pp. 66–8.
31. Ibid., p. 195.

32. Ibid., p. 84.
33. See Joseph Priestley, *An Essay on the First Principles of Government* (1771), in *Priestley's Writings on Philosophy, Science and Politics*, ed. John A. Passmore (New York, 1965) p. 227: 'The most important question concerning the extent of civil government is, whether the civil magistrate, ought to extend this authority to matters of religion.'
34. *Lectures 1795*, p. 84.
35. Ibid., p. 217.
36. *Notebooks*, I, no. 81.
37. *Lectures 1795*, p. 219.
38. Ibid., pp. 219–20, n. 3; cf. Godwin, *Enquiry*, I, 124, citing Thomas Paine, *Common Sense* (1776).
39. Ibid., p. 220.
40. Ibid., p. 221.
41. Ibid., p. 227.
42. Ibid., p. 229.
43. J. Robert Barth, *Coleridge and Christian Doctrine* (Cambridge, Mass., 1969) p. 7.
44. *Lectures 1795*, p. 135. References to the Jewish constitution were fairly common in contemporary literature; see for example Joel Barlow, *Advice to the Privileged Orders in the Several States of Europe Part . . . I*, 2nd edn (1792) p. 39ff; Paine, *Letter Addressed to the Addressers*, pp. 8–9. High Tories derived a more absolutist message from their reading of Hebrew history; see Gunn, *Beyond Liberty and Property*, pp. 165–6.
45. *Lectures 1795*, p. 145.
46. Ibid., p. 126.
47. Ibid., pp. 126–40.
48. See ibid., p. 122 for a note on Coleridge's sources.
49. Ibid., p. 128.
50. Ibid., pp. 132–3. This example was also used by Tom Paine; see note 44 above.
51. Ibid., p. 134.
52. See above, p. 8.
53. Ibid., n. 20.
54. See Mann, Introduction to *Lectures 1795*, pp. viii–lxiii; Leonard W. Deen, 'Coleridge and the Sources of Pantisocracy: Godwin, the Bible, and Hartley', *Boston Studies in English*, 5 (1961) 232–45.
55. Joseph Priestley, *Letters to the Right Honourable Edmund Burke* (1791), cited in Mann's Introduction to *Lectures 1795*, p. lxiv.
56. J. R. MacGillivray, 'The Pantisocracy Scheme and Its Immediate Background', in M. W. Wallace ed, *Studies in English* (Toronto, 1931) p. 155.
57. See *Priestley's Writings on Philosophy, Science and Politics*, pp. 183, 203–4, 267ff.
58. Deen, 'Coleridge and the Sources of Pantisocracy', pp. 236–9.
59. *Lectures 1795*, p. 149.
60. Gunn, *Beyond Liberty and Property*, pp. 165–6.

61. Moses Lowman, *A Dissertation on the Civil Government of the Hebrews*, 2nd edn (1745). Peter Mann has identified the nature and extent of Coleridge's dependence on Lowman in notes to 'Lectures on Revealed Religion', *Lectures 1795*; see particularly the notes to Lecture 2, pp. 123ff.
62. Lowman, *Dissertation*, p. 35ff. Lowman quotes from Harrington's *Art of Law Giving*, which was printed in John Toland's edition of Harrington's writings, *The Oceana and Other Works* (1700). Aspects of Coleridge's use of Harrington and Lowman are discussed in Leask, *The Politics of Imagination*, ch. 3.
63. S. B. Liljegren has argued that Harrington's ideas played an important role in constitutional discussions after the outbreak of the French Revolution, particularly with respect to the Constitution of 1792; see S. B. Liljegren (ed.), 'French Draft Constitution of 1792. Modelled on James Harrington's *Oceana*', *Skrifter utgivna av Kungl. Humanistiska Vetenskapssamfundet i Lund*, XVII, (1932) pp. 3–43. Liljegren points out in *Harrington and the Jews* (Lund, 1932) pp. 6–7, that discussions of the Jewish constitution were common among seventeenth-century Calvinists and sectarians: 'The Levitical legislation was held up as a pattern for England to be instituted there without modifications.' Coleridge's use of the Jewish constitution was more complex than this. For examples of references to Harrington in contemporary literature, see James Mackintosh, *Vindicae Gallicae* (1791) p. 310; and Thomas Spence, *Constitution of a Perfect Commonwealth* (1793), repr. *The Political Writings of Thomas Spence*, ed. H. T. Dickinson (Newcastle upon Tyne, 1982). Spence's commonwealth is very similar to that in Harrington's *Oceana*. Southey used 'Harrington' as a pen name – see *The Life and Correspondence of Robert Southey*, ed. C. C. Southey, 6 vols (1849–50) I, 231 – and Coleridge referred to him on a couple of occasions in the Bristol lectures (*Lectures 1795*, pp. 255, 290). Iain Hampsher-Monk has discussed the use of Harringtonian arguments by the Society of the Friends of Freedom in 'Civic Humanism and Parliamentary Reform: The Case of the Society of the Friends of the People', *Journal of British Studies*, 18 (1979) 70–89.
64. See for example *The Political Works of James Harrington*, ed. J. G. A. Pocock (Cambridge, 1977) pp. 181–5, 213.
65. Ibid., pp. 163–4.
66. See J. G. A. Pocock, *The Machiavellian Moment: Florentine Political Thought and the Atlantic Republican Tradition* (Princeton, NJ, 1977) pt III.
67. Compare this with Priestley's and Price's more conventional views on the relationship between property and political power; see Fruchtman, *Apocalyptic Politics*, pp. 55–6.
68. This formulation comes from J. G. A. Pocock, 'Cambridge Paradigms and Scotch Philosophers', in Istvan Hont and Michael Ignatieff (eds), *Wealth and Virtue: The Shaping of Political Economy in the Scottish Enlightenment* (Cambridge, 1983) p. 248.
69. See above, notes 57 and 67.

70. Godwin, *Enquiry*, II, 431ff. On the juristic nature of this conception of property see Pocock, 'Cambridge Paradigms and Scotch Philosophers', p. 264ff.
71. *PW*, I, 158.
72. *Lectures 1795*, p. 258.
73. Ibid., pp. 261, 270–1.
74. Ibid., p. 275.
75. Ibid., p. xlvii. Harrington was one of Burgh's sources; see James Burgh, *Political Disquisitions*, 3 vols (1774–5), I, xvii– xviii. For Coleridge's borrowings from Burgh see Lucyle Werkmeister, 'Coleridge's *The Plot Discovered*: Some Facts and a Speculation', *Modern Philology*, 56 (1958–9) 254–5. On the dating of this work see P. Kitson, 'Coleridge's *The Plot Discovered*: A New Date', *Notes and Queries*, Mar 1984, pp. 57– 8.
76. *Lectures 1795*, p. 306, n. 4.
77. Ibid., pp. 306–7.
78. Gunn, *Beyond Liberty and Property*, p. 172.
79. *Lectures 1795*, pp. 310–11, 312–13.
80. Cf. Colmer, *Coleridge, Critic of Society*, p. 25. John Colmer criticises Crane Brinton, *The Political Ideas of the English Romanticists* (Oxford, 1926) pp. 69–70, for claiming that Coleridge was a supporter of universal suffrage in the 1790s, but he does so by reference to remarks made by Coleridge more than thirty years later; see Coleridge, *Critic of Society*, p. 25, n. 2.
81. *Lectures 1795*, pp. 306–7.
82. Ibid., p. 295.
83. *Watchman*, p. 5.
84. Ibid., pp. 11, 55, 63, 108–10, 205, 67–8, 123–4, 130ff., 150ff.
85. Ibid., pp. 209, 237, 243, 271–2, 290–1.
86. Ibid., pp. 99–100.
87. *CL*, I, 253 (13 Nov 1796). It is not clear to which work Coleridge was referring. He urged Thelwall, '*immediately* write me the size of your intended work', which suggests that he had seen an unpublished outline or fragment. It seems likely that the work in question was a manuscript version of Thelwall's *The Rights of Nature against the Usurpations of Establishments. A Series of Letters to the People, in Reply to the False Principles of Burke* (1796), the advertisement of which is dated 5 Nov. The material on property appears in the third letter and it is possible that it had not gone through the press by the 13th. Coleridge had read and admired the first part of Thelwall's *Rights of Nature* early in the year; see the letter to Thelwall on 22 June (*CL*, I, 221). The reference to Burke in the title of the first part was less assertive than in the second: it referred merely to 'The Recent Effusions of the Right Honourable Edmund Burke'. Nicholas Roe identifies close connections between Thelwall and Coleridge in the years 1795–6; see *Wordsworth and Coleridge*, pp. 148–50.
88. Thelwall, *Rights of Nature*, pt II, pp. 55, 56, 66, 70–3, 70–1.
89. Ibid. This account of the significance of Thelwall's argument is derived from Iain Hampsher-Monk's unpublished study 'Thelwall

and Natural Rights'. I am grateful to the author for making this paper available to me.
90. Thelwall, *Rights of Nature*, pt II, pp. 77, 80–1.
91. *CL*, I, 253 (13 Nov 1796).
92. *Watchman*, pp. 64, 66.
93. Ibid., pp. 224–5.
94. Marilyn Butler's remark in *Romantics, Rebels and Reactionaries: English Literature and its Background 1760–1830* (Oxford, 1981) p. 81, that 'the schism within the radical movement between Christians and Deists compromised' Coleridge's position, seems to pay too little attention to Coleridge's attempt to ground radicalism on Christianity.
95. *Watchman*, pp. 99–100.
96. Alfred Cobban, *A History of Modern France*, 3 vols (Harmondsworth, 1971) I, 250.
97. On Mackintosh see Knud Haakonssen, 'The Science of a Legislator in James Mackintosh's Moral Philosophy', *History of Political Thought*, V, (1984) 255.
98. See Hampsher-Monk, 'Civic Humanism and Parliamentary Reform'.
99. See above, pp. 15–19.

CHAPTER 2   CONSTITUTIONS, CONCORDATS AND COUNTRY PARTY IDEOLOGY: THE REALIGNMENT OF COLERIDGE'S POLITICAL THEORY, 1799–1802

1. David V. Erdman, 'Coleridge as Editorial Writer', in Conor Cruise O'Brien and William Vanech (eds), *Power and Consciousness* (London and New York, 1969) p. 185.
2. *EOT*, I, lx ff.
3. *PW*, I, 243; Erdman, 'Coleridge as Editorial Writer', p. 185.
4. E. P. Thompson, 'Disenchantment or Default? *A Lay Sermon*', in O'Brien and Vanech, *Power and Consciousness*, pp. 167–9.
5. *CL*, I, 343 (21 Aug 1797).
6. Thompson, 'Disenchantment or Default?', p. 168.
7. *EOT*, I, 53.
8. For example, in the *Monthly Magazine*, IX (Feb 1800) 75.
9. *EOT*, I, 54, 50.
10. *Notebooks*, I, no. 600.
11. *EOT*, I, 32.
12. Ibid., pp. 32–3, 50.
13. Ibid., p. 36.
14. Ibid., p. 48.
15. Ibid., p. 53.
16. Ibid.
17. See above, pp. 27–32.
18. See J. G. A. Pocock, *The Machiavellian Moment: Florentine Political*

Thought and the Atlantic Republican Tradition (Princeton, NJ, 1977) pp. 390, 393–4.
19. Ibid., pp. 478ff; see also H. T. Dickinson, Liberty and Property: Political Ideology in Eighteenth-Century Britain (1977) pp. 102–18.
20. EOT, I, 57.
21. J. A. W. Gunn, Beyond Liberty and Property: The Process of Self-Recognition in Eighteenth-Century Political Thought (Kingston, Ont., and Montreal, 1983) pp. 171–2, 186–7.
22. Dickinson, Liberty and Property, pp. 102–118; Pocock, The Machiavellian Moment, pp. 478ff.
23. Dickinson, Liberty and Property, pp. 117–18.
24. Notebooks, I, no. 594.
25. EOT, I, 55.
26. Ibid., pp. 55, 48.
27. Ibid., p. 37.
28. See 'On Peace', III and IV, EOT, I, 68–71, 72–5.
29. See above, pp. 29–31.
30. EOT, I, 32.
31. Ibid.
32. Lectures 1795, p. 126.
33. Pocock, The Machiavellian Moment, ch. II.
34. CL, I, 563–4 (25 Jan 1800).
35. John Colmer, Coleridge, Critic of Society (Oxford, 1959) pp. 56–7.
36. EOT, I, 48, 55.
37. Pocock, The Machiavellian Moment, pp. 361ff. On the use of this distinction in the war yearssee J. E. Cookson, The Friends of Peace (Cambridge, 1982) pp. 217–18.
38. EOT, I, 39.
39. Ibid. pp. 143–4.
40. Ibid., pp. 312–39.
41. Ibid., p. 325.
42. Ibid., p. 326.
43. Ibid., pp. 315–16.
44. Ibid., p. 326.
45. Ibid., p. 315.
46. Ibid., p. 326.
47. Ibid.
48. See David P. Calleo, Coleridge and the Idea of the Modern State (New Haven, Conn., 1966) p. 110; John Colmer, 'Coleridge and Politics', in R. L. Brett (ed.), Writers and their Background: S. T. Coleridge (1972) pp. 263–4.
49. EOT, I, 367–73, 370.
50. See above, pp. 19–21.
51. See Basil Willey, Samuel Taylor Coleridge (1972) ch. 10.
52. Biographia Literaria, I, 204–5.
53. E. S. Shaffer, 'Kubla Khan' and the Fall of Jerusalem (Cambridge, 1975) p. 50.
54. Ibid., p. 26. On Coleridge in Germany see Biographia Literaria, I, 207–11.

55. [Samuel Horsley], *A Review of the Case of the Protestant Dissenters: with Reference to the Corporation and Test Acts* (1790) pp. 20–1.
56. *Notebooks*, I, no. 1181.
57. *CL*, II, 806 (1 July 1802).
58. Coleridge's earliest marginalia on Baxter date from 1811; see *CM*, I, 230. The marginalia on Luther have not yet appeared in *CC*, but see *The Literary Remains of Samuel Taylor Coleridge*, ed. H. N. Coleridge, 4 vols (1836–9) IV.
59. Richard Baxter, *Of National Churches: Their Description, Institution, Use, Preservation, Danger, Maladies and Cure: Partly Applied to England* (1691) pp. 41 and 49, and *A Holy Commonwealth, or Political Aphorisms, Opening the True Principles of Government* (1659) pp. 241–2.
60. *Church & State*, chs 7–10; and see below, pp. 145, 153–4.
61. *The Political Works of James Harrington*, ed. J. G. A. Pocock (Cambridge, 1977) pp. 678–9.
62. Ibid.
63. *Notebooks*, I, 639–41.
64. *CL*, II, 803 (3 June 1802).
65. Joel Barlow, *Advice to the Privileged Orders in the Several States of Europe, Part I*, 2nd edn (1792) p. 71. The editors of Coleridge's 1795 lectures point to similarities between his language and that of Barlow; see *Lectures 1795*, p. 30, n. 13. For the role of arguments about standing armies in Country Party ideology see Dickinson, *Liberty and Property*, pp. 104–10; and Pocock, *The Machiavellian Moment*, p. 409 ff.
66. *EOT*, I, 314.
67. *CL*, II, 806 (1 July 1802).
68. See for example Colmer, *Coleridge, Critic of Society*, ch. 3.
69. See above, pp. 19–20.
70. [William Warburton], *The Alliance between Church and State, or the Necessity and Equity of an Established Religion and a Test Act* (1736) pp. 7–8, 53, 69, 70, 75. Coleridge remarked that he 'disliked and suspected' the 'Warburtonian System' (*CL*, II, 803 – 3 June 1802). Hume's remark is cited from the *DNB*. On the Warburtonians in the eighteenth century see Leslie Stephens, *History of English Thought in the Eighteenth Century*, 2nd edn, 2 vols (1881) ch. 7. Horsley used the idea of the alliance in his attack on the Dissenters in 1790; see *A Review of the Case of the Protestant Dissenters*, p. 19.
71. [Warburton], *The Alliance between Church and State*, pp. 70, 53, 69, 70, 75.
72. Ibid., p. 75.
73. Gunn, *Beyond Liberty and Property*, pp. 164ff.
74. Alfred Cobban, *Edmund Burke and the Revolt against the Eighteenth Century* (1960) pp. 167–9.
75. Cobban refers to *The Friend* (1809), *Essays on his Times* (c. 1814), *The Statesman's Manual* (1816), *Biographia Literaria* (1817), and *Table Talk*, based on the last years of Coleridge's life.
76. *Biographia Literaria*, I, 217.
77. *EOT*, I, 370–1.

78. Ibid.
79. Ibid.
80. See J. G. A. Pocock, 'Burke and the Ancient Constitution: A Problem in the History of Ideas', *HJ*, 3 (1960) 125–43.
81. Shaffer, *'Kubla Khan' and the Fall of Jerusalem*, p. 85.
82. See above, pp. 60–1.
83. J. G. A. Pocock, 'The Political Economy of Burke's Analysis of the French Revolution', *HJ*, 25 (1982) 337.
84. Ibid.
85. Edmund Burke, *Reflections on the Revolution in France* (Harmondsworth, 1969) p. 199.
86. Ibid., p. 198.
87. Ibid., p. 206.

CHAPTER 3 PRINCIPLED MORALITY AND PRUDENTIAL POLITICS: *THE FRIEND* (1809–10)

1. David V. Erdman, 'Coleridge as Editorial Writer', in Conor Cruise O'Brien and William Dean Vanech (eds), *Power and Consciousness* (New York, 1969) pp. 197–201, and Introduction to *EOT*, I. On Coleridge's reconciliation with Trinitarianism see *CL*, II, 118–93 [early Oct 1806]; and Basil Willey, *Samuel Taylor Coleridge* (1972) ch. 10.
2. On Coleridge in Malta see Donald Sultana, *Samuel Taylor Coleridge in Malta and Italy* (Oxford, 1969).
3. On 'Comforts and Consolations' see *Notebooks*, I, nos 1646, 1835n; II, 1993, f.31. For the background to *The Friend* see Barbara Rooke's Introduction in vol. I of the *CC* edition. The original (1809–10) version of the periodical appears in vol. II of this edition. The fullest study of the 1809–10 version is Deirdre Coleman's *Coleridge and 'The Friend' (1809–10)* (Oxford, 1988). Coleman stresses the tension between religion and politics in this work, and argues that Coleridge moves between principles and prudence (p. 18). This argument is especially persuasive in relation to Coleridge's treatment of international relations (ch. 8), but I think that in general it can be maintained that Coleridge's theory is rather more coherent than Coleman at times allows. Moreover, the distinction between principle and prudence plays a significant role in the development of Coleridge's political theory, especially in relation to property.
4. *CL*, III, 143 (14 Dec 1808); Willey, *Samuel Taylor Coleridge*, p. 123. One important source of Coleridge's unease (namely, the relatively large number of Quakers who subscribed to, or otherwise supported, *The Friend*) is most convincingly presented in ch. 5 of Coleman's *Coleridge and 'The Friend'*.
5. *Friend*, II, 140.
6. Ibid., pp. 76–84.
7. *Notebooks*, III, no. 3581.
8. See above, p. 61.

9. *Notebooks*, II, no. 2983.
10. *Friend*, II, 72.
11. Ibid., p. 314.
12. Ibid., p. 40.
13. Ibid., p. 314.
14. Ibid., p. 125.
15. Ibid., p. 128. For a full discussion of the role played by Coleridge's understanding of Kant see Coleman, *Coleridge and 'The Friend'*, chs 4 and 7; these chapters are particularly interesting on Kant's influence on Coleridge's critique of Rousseau.
16. *Friend*, II, 104n. See also Willey, *Samuel Taylor Coleridge*, p. 128: 'Reason seeks ultimate ends; Understanding studies means. . . . Reason is the eye of the spirit, the faculty whereby spiritual reality is spiritually discerned; Understanding is the "mind of the flesh".'
17. René Wellek, *Immanuel Kant in England 1793–1838* (Princeton, NJ, 1931) pp. 104–8.
18. *Friend*, II, 295.
19. Ibid., p. 315.
20. *EOT*, II, 81.
21. *Friend*, II, 98.
22. Ibid., p. 101.
23. *The Political Works of James Harrington*, ed. J. G. A. Pocock (Cambridge, 1977) p. 162. Sultana (*Coleridge in Malta and Italy*, p. 174) shows that Coleridge read Harrington and made notes in Malta in 1804.
24. *The Political Works of James Harrington*, p. 163.
25. Ibid., p. 169.
26. *Friend*, II, 102.
27. R. Cudworth, DD, *The True Intellectual System of the Universe: The First Part; Wherein, All the Reasons and Philosophy of Atheism is Confuted; and Its Impossibility Demonstrated* (1678) pp. 890–1.
28. Ibid., pp. 895–6.
29. *Friend*, II, 102.
30. Edmund Burke, *Reflections on the Revolution in France* (Harmondsworth, 1969) pp. 149–51. J. D. Coates points out in 'Coleridge's Debt to Harrington: A Discussion of *Zapolya*', *JHI*, 38 (1977) 502, that Coleridge's view of the state was far more progressive than that of Burke; this can be seen by a comparison between Burke's image of the Constitution as the 'proud Keep of Windsor', and Coleridge's view of it as a river and its embankment. Cf. Coleman, *Coleridge and 'The Friend'*, ch. 6.
31. *Notebooks*, II, no. 2223, f.19.
32. *Friend*, II, 125.
33. Ibid., p. 126.
34. *Notebooks*, II, no. 2223, f.17.
35. Ibid.
36. David Newsome, *Two Classes of Men: Platonism and English Romantic Thought* (1974) p. 16. Coleridge claimed that 'Pythagoras, the proper founder of philosophy, proposed the whole problem . . . namely the

connection of the visible things with the invisible thing' – *The Philosophical Lectures of Samuel Taylor Coleridge*, ed. Kathleen Coburn (1949) p. 145.
37. See above, pp. 27–32.
38. J. G. A. Pocock, *The Machiavellian Moment: Florentine Political Thought and the Atlantic Republican Tradition* (Princeton, NJ, 1977) pp. 385–7; cf. Pocock, 'Contexts for the Study of James Harrington', *Il Pensiero Politico*, XI (1978) 20–35. On Harrington's Platonism see W. G. Diamond 'Natural Philosophy and Harrington's Political Thought', *Journal of the History of Philosophy*, XVI (1978) 387–98.
39. On the contrast between Aristotle and Plato see Coates, 'Coleridge's Debt to Harrington', p. 505. The mechanical aspects of Harrington's constitutional forms have been discussed in J. C. Davis, 'Pocock's Harrington: Grace, Nature and Art in the Classical Republicanism of James Harrington', *HJ*, 24 (1981) 683–97.
40. *Notebooks*, III, no. 3293, f.14.
41. *Friend*, II, 127.
42. Ibid.
43. Ibid., p. 128.
44. Ibid., pp. 322, 103–4.
45. Ibid., p. 321.
46. Ibid., p. 105.
47. *Notebooks*, III, no. 3294.
48. *Friend*, II, 61.
49. Ibid., p. 83.
50. Ibid., pp. 323–4.
51. Ibid., p. 325.
52. *EOT*, II, 95–6. For an extended and critical treatment of Coleridge's views on patriotism at this time see Coleman, *Coleridge and 'The Friend'*, ch. 8.
53. *Friend*, II, 129.
54. Thomas De Quincey, 'Samuel Taylor Coleridge', *The Collected Writings of Thomas De Quincey*, ed. David Masson, 14 vols (Edinburgh, 1896) II, 185.
55. *Friend*, II, 101, 288–9. Coleman (*Coleridge and 'The Friend*, p. 110ff) identifies Richard Hooker as an important source for Coleridge's ideas on the relationship between general rules and particular applications.
56. *Friend*, II, 141.
57. Ibid., pp. 131–2.
58. Ibid., p. 132; *Notebooks*, III, no. 3835.
59. *Friend*, II, 132.
60. John Cartwright, *The People's Barrier against Undue Influence and Corruption: or the Common's House of Parliament According to the Constitution* (1780) pp. iv, v–vi, 7, 28. See also Coleman, *Coleridge and 'The Friend'*, pp. 125–6, which argues that Cartwright's social standing and the fact that he was not a Dissenter explain why Coleridge singled him out for treatment.
61. *Friend*, II, 137.

62. Ibid., II, 135.
63. *Friend*, II, 133.
64. *Notebooks*, III, no. 3742.
65. See J. G. A. Pocock, *The Ancient Constitution and the Feudal Law* (Cambridge, 1957) ch. 2. On the use of these arguments in the period see E. P. Thompson, *The Making of the English Working Class* (Harmondsworth, 1972) pp. 94–7.
66. *Friend*, II, pp. 197–8.
67. *Notebooks*, III, no. 3840. Elsewhere Coleridge associated ancient constitutionalism with a failure to distinguish between personal rights and those of a political and social nature; see *Notebooks*, III, nos 3840, 3843.
68. *EOT*, II, 66–7, 68.
69. *Friend*, II, 143.
70. Ibid., p. 141.
71. Ibid., p. 167. In *Notebooks*, III, no. 3832, Coleridge expressed his reservations about Blackstone's theory of the Constitution.
72. See above, pp. 49–52.
73. *Friend*, II, 164–5.
74. See *CL*, II, 710 (23 Mar 1801), 721 (18 Apr 1801); *Notebooks*, II, nos 2488, 2506.
75. *Friend*, II, 140.
76. Ibid., p. 160.
77. Ibid., p. 161.
78. Ibid., p. 162.
79. Sir James Steuart, *An Inquiry into the Principles of Political Oeconomy* (1767), ed. Andrew S. Skinner (Edinburgh, 1966) I, 89. For a different use of this passage see William F. Kennedy, *Humanist versus Economist: The Economic Thought of Samuel Taylor Coleridge* (Berkeley, Calif., 1958) p. 22. For Coleridge's knowledge of Steuart's work see *Notebooks*, I, nos. 308–10; Professor Coburn dates these entries to Dec 1797 and Jan 1805. The phrase 'cement' appeared in Berkeley's *A Discourse Addressed to Magistrates or Men in Authority*, which Coleridge knew of (see *Notebooks*, I, no. 59). Berkeley used it with reference to religion: 'the cement that connects the several parts or members of the political body' – *The Works of George Berkeley, D.D.*, 2 vols (1794) II, 302). This provides an interesting connection with Albert O. Hirschman's claim in *The Passions and the Interests: Political Arguments for Capitalism before its Triumph* (Princeton, NJ, 1977), that commerce came to be seen as a substitute for bonding forces of a weakened morality based on religious sanctions.
80. Steuart, *Inquiry*, I, 24, 208–9, 216.
81. *Friend*, II, 161–2.
82. Ibid., p. 63 n.
83. Coates (Coleridge's Debt to Harrington', p. 507), seems to place too much stress on Coleridge's later attachment to the agrarian ideal, and ignores his development of a guarded, though generally favourable, perspective on commerce.
84. *Friend*, II, 199.

85. Ibid., p. 200.
86. See above, p. 89.
87. *Friend*, II, 201.
88. See John Colmer, *Coleridge, Critic of Society* (Oxford, 1959) p. 109.
89. *Friend*, II, pp. 201–2.
90. Ibid., p. 207.
91. Colmer, *Coleridge, Critic of Society*, p. 110.
92. *EOT*, II, 94–5. See also the critical reference to Steuart in *Friend*, II, 326–7 where he is accused of providing a purely mechanical view of social interaction and human welfare.

CHAPTER 4   POLITICS, PROPERTY AND POLITICAL ECONOMY, 1810–19

1. See above, pp. 88–93.
2. Coleridge's 'Lay Sermons' of 1816 and 1817 were published as *The Statesman's Manual or The Bible the Best Guide to Political Skill and Foresight*, and *A Lay Sermon Addressed to the Higher and Middle Classes on the Existing Distresses and Discontents*. They appear in the Princeton edition of Coleridge's works (*CC*) in a single volume entitled *Lay Sermons*; in the text this phrase is used without italics to refer to both sermons, but where only one or other is mentioned they appear as *The Statesman's Manual*, or *A Lay Sermon*. In addition to Coleridge's letters and notebooks, the major sources for this chapter are articles contributed to the *Courier* between 1810 and 1819 and the rifacciamento of *The Friend* published in 1818.
3. See R. J. White's Introduction to *Lay Sermons*, pp. xli–xlii; Arthur S. Link, 'Samuel Taylor Coleridge and the Economic and Political Crisis in Great Britain, 1816–1820', *JHI*, 9 (1948) 323–38; William Stafford, *Socialism, Radicalism, and Nostalgia* (Cambridge, 1987) ch. 8; and E. P. Thompson, *The Making of the English Working Class* (Harmondsworth, 1972) chs. 15–16.
4. Thompson, *The Making of the English Working Class*, ch. 15. In the *Edinburgh Review* Francis Jeffrey claimed that Cobbett's position could be reduced to the proposition that 'all evils in the state were produced by the corrupt composition of a legislative body not choosen by the people'. See John Clive, *Scotch Reviewers: The 'Edinburgh Review'*, *1802–1815* (1957) pp. 105–6.
5. Coleridge's busiest journalistic year was 1811, when he wrote dozens of pieces for the *Courier*, some of which dealt with issues discussed in the present chapter. The 1814 series 'To Mr Justice Fletcher', I–VI, on disaffection in Ireland, also touches on the question of working-class combinations and is especially important. See *EOT*, II and III.
6. Cited in *CL*, IV, 757 (28 July 1817).
7. *Lay Sermons*, p. 124.
8. The phrase is from *Lay Sermons*, p. 140.
9. See Biancamaria Fontana, *Rethinking the Politics of Commercial Society*

Notes

(Cambridge, 1985) pp. 7–8; J. G. A. Pocock, 'The Political Economy of Burke's Analysis of the French Revolution', *HJ,* 25 (1982) 332–3.

10. See Fontana, *Rethinking the Politics,* pp. 79–111. Dr Fontana also points out that there were significant connections between the ideas of the Edinburgh Reviewers and those of the physiocrats; see pp. 14, 15, 29.
11. *CL,* IV, 856 [early May 1818].
12. *Friend,* I, 459.
13. *Lay Sermons,* pp. 28–9, 28.
14. Anthony John Harding, *Coleridge and the Inspired Word* (Kingston, Ont., and Montreal, 1986), pp. 77–9.
15. *Lay Sermons,* p. 29.
16. Ibid., p. 74.
17. Ibid., p. 25.
18. *Friend,* I 439.
19. *Lay Sermons,* pp. 206–7. Coleridge is probably referring to Adam Smith's *An Inquiry into the Nature and Causes of the Wealth of Nations* (1776) bk I, chs 7–8.
20. A possible source for Coleridge's views on Smith is [Sir] James Grahame, *An Inquiry into the Principles of Population . . .* (Edinburgh, 1816). In response to Smith's claim that 'the demand for *men,* like that for *any other commodity,* necessarily regulates the production of men, quickens it when it goes too slowly, and stops it when it advances too fast' (*Wealth of Nations,* bk I, ch. 8), Grahame commented that 'there is something disgustful and grovelling in the idea presented by this passage, as well as something at once harsh and indefinite in the language in which it is conveyed. It is painful and humiliating to be told, that [man] . . . is *one of the commodities* of a manufacturing country; entirely dependent for his production, like the spade or plough he is to hold, on a certain commercial demand . . .' (*Inquiry,* p. 16).
21. See J. L. and Barbara Hammond, *The Town Labourer 1760–1832,* 2 vols (1949) I, 164–5.
22. *CL,*IV, 855–6 [early May 1818].
23. *EOT,* II, 488.
24. On Coleridge and animal legislation see John Colmer, *Coleridge, Critic of Society* (Oxford, 1959) pp. 92–3.
25. See George Reuben Potter, 'Unpublished Marginalia in Coleridge's Copy of Malthus' Essay on Population', *Proceedings of the Modern Language Society of America,* LI (Dec 1936) 1061–8. For parallels between aspects of Coleridge's and Malthus's economic thought see William F. Kennedy, *Humanist versus Economist: The Economic Thought of Samuel Taylor Coleridge* (Berkeley, Calif., 1958) pp. 24–6.
26. *Friend,* II, 167.
27. Patricia James, *Population Malthus* (1978) pp. 103, 121, points out that Coleridge 'inspired' Southey's attack on Malthus in the *Annual Review* for 1804.
28. See above, pp. 75–6.
29. *Lay Sermons,* pp. 168, 169n.

30. *CM*, II, 616, 622.
31. *EOT*, II, 389.
32. Ibid., pp. 388–9.
33. *CL*, IV, 710–11 (15 Mar 1817).
34. *Biographia Literaria*, I, 192.
35. *Lay Sermons*, p. 143ff.
36. Cf. *Friend*, II, pp. 52ff.
37. See J. D. Coates, 'Coleridge's Debt to Harrington: A Discussion of *Zapolya*', *JHI*, 38 (1977) 505.
38. *Lay Sermons*, p. 142.
39. *EOT*, II, 165; for Coleridge's critique of the idea of the general will see above, p. 84.
40. *Lay Sermons*, p. 151. Robert R. Dozier has argued that one of the purposes of Thomas Paine's writings from the 1790s was to weaken the structure of society by subjecting it to ridicule; see *For King, Constitution, and Country: The English Loyalists and the French Revolution* (Lexington, Mass., 1983) p. 8.
41. *Notebooks*, III, no. 4311.
42. *Lay Sermons*, p. 148. Earlier, on 1 Dec 1808, the *Courier* had connected the two, describing the *Edinburgh Review* as 'a quarterly Cobbett'.
43. On Cobbett see Fontana, *Rethinking the Politics*, pp. 128–9.
44. Cited in Noel W. Thompson, *The People's Science* (Cambridge, 1984), p. 193. Thompson argues (ch. 1) that the years after the Napoleonic Wars saw an attempt by radicals to develop an alternative economic theory to that of the classical political economists.
45. See above, pp. 93–4.
46. *Lay Sermons*, p. 157.
47. Ibid., pp. 158–9; see also Kennedy, *Humanist versus Economist*, pp. 22–9.
48. *Lay Sermons*, p. 167.
49. Ibid., p. 168. Coleridge's views on this issue were distinctly 'liberal'. Cf.the more traditional 'Christian and paternalist' position attacked by Sydney Smith in ('Nares' Sermon', *Edinburgh Review*, I, (1802) 128·30; see Fontana, *Rethinking the Politics*, p. 56.
50. Ibid., p. 162.
51. See Fontana, *Rethinking the Politics*, p. 32. This position was advanced by Sir James Mackintosh in 'France', *Edinburgh Review*, XXIV (1814) 528–9.
52. See below, p. 115. In a note added to part IV of 'To Mr Justice Fletcher' in 1832, Coleridge commented that 'the Working Classes did not substitute Rights for Duties, and take the former into their own guardianship, till the higher Classes, their legitimate protectors, had subordinated *Persons* to *Things*, and systematically perverted the former into the latter' (*EOT*, II, 393).
53. *CL*, IV, 710–11 [15 Mar 1817].
54. See for example *Notebooks*, III, nos 3325, 3327.
55. On cash payments see Boyd Hilton, *Corn, Cash, Commerce: The Economic Policies of the Tory Governments 1815–1830* (Oxford, 1977) ch. 2.

56. *EOT*, II, 124–7, 129, 131–3, 228–30.
57. Ibid., III, 121; II, 249–54.
58. On the Corn Law see Hilton, *Corn, Cash, Commerce*, ch. 1.
59. Ibid., pp. 15–26.
60. Robert Blake, *The Conservative Party from Peel to Churchill* (1970) p. 15.
61. *CL*, III, 497 (23 May 1914).
62. *CL*, IV, 549 [10 Mar 1815]. Hilton points out (*Corn, Cash, Commerce*, p. 8) that Wiltshire was an area where agricultural producers were not immediately affected by the end of the war, and where there were, in any case, large numbers of people employed in non-agricultural activities.
63. *CL*, IV, 549–50 [10 Mar 1815]. On this issue Coleridge shared common ground with philosophical radicals whom he otherwise despised; see William Thomas, *The Philosophical Radicals: Nine Studies in Theory and Practice, 1817–1841* (Oxford, 1979) p. 50.
64. *CL*, IV, 854 (2 May 1818). James Maitland (1759–1839), eighth Earl of Lauderdale. Coleridge's contempt for Lauderdale illustrates one of the major themes of the 'Lay Sermons'. Lauderdale was both a peer of the realm and a political economist; his *Inquiry into the Nature and Origin of Public Wealth* was published in 1804. He makes an appearance in Karl Marx's *Economic and Philosophical Manuscripts* as a proponent of the view that luxury is an important spur of economic activity.
65. Lauderdale thought that factory legislation involved an attempt to 'encroach upon that great principle of political economy, that labour ought to be left free' – cited in Hammond and Hammond, *The Town Labourer*, I, 166.
66. *CL*, IV, 856 [early May 1818].
67. See Hilton, *Corn, Cash, Commerce*, p. 26ff.
68. See below, pp. 119–20. In 1834 Coleridge reconsidered the Corn Law, and seemed to think it might be necessary to maintain the agricultural base of the country; earlier, in 1828–9, he suggested that a corn law may be necessary to maintain the aristocracy. See *Table Talk*, pp. 317 (3 May 1834) and 324 (20 June 1834); and the manuscript material cited in *Church & State*, p. 90, n 2. In both cases, however, the virtues of the law in question are related to the interests of the state, not to the narrow, material concerns of a section of the population.
69. *Lay Sermons*, p. 169.
70. *Friend*, I, 228n.
71. *Lay Sermons*, pp. 108–9.
72. Ibid., p. 170.
73. See above, pp. 93–9.
74. *Lay Sermons*, pp. 210–11.
75. See Adam Ferguson, *An Essay on the History of Civil Society* (1767), ed. Duncan Forbes (Edinburgh, 1966) pp. 19, 61–7, 145, 218–20, 231. Coleridge had first-hand knowledge of Ferguson's *Essay*; see *Notebooks*, II, no. 1847.
76. *Lay Sermons*, p. 216.

77. The idea of 'ancient prudence' played a central role in Harrington's *Oceana* and was recorded by Coleridge in a notebook entry from 1804 (*Notebooks*, II, no. 2223). Coleridge's use of the term is, however, only vaguely related to Harrington's. For Harrington, 'ancient prudence' was derived from a view of the republic as a 'positively functioning relationship between the Few and the Many . . . and . . . an agrarian law was designed to control the distribution of land in such a way that there should always be enough free proprietors to constitute a Many' – *The Political Works of James Harrington*, ed. J. G. A. Pocock (Cambridge, 1977) p. 47. Moreover, since Harrington thought that states were based upon land, he mentioned an 'overbalance of riches in money or goods' (ibid., p. 835) as something which he would not discuss: a nation depending more on money than on land 'is not to be found'. However, Coleridge's view on the connection between property-holding and political personality and his moral conception of the state have a distinctly Harringtonian flavour; see above, p. 81.
78. *Lay Sermons*, pp. 216–17.
79. See the series of articles 'Comparison between France and Rome', discussed above, pp. 58–61.
80. *Lay Sermons*, p. 215 and n.
81. Ibid., p. 229. For an interesting account of this aspect of Coleridge's theory see David Roberts, *Paternalism in Early Victorian England* (New Brunswick, NJ, 1979) pp. 32–5.
82. *Lay Sermons*, pp. 216–17. Coleridge's attack on gambling in *A Lay Sermon* was related to his views on the importance of hope. See *Notebooks*, III, no. 3343, where he wrote that the purchase of a lottery ticket indicated 'a strong desire in spite of all rational Hope'.
83. *Lay Sermons*, pp. 220–1.
84. Ibid., p. 218.
85. George Finch, ninth Earl of Winchelsea and fifth Earl of Nottingham (1752–1826); in the *DNB* Finch's first title is spelt 'Winchilsea'. Originally appearing in 1797, Winchelsea's communication was republished in *Agricultural State of the Kingdom, in February, March and April, 1816; Being the Substance of the Replies to a Circular Letter Sent by the Board of Agriculture to Every Part of the Kingdom* (1816). For details see *Lay Sermons*, p. 219, n.1; Appendix D, pp. 263–4, gives Winchelsea's statement.
86. 'Great as "their almost magical effects" on the increase of prices were in the necessaries of life, they were still greater, disproportionately greater, in all articles of shew and luxury. With few exceptions, it soon became difficult, and at length impracticable, for the gentry of the land, for the possessors of fixed property to retain the rank of their ancestors, or their own former establishments, without joining in the general competition under the influence of the same trading spirit' (*Lay Sermons*, pp. 212–13).
87. Winchelsea argued that labourers should be able to rent land from those who employed them, so that they could, depending on the circumstances, keep livestock or a garden. He was keen to show

88. *Lay Sermons*, p. 212.
89. Ibid., pp. 194–5.
90. See above, p. 119.
91. *Lay Sermons*, p. 195.
92. Ibid., p. 229 (emphasis added).
93. *CL*, IV, 919 (9 Feb 1819).
94. The 'poor visionaries called SPENCEANS', as Coleridge called them, were followers of Thomas Spence (1750–1814), a schoolmaster, publisher, and bookseller. After Spence's death a society of Spencean Philanthropists was established by Thomas Evans in London. E. P. Thompson argues (*The Making of the English Working Class*, p. 672) that they were a real force in radical London politics in 1816–17, providing an alternative to the working-class philosophic radicalism of such men as Frances Place. Coleridge's half-sympathetic reference to the Spenceans may have reflected Evans' habit of carrying a Bible and reading from it in public houses, and the fact that his published statement of the Spencean position was entitled *Christian Policy the Salvation of the Empire* (1816). However, the Spenceans' claim that 'Landholders are not Proprietors in chief, they are but stewards of the Public' (cited in *Lay Sermons*, p. 228, n.2) ran contrary to Coleridge's view that land was held as a trust.
95. *Lay Sermons*, pp. 217–18; see also *Notebooks*, III, no. 3825.
96. *Lay Sermons*, p. 24.
97. Ibid., p. 17; see also *Friend*, II, 85.
98. *Lay Sermons*, p. 39.
99. *CL*, III, 414 (17 July 1812); IV, 554 [13 Mar 1815].
100. Ibid., IV, 762 (28 July 1817).
101. *Lay Sermons*, p. 25.
102. *Lay Sermons*, pp. 105–7. See also Ben Knights, *The Idea of the Clerisy in the Nineteenth Century* (Cambridge, 1978) ch. 2; J. H. Muirhead, *Coleridge as Philosopher* (1930) pp. 115–17; and David Newsome, *Two Classes of Men*: *Platonism and English Romantic Thought* (1974) chs 1 and 4. In light of Coleridge's subsequent attempt to identify the Church of England as the carrier of this philosophy, it is significant that he attributed its apathy in the eighteenth century in part to the impact of Lockean materialism; see *Notebooks*, III, no. 3749.
103. *Lay Sermons*, p. 199.
104. Ibid., pp. 194–5.
105. Ibid., p. 193.
106. Ibid., p. 90.
107. Ibid., pp. 229–30.
108. See below, pp. 126ff.

CHAPTER 5   PROPERTY, POLITICS AND CULTIVATION: *ON THE CONSTITUTION OF THE CHURCH AND STATE* (1829)

1. CL, VI, 913 (26 May 1832); *The Eclectic Review*, n.s., VI (July 1832) 1.
2. *Lay Sermons*, p. 170.
3. On the issue of Catholic Emancipation see G. I. T. Machin, *The Catholic Question in English Politics, 1820 to 1830* (Oxford, 1964).
4. *Table Talk*, p. 154 (17 Dec 1831).
5. *Church & State*, p. xxxvi, n. 1.
6. Machin, *The Catholic Question*, p. 1.
7. Ibid., p. 52.
8. See *Church & State*, pp. li–lvii. Coleridge mentioned this work in *Aids to Reflection*, p. 260.
9. *Church & State*, pp. 156–7.
10. Ibid., pp. 106–7.
11. CL, V, 228 [28 May 1822]. Southey's private views of emancipation were phrased in the intemperant language of loathing; see for example the letters to Blanco White in *The Life of the Rev. Joseph Blanco White*, ed. John Hamilton Thorn, 3 vols (1845) I, 410–15, 434. His public statements on the issue were more extreme than those of the Tory *Quarterly Review*; see Scott Bennett, 'Catholic Emancipation, the *Quarterly Review* and Britain's Constitutional Revolution', *Victorian Studies*, XII (1969) 285–304. There is a particularly good account of Southey's views in the 1820s in Sheridan Gilley, 'Nationality and Liberty, Protestant and Catholic: Robert Southey's *Book of the Church*', *Studies in Church History*, 18 (1982) 409–32.
12. See G. F. A. Best, 'The Protestant Constitution and its Supporters, 1800–1829', *Transactions of the Royal Historical Society*, 5th ser., VIII (1958) 105–27; Machin, *The Catholic Question*, pp. 16–17; and E. R. Norman, *Church and Society in England 1770–1970* (Oxford, 1976) p. 81.
13. Best, 'The Protestant Constitution', p. 109.
14. Cited in J. C. D. Clark, *English Society 1600–1832* (Cambridge 1985) p. 351.
15. Ibid., p. 350.
16. See G. F. A. Best, *Temporal Pillars: Queen Anne's Bounty, the Ecclesiastical Commissioners, and the Church of England* (Cambridge, 1964) chs 4 and 6; Norman, *Church and Society*, pp. 41–102.
17. See for example, *Edinburgh Review*, XLIV (Sep 1826) 490–513.
18. Cited in Norman, *Church and Society*, p. 83. This remark was made in a speech to the House of Lords. In annotations to Blomfield's *A Charge Delivered to the Clergy of his Diocese* (1830), Coleridge was critical of his failure to separate the Church of England from the Church of Christ; see *CM*, I, 526–34.
19. Best, *Temporal Pillars*, p. 164.
20. [Richard Whately], *Letters on the Church: by an Episcopalian* (1826). Whately was Professor of Political Economy at Oxford and then Archbishop of Dublin.
21. Whately's *Letters* was reviewed by Thomas Arnold in the *Edinburgh Review*, XLIV, (Sep 1826) 490–513.

22. *Church & State*, p. 12. Elsewhere Coleridge wrote that *'Ideas*, known to be unapproachable as to realization, but [they served as] . . . a polar star, guiding a man's mind by approximation' – *The Philosophical Lectures of Samuel Taylor Coleridge*, ed. Kathleen Coburn (1949) p. 164.
23. CM, II, 1134.
24. *Church & State*, p. 13.
25. Ibid., p. 19.
26. Ibid., p. 20.
27. Ibid., p. 22. On Davies and the ancient constitution see J.G.A. Pocock, *The Ancient Constitution and the Feudal Law* (Cambridge, 1957) pp. 32–5.
28. *Zapolya*, Prelude, ll. 369–72, cited in J. D. Coates, 'Coleridge's Debt to Harrington: A Discussion of *Zapolya*', *JHI*, 38 (1977) 502.
29. *Church & State*, p. 31, n. 2.
30. Ibid., pp. 18–19.
31. Ibid., p. 19.
32. Ibid., p. 65, n. 5. On *The Friend*, see above, pp. 97–8.
33. Ibid., p. 15.
34. G. H. C. Le May, *The Victorian Constitution* (1979) p. 51.
35. *Church & State*, p. 23.
36. Ibid.
37. Ibid.
38. For contemporary examples see Francis Gould Leckie, *Essay on the Principles of British Government* (1817), in *Pamphleteer*, XI, xxi (1818) 56–87; J. J. Park, *The Dogmas of the Constitution. Four Lectures . . . on the Theory and Practice of the Constitution* (1832) p. 98; [Robert Southey], 'Parliamentary Reform', *Quarterly Review*, XVI, xxxi (1816) 252.
39. CL, V, 35 [8 Apr 1820].
40. *Church & State*, p. 82.
41. Ibid., p. 24n.
42. Ibid., p. 25.
43. Ibid., p. 41. Cf. Nigel Leask, *The Politics of Imagination in Coleridge's Critical Thought* (1988), which argues that Coleridge 'awarded' a 'somewhat vestigial role . . . to the civic idealization of landed property in Church and State' (p. 213). This interpretation rests on a claim about the moral elevation of the commercial order that is based on a passage in *Church & State* (p. 72) which in Leask's opinion shows that the commercial order emerged from 'the nationalty' or 'Christian cultivation'. This reading seems dubious. The passage in question occurs in the course of a discussion of 'hope'. Coleridge wrote that the Church acted as a 'breathing hole of hope' in feudal society and thus provided a 'fostering wing' under which 'free citizens and burghers were reared'; there is no suggestion that the Church *directly* nurtured commerce, and given Coleridge's views on the values of commerce it is unlikely that he would have thought of these as derived from 'Christian cultivation'.
44. Ibid., p. 25.

45. Ibid., p. 31, n.2; and see above, note 29.
46. Cited ibid., p. lx; see also *The Friend*, above, pp. 76, 80.
47. *Table Talk.*, p. 120 (21 Nov 1830).
48. Ibid., pp. 124–5 (25 Aug 1831).
49. For Coleridge's criticism of proposals for the reform of Parliament, see *Table Talk*, citations in notes 47 and 48 above.
50. *Church & State*, pp. 26–9.
51. Ibid., p. 29–30.
52. Ibid., pp. 41–2.
53. Leckie, *Essay on the Practice of British Government*, p. 56. This work was savaged by Francis Jeffrey in the *Edinburgh Review* in Nov 1812; see 'Essay on British Government', *Contributions to the 'Edinburgh Review'*, (1853) pp. 724–41.
54. *Table Talk*, p. 110 (19 Sep 1830).
55. *CM*, II, 1200–1. In a comment on a verse from Isaiah, 'And Kings shall be their nurses', cited in Martin Luther's *Table Talk*, Coleridge remarked, 'Corpulent nurses too often, that overlay the babe; distempered nurses, that convey poison in their milk' – *The Literary Remains of Samuel Taylor Coleridge*, ed. H. N. Coleridge, 4 vols (1836–9) IV, 31.
56. For Tory views of monarchy, and Charles I as martyr, see Clark, *English Society*, chs 3 and 4; and J. A. W. Gunn, *Beyond Liberty and Property: The Process of Self-Recognition in Eighteenth-Century Political Thought* (Kingston, Ont., and Montreal, 1983) ch. 4. For an account of Coleridge's view of the Stuarts in general, and Charles I in particular, see John Morrow, 'Coleridge and the English Revolution', *Political Science*, 40 (1988) 129–31.
57. In an annotation to Southey's *Life of Wesley* Coleridge described the interregnum as the 'alas! too brief substitution of a hero for an imbecile would-be despot' – Robert Southey, *The Life of Wesley and the Rise and Progress of Methodism* (1820), ed. Maurice H. Fitzgerald, 2 vols (Oxford, 1925) I, 106.
58. *Church & State*, p. 86.
59. Ibid., pp. 88, 87.
60. Ibid., p. 90.
61. Ibid., p. 86.
62. See above, pp. 60–1, 116–17.
63. *NTP*, p. 211. Cf. Harold Beeley, 'The Political Thought of Coleridge', in Edmund Blunden and Earl Leslie Griggs (eds), *Coleridge Studies by Several Hands on the Hundredth Anniversary of his Death* (1934) p. 163.
64. *Church & State*, p. 96.
65. *Table Talk*, p. 110 (19 Sep 1830).
66. Ibid., p. 176 (21 May 1832).
67. Ibid. On the connection between Platonism and aristocratic virtue in Sidney's writings see Jonathan Scott, *Algernon Sidney and the English Commonwealth* (Cambridge, 1988) ch. 2. I am grateful to the author for allowing me to see the typescript of his book.
68. *Church & State*, p. 95.

69. Ibid., p. 99. See also *CM*, II, pp. 113–15, for Coleridge's marginalia on Dallison's work.
70. *Church & State*, p. 101.
71. John Colmer, *Coleridge, Critic of Society* (Oxford, 1959) p. 163. Both Blackstone and De Lolme took the omnipotence of parliament for granted; see Mark Francis with John Morrow, 'After the Ancient Constitution: Political Theory and English Constitutional Writings, 1765–1832', *History of Political Thought*, IX (1988) 280–301.
72. See above, pp 77–82.
73. *Church & State*, p. 103.
74. Henry Phillpotts, *A Letter to an English Layman, on the Coronation Oath* ... (1828) pp. 7–8. Phillpotts (1778–1868) was Bishop of Exeter from 1830, having been Dean of Chichester from 1828 to 1830.
75. *Church & State*, p. 104. See Phillpott's *A Letter*, p. 83, for a similar remark about the Coronation Oath, but one which is part of an argument suggesting that Parliament is the 'King's Great Council'.
76. Ibid., p. 31.
77. Ibid.
78. See Clark, *English Society*, pp. 216–35 for a discussion of the ideology of the eighteenth-century Anglican Church-state.
79. *Church & State*, p. 32.
80. Ibid., p. 35.
81. See William Paley, *Moral and Political Philosophy*, in *The Works of William Paley DD* (1838) pp. 670–81.
82. *CM*, II, 943.
83. Best, *Temporal Pillars*, p. 254.
84. *Church and State*, p. 42. Henry Phillpotts identified the statute in which the Church was mentioned in these terms as 8 Eliz. c.1 (*A Letter*, p.10).
85. See above, ch. 4.
86. *Lay Sermons*, p. 170.
87. See above, p. 66. The importance Coleridge ascribes to the Church's possession of independent property provides an apparent contrast between his views and those of James Harrington. Harrington believed that the clergy had been an 'estate' under the feudal monarchy, but at the same time had constituted a corrupt 'priesthood'. Coleridge argues, however, that if the clergy and their property were placed at the service of a critical and humanising philosophy they could make an essential contribution to the commonweal. It remains true that Coleridge's treatment of the National Church has some connections with concerns which informed Harrington's views on the matter. Harrington associated 'priesthood' with the corrupt displacement of the public interest by private concerns, and with a form of tyranny that was reinforced by the misuse of supposedly 'spiritual' powers. On this see Mark Goldie, 'The Civil Religion of James Harrington', in Anthony Pagden (ed.), *The Language of Political Theory in Early-Modern Europe* (Cambridge, 1987) pp. 212–13. Coleridge stripped the clergy of

spiritual authority derived from their position in the Church, and tried to show that under existing conditions the independence of the clergy contributed to the fulfilment of the ends of the state.

88. For recent discussions of Coleridge's clerisy see Ben Knights, *The Idea of the Clerisy in Nineteenth Century Britain* (Cambridge, 1978) ch. 2; and Peter Allen, 'S. T. Coleridge's *Church and State* and the Idea of an Intellectual Establishment', *JHI*, 46 (1985) 87–106. Cf. John Morrow, 'The National Church in Coleridge's *Church and State*: A Response to Allen', *JHI*, 47 (1986) 640–52.

89. *Church & State*, pp. 42–3. In a work that went through the press while Coleridge was in the early stages of writing *Church & State*, he praised the educational work of the early Reformed Church in England: 'The diffusion of light and knowledge through this kingdom, by the exertions of the Bishops and clergy, by Episcopalians and Puritans, from Edward VI to the Restoration, was as wonderful as it is praiseworthy, and may be justly placed among the most remarkable facts of history' (*Aids to Reflection*, p. 6, n.2).

90. *Church & State*, p. 76. See also *CL*, VI, 903 [7 May 1832], where Coleridge objected to the idea that the clerisy were 'neither more nor less than Government Cooks in office, to be kept, or dismissed, by the Ministers & Majority of the Houses for the time being'.

91. *Church & State*, pp. 75–6.

92. See Best, *Temporal Pillars*, pp. 62–77.

93. *Table Talk*, p. 109 (8 Sep 1830). Many clergymen were in fact strong proponents of political economy; see Norman, *Church and Society*, pp. 42–5; R. A. Solway, *Prelates and People: Ecclesiastical Social Thought in England, 1783–1852* (1969) ch. 3; and A. M. C. Waterman, 'The Ideological Alliance of Political Economy and Christian Theology, 1798–1833', *Journal of Ecclesiastical History*, 34 (1983) 231– 44.

94. See Clark, *English Society*, ch. 4; [William Warburton], *The Alliance between Church and State, or the Necessity and Equity of an Established Religion and a Test Act* (1736) pp. 7–8, 53, 69, 70, 75. Coleridge had earlier remarked that he 'disliked' and suspected' the 'Warburtonian System' (*CL*, II, 803 – 3 June 1802). Warburton explicitly rejected the idea that the Church formed an estate of the realm (*The Alliance*, p. 75), as did Coleridge's old friend George Dyer – see his *Four Letters on the English Constitution* (1812), 3rd edn (1817) p. 54.

95. *Church & State*, p. 68. On the connection between property and an independent National Church see John Morrow, 'The National Church in Coleridge's *Church & State*'.

96. *Church & State*, pp. 83 99 and n.3. Best comments that 'The end of sitting Convocations removed the thin screen that had, sometimes, stood between the clergy and the mixed supremacy of monarch and parliament' (*Temporal Pillars*, p. 60). He also pointed out that by the early nineteenth century the idea of a clerical estate had virtually 'evaporated' (ibid., and n. 2). Coleridge's discussion involved an attempt to revive the idea of a clergy as an estate in order to emphasis and reinforce its independence. The restitution

Notes

of Convocation was a corollary of this. The proposal that clergymen should sit in the House of Commons involved an innovation, for, as the Duke of York pointed out in a much-applauded speech, clergymen were excluded from the Commons. Emancipation thus seemed to grant those who were hostile to the Church a right which its own clergy lacked. See E. R. Norman, *Anti–Catholicism in Victorian England* (1968) p. 127.

97. Mill's comment appeared in his 'Corporation and Church Property' (1833), in *Collected Works of John Stuart Mill*, IV: *Essays on Economics and Society*, ed. J. M. Robson (Toronto, 1967) p. 220.
98. [Warburton], *The Alliance*, p. 111.
99. *Church & State (CC)*, p. 75; see also *Aids to Reflection*, p. 239, n.1. In a marginal comment on Blanco White's *Practical Evidence against Catholicism* (1825) Coleridge related the emergence of commercial society to the 'mental emancipation' achieved by Protestantism ('increase of *popular* knowledge, arts, industry, trade, commerce, civil & political Liberty, all tending to an exclusive exercise and cultivation of the *Understanding* and the prudential habit, to the bedimming of the Reason and the Spiritual Light' – *CM*, I, 515), but implied that, because it cherished national churches, it could overcome the problematic results of such emancipation.
100. Ibid.
101. *Aids to Reflection*, p. 141 n; see also above, p. 64.
102. See William Stafford, 'Religion and the Doctrine of Nationalism in England at the Time of the French Revolution and Napoleonic Wars', *Studies in Church History*, 18 (1982) 391–5.
103. *Church & State*, p. 69. For an account of the struggle between the British and Foreign and the National Bible Societies see Solway, *Prelates and People*, pp. 370–9. Coleridge's views on the educational role of the Church explains his position on the Lancaster–Bell controversy. Like Robert Southey, Coleridge associated non-Anglican educational initiatives with hostility towards the Church; see 'Mr. Brougham-Education', *Quarterly Review*, X, xxxviii (1818) 492–517.
104. *CM*, I, 275.
105. Ibid., I, 809; II, 747.
106. See *CL*, V, 51 [31 May 1820] for an earlier expression of this. In a letter to Blanco White on 20 July 1825 (*CL*, V, 485) Coleridge again mentioned this subject, and, when White incurred the displeasure of some of his friends by supporting Sir Robert Peel, the pro-emancipation candidate, in the Oxford election of February 1829, he used the distinction between 'the *spiritual* part of the Church' and 'external establishment by law' as one of the grounds for so doing. See *The Life of the Rev. Blanco White*, I, 462.
107. *Church & State*, p. 116. The visible and public character of Coleridge's 'Church of Christ' distinguished it from that advanced by Benjamin Hoadley, Bishop of Bangor, in his famous sermon of 1717, *The Nature of the Kingdom, or Church of Christ* (1717). Hoadley's text was John 18:36: 'Jesus answered, "My kingdom is not of this

world"'. Hoadley's critics thought that his argument implied that the 'visible' and 'invisible' churches were opposed to one another; see, for example, William Law, *A Reply to the Bishop of Bangor's Answer to the Representation of the Committee of Convocation* (1719) pp. 29–30. The Committee took the view that Hoadley's argument reduced the 'Church and Kingdom of Christ . . . to a mere State of Anarchy and Confusion'.

108. *Church & State*, pp. 115–24.
109. Ibid., pp. 114–15.
110. *Table Talk*, p. 110 (19 Sep 1830).
111. *Church & State*, p. 45. The popularist conception of the Church as *ecclesia* was raised by Thomas Arnold in a review of Whately's *Letters on the Church*; see *Edinburgh Review*, XLIV, (Sep 1826) 507. The idea of the Church as an 'Ecclesia, a multitude called out', appeared in Richard Field's *Of the Church, Five Books*, 3rd edn (Oxford, 1635) p. 11, a work which Coleridge admired; see *CM*, II, 650ff., for Coleridge's marginalia on Field's book, and *Lay Sermons*, p. 107, for an approving comment.
112. *Church & State*, p. 116.
113. *CM*, I, 531.
114. See above, p. 20.
115. *CM*, I, 531. Grindal had advised Elizabeth not to act 'resolutely and peremptorily . . . as ye may do in Civil and External Matters' – John Strype, *The History of the Life and Acts of the Most Reverend Father in God, Edmund Grindal* (1710) Appendix IX, p. 83. See also Coleridge, *Literary Remains*, III, 27–8.
116. *CM*, I, 247–8. See also Morrow, 'Coleridge and the English Revolution'.
117. *CM*, I, 311.
118. *Coleridge on the Seventeenth Century*, ed. R. F. Brinkley (Durham, NC, 1955) p. 270.
119. *CM*, I, 293, 313.
120. *NTP*, p 149; also *CM*, II, 1104. See also the criticism of Southey's sympathy with 'popestical clergy' of Elizabeth I's reign in marginalia in Southey's *Life of Wesley*, I, 227, 230.
121. *CM*, II, 1136; see also pp. 1138–9, 1142.
122. *Church & State*, pp. 55–6.
123. *CM*, I, 530.
124. *Table Talk*, p. 322 (31 May 1834). See also an earlier (1812) remark on toleration: 'The state, with respect to the different sects of religion under its protection should resemble a well drawn portrait. Let there be half a score individuals looking at it, every one sees its eyes and its benignant smile directed towards himself' (Coleridge, *Literary Remains*, I, 288).
125. Coleridge had, of course, held this sort of position in 1795; see above, p. 19ff.
126. *Table Talk*, p. 159 (22 Feb 1832).

CONCLUSION: LAND, COMMERCE AND THE LIMITS OF TRADITION

1. *Biographia Literaria*, I, 217.
2. Ibid., p. 173. For this interpretation of Coleridge's use of Kant see D. M. MacKinnon, 'Coleridge and Kant', in John Beer (ed.), *Coleridge's Variety* (1974) p. 191.
3. For an account of the political implications of Coleridge's interest in the seventeenth century see John Morrow, 'Coleridge and the English Revolution', *Political Science*, 40 (1988) 128–41.
4. David Newsome, *Two Classes of Men: Platonism and English Romantic Thought* (1974) p. 17; Robert O. Preyer, 'Coleridge's Historical Thought', in Kathleen Coburn (ed.), *Coleridge: A Collection of Critical Essays* (Englewood Cliffs NJ, 1967) p. 152.
5. Newsome, *Two Classes of Men*, p. 118.
6. *CM*, II, 115.
7. Thomas Arnold, 'National Church Establishments' and 'Church Politics', in *The Miscellaneous Works of Thomas Arnold D. D.* (New York, 1845) pp. 510, 437, 493.
8. Ibid., p. 495.
9. See above, p. 75.
10. Edmund Burke, *An Appeal from the New to the Old Whigs*, in *Works of the Rt Hon. Edmund Burke*, 16 vols (1826) VI, 218. The argument of the following passage (and indeed of the preceding chapter as well) is at odds with that presented in the concluding chapter of Nigel Leask's *The Politics of Imagination in Coleridge's Critical Thought* (1988). Leask argues that Coleridge was primarily interested in moralising members of the commercial order, the landed classes having become increasingly marginalised in an emerging liberal-democratic society; see especially p. 216. This interpretation is difficult to square with accounts of English society at the time, with what Coleridge actually says in *Church & State*, with his critical (but not dismissive) statements about the landed classes, and with his views on the necessarily morally ambivalent character of commerce.
11. See above, pp. 46–52.
12. *Biographia Literaria*, I, ch. 3.
13. Ibid., p. 58.
14. Ibid., p. 54.
15. Ibid., p. 62.
16. James K. Chandler, *Wordsworth's Second Nature: A Study of the Poetry and Politics* (Chicago, 1984) p. 67.
17. Ibid., ch. 10.
18. See for example Charles Smith, *Seven Letters on National Religion* (1833). Smith mentions Coleridge on pp. 46–7, but his argument seems to depend on an un-Coleridgean conflation of the National Church and the Church of Christ; his *Letters* are virulently anti-Catholic and anti-Dissenter, and are ranting in tone.

19. For Coleridge's connection with the British Association see Jack Morrell and A. Thackray, *Gentlemen of Science* (Oxford, 1984); on the moderation of this body see ch. 6.
20. See Charles Richard Sanders, *Coleridge and the Broad Church Movement* (Durham, NC, 1942); and Duncan Forbes, *The Liberal Anglican Idea of History* (Cambridge, 1952).
21. J. S. Mill, 'Coleridge', in *Mill on Bentham and Coleridge*, ed. F. R. Leavis (1965) p. 155.
22. Ibid., p. 151.
23. See for example T. H. Green, *Lectures on the Principles of Political Obligation and Other Writings*, ed. Paul Harris and John Morrow (Cambridge, 1986) pp. 5, 8, 328, 360–6; and J. H. Muirhead, *Coleridge as Philosopher* (1930) *passim*.

Bibliography

WORKS BY SAMUEL TAYLOR COLERIDGE

Aids to Reflection and the Confessions of an Inquiring Spirit, new edn (1884).

Biographia Literaria, ed. James Engell and W. Jackson Bate, 2 vols, CC, VII (Princeton, NJ, 1983).

Coleridge on the Seventeenth Century, ed. R. F. Brinkley (Durham, NC, 1955).

Collected Letters of Samuel Taylor Coleridge, ed. Earl Leslie Griggs, 6 vols (Oxford, 1956–71).

The Complete Poetical Works of Samuel Taylor Coleridge, ed. E. H. Coleridge, 2 vols (Oxford, 1912).

Essays on his Times in 'The Morning Post' and 'The Courier', ed. David V. Erdman, 3 vols, CC, III (Princeton, NJ, 1977).

The Friend, ed. Barbara E. Rooke, 2 vols, CC, IV (Princeton, NJ, 1969).

Lay Sermons, ed. R. J. White, CC, VI (Princeton, NJ, 1972).

Lectures 1795: On Politics and Religion, ed. Lewis Patton and Peter Mann, CC, I (Princeton, NJ, 1971).

The Literary Remains of Samuel Taylor Coleridge, ed. H. N. Coleridge, 4 vols (1836–9).

Marginalia, ed. George Whalley, 2 vols so far published, CC, XII (Princeton, 1980–   ).

Notebooks of Samuel Taylor Coleridge, ed. Kathleen Coburn, 3 vols so far published (New York and Princeton, NJ, 1957–   ).

Notes, Theological, Political and Miscellaneous, ed. Derwent Coleridge (1853).

On the Constitution of the Church and State, According to the Idea of Each, ed. John Colmer, CC, X (Princeton, NJ, 1976).

The Philosophical Lectures of Samuel Taylor Coleridge, ed. Kathleen Coburn (1949).

Specimens of the Table Talk of Samuel Taylor Coleridge, ed. H. N. Coleridge, 2nd edn (1870).

The Watchman, ed. Lewis Patton, CC, II (Princeton, NJ, 1970).

OTHER PRIMARY WORKS

[Arnold, Thomas], 'Church of England', *Edinburgh Review*, XLIV (Sep 1826) 490–513.

——, *The Miscellaneous Works of Thomas Arnold D. D.* (New York, 1845).

Joel Barlow, *Advice to the Privileged Orders in the Several States of Europe, Part 1*, 2nd edn (1792).

Baxter, Richard, *A Holy Commonwealth, or Political Aphorisms, Opening the True Principles of Government* (1659).

——, *Of National Churches: Their Description, Institution, Use, Preservation, Danger, Maladies and Cure: Partly Applied to England* (1691).

Berkeley George, *The Works of George Berkeley, D. D.*, 2 vols (1794).

Blanco White, Joseph, *The Life of the Rev. Joseph Blanco White*, ed. John Hamilton Thorn, 3 vols (1845).

——, *Practical Evidences against Catholicism* (1825).

Burgh, James, *Political Disquisitions*, 3 vols (1774–5).

Burke, Edmund, *Reflections on the Revolution in France* (1790) (Harmondsworth, 1969).

——, *An Appeal from the New to the Old Whigs*, in *Works of the Rt Hon. Edmund Burke*, 16 vols (1826) VI.

[Callender, John Thompson], *The Political Progress of Great Britain . . .* (1795).

Cartwright, John, *The People's Barrier against Undue Influence and Corruption: or the Common's House of Parliament According to the Constitution* (1780).

Cudworth, Richard, DD, *The True Intellectual System of the Universe: The First Part: Wherein, All the Reasons and Philosophy of Atheism is Confuted; and its Impossibility Demonstrated* (1678).

Curry, Keith (ed.), *New Letters of Robert Southey*, 2 vols (New York, 1965).

De Quincey, Thomas, 'Samuel Taylor Coleridge', *The Collected Writings of Thomas de Quincey*, ed. David Masson, 14 vols (Edinburgh, 1896) II.

Dickinson, H. T. (ed.), *The Political Works of Thomas Spence* (Newcastle upon Tyne, 1982).

Dinmore, Richard, Jr, *An Exposition of the Principles of English Jacobins* (Norwich, 1796).

Dyer, George, *Complaints of the Poor People of England* (1793).

——, *Four Letters on the English Constitution*, 3rd edn (1817).

Eaton, Daniel, *The Philanthropist*, nos 1 and 5 (1795).

Ferguson, Adam, *An Essay on the History of Civil Society* (1767), ed. Duncan Forbes (Edinburgh, 1966).

Field, Richard, *Of the Church, Five Books* (1606), 3rd edn (Oxford, 1635).

Flower, Benjamin, *The French Constitution: with Remarks on Some of its Principle Articles* (1792).

Gerrald, Joseph, *A Convention the Only Means of Saving Us All from Ruin* (1793).

Godwin, William, *An Enquiry Concerning Political Justice* (1793), 3rd edn (1798), ed. F. E. L. Priestley, 3 vols (Toronto, 1946).

Grahame, Sir James, *An Inquiry into the Principles of Population . . .* (Edinburgh, 1816).

Green, T. H., *Lectures on the Principles of Political Obligation and Other Writings*, ed. Paul Harris and John Morrow (Cambridge, 1986).

Hall, Robert, *An Apology for the Freedom of the Press and for General Liberty* (1793).

Harrington, James, *The Political Works of James Harrington*, ed. J. G. A. Pocock (Cambridge, 1977).

[Hoadley, Benjamin], *The Nature of the Kingdom, or Church of Christ* (1717).

Holcroft, Thomas, *A Narrative of Facts Relating to a Prosecution for High Treason* (1795).

Horsley, Samuel, *A Review of the Case of the Protestant Dissenters: with Reference to the Test and Corporation Acts* (1790).

———, *A Sermon Preached . . . on Wednesday, January 30, 1793: Being the Anniversary of the Martyrdom of King Charles the First* (1793).

Jeffrey, Francis, 'Essay on British Government' (1812), in *Contributions to the 'Edinburgh Review'* (1853), pp. 724–41.

Law, William, *A Reply to the Bishop of Bangor's Answer to the Representation of the Committee of Convocation* (1719).

Leckie, Francis Gould, *Essay on the Principles of British Government* (1817), in *Pamphleteer*, XI, xxi (1818) 56–87.

Lowman, Moses, *A Dissertation on the Civil Government of the Hebrews* (1740), 2nd edn (1745).

Mackintosh, James, *Vindicae Gallicae* (1791).

Mill, John Stuart, 'Coleridge', in *Mill on Bentham and Coleridge*, ed. F. R. Leavis (1967).

———, 'Corporation and Church Property' (1833), in *Collected Works of John Stuart Mill*, IV: *Essays on Economics and Society*, ed. J. M. Robson (Toronto, 1967).

Ogilvie, William, *The Rights of Property in Land* (1781), in M. Beer

(ed.), *The Pioneers of Land Reform* (1920).
Paine, Thomas, *Agrarian Justice* (1795–6).
———, *Letter Addressed to the Addressers on the Late Proclamation* (1792).
———, *The Rights of Man* (1791–2; Harmondsworth, 1969).
Paley, William, *Moral and Political Philosophy*, in *The Works of William Paley D. D.* (1838).
Park. J. J., *The Dogmas of the Constitution. Four Lectures . . . on the Theory and Practice of the Constitution* (1832).
Phillpotts, Henry, *A Letter to an English Layman, on the Coronation Oath . . .* (1828).
Priestley, Joseph, *An Essay on the First Principles of Government* (1771), in *Priestley's Writings on Philosophy, Science and Politics*, ed. John A. Passmore (New York, 1965).
———, *Letters to the Right Honourable Edmund Burke* (1791).
———, *Memoirs of Dr. Joseph Priestley Written by Himself* (1809).
[Reeve, James], *Thoughts on English Government Addressed to the Quiet Good Sense of the People of England* (1795).
Sandford, M. E., *Thomas Poole and his Friends*, 2 vols (1888).
Smith, Adam, *An Inquiry into the Nature and Causes of the Wealth of Nations* (1776).
Southey, C. C. (ed.), *The Life and Correspondence of Robert Southey*, 6 vols (1849–50).
Southey, Robert, *The Life of Wesley and the Rise and Progress of Methodism* (1820), ed. Maurice H. Fitzgerald, 2 vols (Oxford, 1925).
———, 'Mr Brougham–Education', *Quarterly Review*, x, xxxviii (1818) 492–517.
———, *New Letters of Robert Southey*, ed. Kenneth Curry, 2 vols (New York, 1965).
———, 'Parliamentary Reform', *Quarterly Review*, xvi, xxxi (1816) 225–78.
Steuart, Sir James, *An Inquiry into the Principles of Political Oeconomy* (1767), ed. Andrew S. Skinner, 2 vols (Edinburgh, 1966).
Strype, John, *The History of the Life and Acts of the Most Reverend Father in God, Edmund Grindal* (1710).
Thelwall, John, *The Rights of Nature against the Usurpations of Establishments. A Series of Letters to the People of England, in Reply to the False Principles of Burke* (1796).
———, *The Tribune. A Periodical Publication Consisting Chiefly of the Political Lectures of J. Thelwall*, 3 vols (1795).
[Warburton, William], *The Alliance between Church and State, or the Necessity and Equity of an Established Religion and a Test Act* (1736).

[Whately, Richard], *Letters on the Church of England by an Episcopalian* (1826).

SECONDARY WORKS

(a) BOOKS

Appleyard, J. A., *Coleridge's Philosophy of Literature* (Cambridge, Mass., 1965).
Barth, J. Robert, *Coleridge and Christian Doctrine* (Cambridge, Mass., 1969).
Best, G. F. A., *Temporal Pillars: Queen Anne's Bounty, the Ecclesiastical Commissioners, and the Church of England* (Cambridge, 1964).
Blake, Robert, *The Conservative Party from Peel to Churchill* (1970).
Bowle, John, *Politics and Opinion in the 19th Century* (1954).
Brinton, Crane, *The Political Ideas of the English Romanticists* (Oxford, 1926).
Butler, Marilyn, *Romantics, Rebels and Reactionaries: English Literature and its Background 1760–1830* (Oxford, 1981).
Calleo, David P., *Coleridge and the Idea of the Modern State* (New Haven, Conn., 1966).
Chandler, James K., *Wordsworth's Second Nature: A Study of the Poetry and Politics* (Chicago, 1984).
Clark, J. C. D., *English Society, 1660–1832* (Cambridge, 1985).
Clive, John, *Scotch Reviewers: The 'Edinburgh Review', 1802–1815* (1957).
Cobban, Alfred, *Edmund Burke and the Revolt against the Eighteenth Century* (1929), 2nd edn (1960).
Coleman, Deirdre, *Coleridge and 'The Friend' (1809–10)* (Oxford, 1988).
Colmer, John, *Coleridge, Critic of Society* (Oxford, 1959).
———, *From Coleridge to Catch-22* (1978).
Cone, Carl B., *The English Jacobins* (New York, 1968).
Cookson, J. E., *The Friends of Peace* (Cambridge, 1982).
Dickinson, H. T., *Liberty and Property: Political Ideology in Eighteenth Century England* (1977).
Dozier, Robert R., *For King, Constitution, and Country: The English Loyalists and the French Revolution* (Lexington, Mass., 1983).
Everest, Kelvin, *Coleridge's Secret Ministry* (Hassocks, 1979).
Fontana, Biancamaria, *Rethinking the Politics of Commercial Society* (Cambridge, 1985).

Forbes, Duncan, *The Liberal Anglican Idea of History* (Cambridge, 1952).
Fruchtman, Jack Jr, *The Apocalyptic Politics of Richard Price and Joseph Priestley* (Philadelphia, 1983).
Garrett, Clarke, *Respectable Folly: Millenarians and the French Revolution in France and England* (Baltimore, 1975).
Gillman, James, *The Life of Samuel Taylor Coleridge* (1838).
Gunn, J. A. W., *Beyond Liberty and Property: The Process of Self-Recognition in Eighteenth-Century Political Thought* (Kingston, Ont., and Montreal, 1983).
Gunning, H., *Reminiscences of Cambridge* (1854).
Hammond, J. L. and Barbara, *The Town Labourer, 1760–1832*, 2 vols (1949).
Harding, Anthony John, *Coleridge and the Idea of Love* (Cambridge, 1974).
――――, *Coleridge and the Inspired Word* (Kingston, Ont., and Montreal, 1986).
Hilton, Boyd, *Corn, Cash, and Commerce: The Economic Policies of the Tory Governments, 1815–1830* (Oxford, 1977).
Hirschman, Albert O., *The Passions and the Interests: Political Arguments for Capitalism before its Triumph* (Princeton, NJ, 1977).
James, Patricia, *Population Malthus* (1978).
Kelly, Gary, *The English Jacobin Novel 1780–1805* (Oxford, 1976).
Kennedy, William, F., *Humanist versus Economist: The Economic Thought of Samuel Taylor Coleridge* (Berkeley, Calif., 1958).
Knight, Frida, *University Rebel: The Life of William Frend 1751–1841* (1971).
Knights, Ben, *The Idea of the Clerisy in the Nineteenth Century* (Cambridge, 1978).
Leask, Nigel, *The Politics of Imagination in Coleridge's Critical Thought* (1988).
Le May, G. H. C., *The Victorian Constitution* (1979).
Liljegren, S. B., *Harrington and the Jews* (Lund, 1932).
Machin, G. I. T., *The Catholic Question in English Politics, 1820–1830* (Oxford, 1964).
Manuel, Frank E. and Fritzie P., *Utopian Thought in the Western World* (Cambridge, Mass., 1979).
Morrell, Jack, and Thackray, A., *Gentlemen of Science* (Oxford, 1984).
Muirhead, J. H., *Coleridge as Philosopher* (1930).
Newsome, David, *Two Classes of Men: Platonism and English Romantic Thought* (1974).

Norman, E. R., *Anti-Catholicism in Victorian England* (1968).
_____, *Church and Society in England 1770–1970* (Oxford, 1976).
Oliver, W. H., *Prophets and Millennialists* (Auckland and Oxford, 1978).
Orsini, G., *Coleridge and German Idealism* (Carbondale, Ill., 1969).
Pocock, J. G. A., *The Ancient Constitution and the Feudal Law* (Cambridge, 1957).
_____, *The Machiavellian Moment: Florentine Political Thought and the Atlantic Republican Tradition* (Princeton, NJ, 1977).
_____, *Virtue, Commerce and History* (Cambridge, 1985).
Quinton, Anthony, *The Politics of Imperfection* (1978).
Roberts, David, *Paternalism in Early Victorian England* (New Brunswick, NJ, 1979).
Roe, Nicholas, *Wordsworth and Coleridge: The Radical Years* (Oxford, 1988).
Sanders, Charles Richard, *Coleridge and the Broad Church Movement* (Durham, NC, 1942).
Scott, Jonathan, *Algernon Sidney and the English Commonwealth* (Cambridge, 1988).
Shaffer, E. S., *'Kubla Khan' and the Fall of Jerusalem* (Cambridge, 1975).
Smith, Olivia, *The Politics of Language 1791–1819* (Oxford, 1984).
Solway, R A., *Prelates and People: Ecclesiastical Social Thought in England, 1783–1852* (1969).
Stafford, William, *Socialism, Radicalism, and Nostalgia* (Cambridge, 1987).
Sultana, Donald, *Coleridge in Malta and Italy* (Oxford, 1969).
Thomas, D. O., *The Honest Mind: The Thought and Work of Richard Price* (Oxford, 1977).
Thomas, William, *The Philosophical Radicals: Nine Studies in Theory and Practice, 1817–1841* (Oxford, 1979).
Thompson, E. P., *The Making of the English Working Class* (Harmondsworth, 1972).
Thompson, Noel W., *The People's Science* (Cambridge, 1984).
Wellek, René, *Immanuel Kant in England 1793–1838* (Princeton, NJ, 1931).
Willey, Basil, *Nineteenth-Century Studies* (1949).
_____, *Samuel Taylor Coleridge* (1972).
Williams, Raymond, *Culture and Society* (1960).
Woodring, Carl R., *Politics in the Poetry of Coleridge* (Madison, Wis., 1961).

(b) BOOK CHAPTERS AND JOURNAL ARTICLES

Allen, Peter, 'S. T. Coleridge's *Church and State* and the Idea of an Intellectual Establishment', *JHI*, 46 (1985) 89–106.

Beeley, Harold, 'The Political Thought of Coleridge', in Edmund Blunden and Earl Leslie Griggs (eds), *Coleridge Studies by Several Hands on the Hundredth Anniversary of his Death* (1934) pp. 159–75.

Beer, John, 'The "Revolutionary Youth" of Wordsworth and Coleridge: Another View', *Critical Quarterly*, 19, ii (1977) 79–87.

Bennett, Scott, 'Catholic Emancipation, the *Quarterly Review* and Britain's Constitutional Revolution', *Victorian Studies*, XII (1969) 285–304.

Best, G. F. A., 'The Protestant Constitution and its Supporters, 1800–1829', *Transactions of the Royal Historical Society*, 5th ser., VIII (1958) 105–27.

Coates, J. D., 'Coleridge's Debt to Harrington: A Discussion of *Zapolya*', *JHI*, 38 (1977) 501–8.

Colmer, John, 'Coleridge and Politics', in R. L. Brett (ed.), *Writers and their Background: S. T. Coleridge* (1972) pp. 244–70.

Davis, J. C., 'Pocock's Harrington: Grace, Nature and Art in the Classical Republicanism of James Harrington', *HJ*, 24 (1981) 683–97.

Deen, Leonard W., 'Coleridge and the Sources of Pantisocracy: Godwin, the Bible and Hartley', *Boston University Studies in English*, 5 (1961) 232–45.

———, 'Coleridge and the Radicalism of Religious Dissent', *Journal of English and Germanic Philology*, 61 (1962) 496–510.

Diamond, W. G., 'Natural Philosophy and Harrington's Political Thought', *Journal of the History of Philosophy*, XVI (1978) 387–98.

Erdman, David V., 'Coleridge as Editorial Writer', in Conor Cruise O'Brien and William Dean Vanech (eds), *Power and Consciousness* (New York, 1969) pp. 183–201.

Eugenia, Sister, 'Coleridge's Scheme of Pantisocracy and American Travel Accounts', *Proceedings of the Modern Language Association of America*, XLV (Dec 1930) 1069–84.

Francis, Mark, with Morrow, John, 'After the Ancient Constitution: Political Theory and English Constitutional Writings, 1765–1832', *History of Political Thought*, IX (1988) 280–301.

Gilley, Sheridan, 'Nationality and Liberty, Protestant and Catholic: Robert Southey's *Book of the Church*', *Studies in Church History*, 18 (1982) 409–32.

Goldie, Mark, 'The Civil Religion of James Harrington', in Anthony Pagden (ed.), *The Languages of Political Theory in Early-Modern Europe* (Cambridge, 1987) pp. 197–222.

Haakonssen, Knud, 'The Science of a Legislator in James Mackintosh's Moral Philosophy', *History of Political Thought*, v (1984) 245–80.

Hampsher-Monk, Iain, 'Civic Humanism and Parliamentary Reform: The Case of the Society of the Friends of the People', *Journal of British Studies*, 18 (1979) 70–89.

―――, 'Thelwall and Natural Rights' (unpublished paper).

Kitson, P., '*The Plot Discovered*: A New Date', *Notes and Queries*, Mar 1984, pp. 57–8.

Kramnick, Isaac, 'Religion and Radicalism: English Political Theory in the Age of Revolution', *Political Theory*, 5 (1977) 505–34.

Landess, Thomas H., 'The Politics of Samuel Taylor Coleridge', *Sewanee Review*, 81 (1973) 847–59.

Levy, David, 'S. T. Coleridge Replies to Adam Smith's "Pernicious Opinion": A Study in Hermetic Social Engineering', *Interpretation*, 14 (1986) 89–114.

Liljegren, S. B. (ed.), 'French Draft Constitution of 1792 Modelled on James Harrington's *Oceana*', *Skrifter utgivna av Kungl. Humanistiska Vetenskapssamfundent i Lund*, xvii (1932) 3–43.

Link, Arthur S., 'Samuel Taylor Coleridge and the Economic and Political Crisis in Great Britain, 1816–1820', *JHI*, 9 (1948) 323–38.

MacGillivray, J. R., 'The Pantisocracy Scheme and its Immediate Background', in M. W. Wallace (ed.), *Studies in English* (Toronto, 1931) pp. 131–69.

MacKinnon, D. M., 'Coleridge and Kant', in John Beer (ed.), *Coleridge's Variety* (1974) pp. 183–203.

Morrow, John, 'Coleridge and the English Revolution', *Political Science*, 40 (1988) 128–41.

―――, 'The National Church in Coleridge's *Church and State*: A Response to Allen', *JHI*, 47 (1986) 640–52.

Pocock, J. G. A., 'Burke and the Ancient Constitution: A Problem in the History of Ideas', *HJ*, iii (1960) 125–43.

―――, 'Cambridge Paradigms and Scotch Philosophers', in Istvan Hont and Michael Ignatieff (eds), *Wealth and Virtue: The Shaping of Political Economy in the Scottish Enlightenment* (Cambridge, 1983) pp. 235–52.

―――, 'The Political Economy of Burke's Analysis of the French Revolution', *HJ*, 25 (1982) 331–49.

Pollin, Burton R., and Burke, R., 'John Thelwall's Marginalia in a Copy of Coleridge's *Biographia Literaria*', *Bulletin of the New York Public Library*, LXXIV (Feb 1970) 73–94.

Potter, George Reuben, 'Unpublished Marginalia in Coleridge's Copy of Malthus' *Essay on Population*', *Proceedings of the Modern Language Society of America*, LI (Dec 1936) 1061–8.

Sanderson, David R., 'Coleridge's Political "Sermons": Discursive Language and the Voice of God', *Modern Philology*, 70 (1972–3) 318–30.

Stafford, William, 'Religion and the Doctrine of Nationalism in England at the Time of the French Revolution and Napoleonic Wars', *Studies in Church History*, 18 (1982) pp. 381–95.

Thompson, E. P., 'Disenchantment or Default? *A Lay Sermon*', in Conor Cruise O'Brien and William Dean Vanech (eds), *Power and Consciousness* (New York, 1969) pp. 149–81.

Waterman, A. M. C., 'The Ideological Alliance of Political Economy and Christian Theology, 1798–1833', *Journal of Ecclesiastical History*, 34 (1983) 231–44.

Watson, George, 'The Revolutionary Youth of Wordsworth and Coleridge', *Critical Quarterly*, 18, iii (1976) 49–66.

Werkmeister, Lucyle, 'Coleridge's *The Plot Discovered*: Some Facts and a Speculation', *Modern Philology*, 56 (1958–9) 254–63.

———, 'Coleridge and Godwin on the Communication of Truth', *Modern Philology*, 55 (1957–8) 170–7.

Whalley, George, 'Coleridge and Southey in Bristol, 1795', *Review of English Studies*, n.s., 1 (1950) 324–40.

Index

Akenside, M., 12–13
Allen, P., 192
Aristocracy, 8, 15, 59–61, 111–21, 161–3
  ancestry and, 53, 117, 161–2
  and their estates, 50–1, 117–21
  Bullion Controversy and the, 112–13
  Burke on, 161–2
  Corn Laws and, 113–14, 185
  education of, 101, 122–4, 162–3
  English, 59, 111–21, 123, 161–3
  feudal, 37, 59–61
  French, 59–61
  natural, 60
  non-traditional, 161–3
  responsibilities of, 111–21
Arnold, T., 160, 164, 194, 195

Bacon, F., 122, 162
Ball, Sir A., 73, 87–8
Barlow, J., 65, 172, 177
Barth, J. R., 168
Baxter, R., 63–4, 153–4, 177
Beccaria, C., 90
Beer, J., 168, 195
Berkeley, G., 181
Best, G. F. A., 144, 192
Bible, the Holy, 28, 101, 122–3
  and: education, 122–3; popular enlightenment, 16–17
  Anglican and Roman Catholic Churches and, 20–1
  as the statesman's manual, 101
  political economy in, 103–4
Blackstone, W., 181, 191
Blomfield, C. J., 129, 151, 188
Bolingbroke, Lord, 33, 68
Brinton, C., 174

British Association for the Advancement of Science, the, 164, 196
British Idealism, 164
Bullion Controversy, the, 112–13
Burdett, Sir F., 108
Burgh, J., 32–3, 68, 174
Burke, E., 6, 12–13, 69–72, 161–3, 178, 195
  views on fixed principles, 12
  on Church of England, 6, 71–2
  on fixed principles, 12
  on natural rights, 37
  on social contract, 79
  on traditional aristocracy, 70, 161–3
Butler, M., 167, 175

Calleo, D., 167, 176
Cambridge Platonists, the, 3, 79
Cartwright, J., 75, 89–91, 160, 180
Chandler, J. K., 195
Charles I (of England), 137–8
Church of England, the, 19, 20, 61ff., 92, 126–31, 141ff., 158, 160
  and: Country Party ideology, 62ff.; cultivation, 145–6; dissenters, 6, 63, 128–9; education, 64, 145–6; Parliament, 127–9, 141–2, 146–7, Protestantism, 128, 148; secular elites, 144–7; the commercial spirit, 145; the constitution of the nation, 142–8; the Nationalty, 143–5, 147; the poor, 146; the Reformation, 129, 146
  as: an estate of the realm, 66, 144; enclesia, 150; National

Church, 62ff., 64–6, 141–9
  Burke on, 71–2
  Catholic emancipation and, 126–31, 142–3, 146–7
  clerisy in, 145–6, 163
  Crown and, 147
  independent property of, 62ff., 71–2, 127–31, 143–7
  'mild and liberal spirit' of, 148
  Mill on, 147
  Warburton on, 67–8, 146–8
Church(es), 19ff., 61ff., 126–33, 142ff.
  church–state alliance, 20, 65, 67–8, 128–30, 142, 146
  Dissenting, 6, 128, 146–7
  Druidical, 149
  established, 61ff., 92, 126–33, 142–9
  Jewish, 149
  National, 62ff., 126–7, 142ff., 158: and the Church of Christ, 149–54; Church of England as, 64–6, 142–9; human law and; Papacy and, 148, 153–4; Parliament and, 142–9; property and, 61–6, 142–9; secular elites and, 145–7; the poor and, 145–6; the state and, 142ff.; toleration and, 151–2; Warburton on, 147–8
  of Christ, 149–54, 160; and the Church of England, 150–1; and the national church, 150–4; as ecclesia, 150, 194
  of Rome, 64–5, 147–8
  oppressive nature of, 19ff.
  'standing', 65–6, 72
Clark, J. C. D., 146, 167, 168, 170, 190, 191
Coates, J. D., 131, 179, 180, 181, 184
Cobban, A., 69, 175
Cobbett, W., 75, 108, 110–11, 129, 160
Coburn, K., 63, 181
Coleman, D., 167, 178, 179, 180
Coleridge, Revd G., 63, 65
Coleridge, S. T. C.
  and:civic humanism, 27–31, 40–2; pantiscocracy, 6–10, 21, 39, 54; revealed religion, 21, 28–9, 37, 75–6; Thelwall, 36–9, 44; Trinitarianism, 20, 72; Unitarianism, 5–7, 20–1, 28–9, 39, 61–2, 73, 75
  biblical criticism of, 62–3, 70
  his Bristol lectures (1795), 11ff.
  his early radicalism, 4–6, 11ff.
  his Platonism, 81–3, 99, 122–3, 125, 158–9, 161
  his republicanism, 137–40, 159
  life of: and Robert Southey, 5–10; at Bristol, 10ff.; at Calne, 113–14; at Cambridge, 4–7; at Nether Stowey, 44; millenarianism, 9–10; pantisocracy, 6–10; the *Morning Post*, 43–5; the Wedgwood annuity, 62; Trinitarianism, 61–3; Unitarianism, 5–7, 28–9, 61–3; visits Germany, 44, 62; visits Malta
views on:
agrarian laws, 59, 60
ancestry, 46, 53, 56, 59, 117, 135, 161–3
Ancient Jews, 24–7, 28–30, 83
aristocracy, 8, 15, 53, 56, 59, 60–1, 111–21, 137, 161–3
atheism, 19, 28, 39
benevolence, 8–9, 14–15, 18, 36, 39
Catholic emancipation, 126–32, 142–3
church establishments, 19ff., 61ff., 92, 126–31, 142–5, 191
civilisation, 58, 96, 145
commerce, 1–2, 23, 56–7, 92–6, 106–111, 123–5, 161–2
Corn Laws, 113–15, 185
cultivation, 145
deference, 60–1, 108, 116–17, 120, 139
democracy, 33–5, 61, 69
education, 81, 121–5, 161–3
enlightenment, 13–14, 15–18, 81
expediency, 75–6, 84–7, 97

Index

feudal institutions, 46, 59–61
'Friends of Freedom', 13ff.
Fichte, 107
freedom, 1, 32ff., 54–5, 58–9, 76–7, 96–7, 106, 144
Godwin, 28, 36, 39
Hobbes, 78–81
Ideas, 130–3
independence, 38, 40–1, 47ff., 57, 142–6
Jacobinism, 54, 61, 69, 107–8, 112
juvenile labour, 105–6, 114
Malthus, 106, 109
mixed government, 33, 93
Napoleon, 45, 54, 58, 61, 65, 86, 95–6
oligarchy, 33–4, 49–50, 52–5, 91
Paley, 7, 74–7, 84, 97, 106
parliamentary reform, 33–5, 36, 40–1, 89–92, 136–7
patriotism, 86
pauperisation, 120
political corruption, 34, 47ff., 57, 92–4
political economy, 102ff.
property, 1–3, 8–9, 36–42, 45ff., 61ff., 88ff., 93ff., 117–21, 124–5
prudence, 83–5, 97
public freedom, 33–5, 54–9, 69, 157
radical reformers, 43, 44, 54, 69, 88, 101, 107–11
reactionaries, 88, 93
reason, 97, 103, 124
religion, 4–7, 16–17, 19ff., 36, 61–2, 75–6, 122–5
Robespierre, 16
Rome, 58ff., 118
Rousseau, 75, 80–1, 84–7, 109
scientific method, 102–3
Switzerland, 43, 69
the Church of Christ, 149–54
the Church of England, 19ff., 43, 61ff., 92, 126–33, 142–54, 158, 192
the commercial spirit, 115–25, 143–5, 161–3
the Crown, 137–8

the *Edinburgh Review*, 3, 76, 102, 106, 111, 150
the English Commonwealth, 137, 139
the franchise, 33–6, 40–1, 89–92, 136–7
the French Constitution of 1799, 45ff., 89, 161
the French Revolution, 16, 36, 43–5, 53–4, 59, 61, 156–7, 161
the general will, 34, 84, 109
the gentry, 111–21, 161–3
the Highland Clearances, 117
the liberty of the press, 34–6
the lower classes, 16–17, 46–7, 107–11, 116–27
the nation, 142ff.
the National Church, 64ff., 126–33, 142ff.
the national debt, 114–5
the social contract, 79–80, 132–3
the state, 21–3, 81–2, 85–7, 97–9, 118–19, 126–33, 142ff.
the understanding, 81–6, 97, 103, 124
the United States, 25, 54, 98
toleration, 148, 151–2, 194
tradition, 70–1, 161–3
tyranny, 32, 58–9, 107
virtual representation, 34
war with France, 20, 36, 43
works:
A Lay Sermon, 101ff., 126, 135, 157
A Moral and Political Lecture, 11ff.
Aids to Reflection, 148
Biographia Literaria, 69, 157, 162, 163
'Comforts and Consolations', 73
'Comparison Between France and Rome', 58ff.
Conciones ad Populum, 11, 16
France: An Ode, 43–4
Lectures 1795, 170–5
'Lectures on Revealed Religion', 19ff.
'Lectures on the Two Bills', 32–3
'Letters on the Spaniards', 86, 92–3

Literary Remains, 177, 190, 194
Marginalia, 184, 189, 190–1, 194
Notebooks, 45–6, 63, 75, 80, 81, 83, 89, 147, 172, 175, 176, 177, 178, 179, 180, 184, 185, 186, 187
Notes, Theological and Political, 190
On the Constitution of the Church and State, 99, 125, 126ff., 157, 163
'On the French Constitution', 46ff.
'On the Present War', 11
'Our Commercial Politicians', 57
Religious Musings, 6, 9–10
Philosophical Lectures, 180, 189
Table Talk, 188, 190, 194
The Friend, 17, 73ff., 110, 117, 127, 132–3, 134–5, 157, 162
The Plot Discovered, 32ff.
The Watchman, 11, 35ff., 43, 53, 54
The Statesman's Manual, 101ff.
Zapolya, 131, 179
Colmer, T., 98, 141, 167, 176, 182, 183
commerce, 1–2, 56–7, 71, 93ff., 106–11, 115–25, 161
  and: coercion, 23; enlightenment, 1–2, 96, 158; freedom, 1, 96, 106–7; hope, 98–9; landed property, 56–7, 115–21; morality, 1, 96, 124–5; political corruption, 30–1, 56–7, 93–4, 136; political economy, 102; the constitution, 30–1, 135–6; the ends of the state, 97–9, 124–5
  Coleridge's reservations about, 56–7, 71
  Napoleon as a threat to, 95–6
  Priestley on, 29
commercial spirit, the, 107, 115ff., 161
  counterweights to, 116–17, 122–5
  gentry and, 115–21, 161–2
Commonwealth, English, 137
  ideology, 33, 40–2, 81

Concordat (of 1802), 65–6, 71
constitution(s), 45ff., 86–7, 126ff.
  and: free and organised powers, 133, 138–40; permanence, 134–5, 137–8; progression, 134–5, 137–8
  actual and potential powers in, 133, 140–2
  ancient, 70, 91–2, 131–2
  as Idea, 130–3
  balanced, 46ff., 71, 93, 133
  British, 32–5, 48–53, 71, 92–3, 121, 131–2
  crown in, 137–8
  democracy in, 139
  French of 1799, 45ff., 87
  Harrington on, 30–1, 50
  improvement of, 34–5
  interests in, 135–6
  mixed mode of, 33–4
  royal veto in, 141–2
  Venetian, 139
  see also Church of England, nation, national church, property, state
Cone, C. B., 170
Convocation, 140, 147, 160
Country party ideology, 30–1, 33, 49–53, 60, 68–71, 81–2, 93–5, 100, 110–44   156–7
  and: Burgh, 33, 50; Harrington, 30–1, 41, 50
  corruption in, 30–1, 47ff., 93–4
  French Church and, 61–6, 70–1
  independence in, 30–1, 40–1, 47ff.
crisis, postwar, 100–2, 107–8
Cromwell, O., 137
Cudworth, R., 79, 182, 179

Dallison, C., 140
Davies, Sir J., 131
Davis, J. C., 180
De Quincey, T., 87, 180
Deen, L. W., 29, 168, 169, 172
Dickinson, H. T., 173, 176
Dinmore, R., 170
Dissent(ers), 2, 14, 27ff., 129–30, 142ff., 153–5; *see also*

Index

church(es), Church of England, radical, Unitarianism
Dozier, R. R., 184
Drummond, H., 128–9
Dyer, G., 168

Eaton, D., 16, 171
education, 81, 121ff., 161–3
   and: philosophy, 122–3, 161–3; Platonism, 81, 122–3, 161–3; the clerisy, 145–6, the lower orders, 125, 145; the National Church, 64, 126; the upper classes, 121–5, 161–3; theology, 122–3
   the decline of, 122ff.
Elizabeth I (of England), 151, 194
emancipation, of Roman Catholics, 126–31, 132
Erdman, D., 43–4, 175, 178

Ferguson, A., 117, 185
Fichte, J. G., 107
Field, R., 194
Fielding, H., 145
Fifth Monarchy Men, 90
Filmer, Sir R., 29, 69
Fontana, B., 167, 182–3, 184
Francis, M., 191
Flower, B., 168
Frend, W., Revd, 4, 5–6
Fruchtman, J., 168, 171, 173

Garrett, C., 169
gentry, the, 113–25, 161–3
George III (of England), 127
Girondists, the, 16
Godwin, W., 2, 9, 12, 15, 16–17, 22, 28, 36, 171, 172, 174
Grahame, Sir J., 183
Green, T. H., 164
Grenville, Ld, 32
Grindal, E., 151
Gunn, J. A. W., 68, 167, 171, 176, 177, 190

Hammond, J. L. and B., 183
Hampsher-Monk, I., 173, 175
Harding, A. J., 167, 183

Hardy, T., 11
Harrington, James, 29, 30–1, 41, 50, 54, 60, 64, 79–82, 88, 96, 99, 122, 162, 173, 186, 191
   and: Aristotle, 82; Christian egalitarianism, 31, 41–2; Country Party ideology, 30–1, 41, 50, 54; Platonism, 82, 159
   civil humanism of, 29–31, 50–1
   Oceana, 29–30, 79
   The Art of Law Giving, 64
   views on: goods of fortune, 79, 88; 'goods of the mind', 79, 81, 88; authority, 79; Hobbes, 78–9; inequality, 30; national religion, 64, 191; participation, 30–1; political power, 30–1; private property, 30–1, 41, 50, 54
Hartley, D., 28
Hilton, B., 184, 185
Hirschman, A., 167, 181
Hoadley B., 193–4
Hobbes, T., 78–82
Holcroft, T., 2, 15, 171
Hooker, R., 152, 180
Horsley, S., 6, 15, 63, 171, 177
House of Commons, the, 50–1, 127, 136–7
   and: landed property, 50–1, 136; threats of oligarchy in, 33–5, 40, 48–52
   forces of: permanance in, 96, 136–7; progression in, 96, 136–7
   reform of elections to, 33–5, 40–1, 89–92, 136–7
House of Lords, the, 136–7
humanism, civic, 27ff.
   commercial, 94–5
Hume, D., 123, 162

Jacobin(ism), 3, 61, 69, 107–11
   English, 6, 107–11
   French, 6, 54
   'new', 107–8
   property in theory of, 61, 69
   'Quality cousins' of, 111ff.

James, P., 183
Jeffrey, F., 182
Jews(ish), 24ff., 83, 85, 173
   and christianity, 24–5
   constitution of, 24–7, 29, 173
   ignorance of, 24, 26, 83
   jubilee of, 25
   laws and the, 83, 85
   state, 24–7
   views on property of, 24–7

Kant, I., 76, 81, 159, 195
Kennedy, W. F., 183, 184
King, Lord, 113
Knight, F., 168, 169
Knights, B., 187, 192

La Grice, C., 4
labour, juvenile, profection of, 105–6, 114, 121
landlords, 117–21
   Highland Clearances and, 117
   responsibilities of, 116–21
   selfishness of, 112–21
   peasantry and, 117–20
Laud, W., 152
Lauderdale, Earl of, 114, 185
Law(s), 27, 78ff.
   and: custom, 85–6; expediency, 84–5; moral personality, 84–6; morality, 27, 78–80; prudence, 85–6
   Harrington on, 78–9
   Hobbes on, 78–9
Leask, N., 167, 170, 189, 195
Leckie, F., 137, 189, 190
Lessing, G. E., 132
Liljegren, S. B., 173
Liverpool, Lord, 101, 122–3
Locke, J., 3, 23
Lockean philosophy, 123, 125, 158–9, 162–3, 187
Louis XIV (of France), 99
Lowman, Revd. M., 29–31, 55, 173
Luther, M., 86, 190

MacGillivray, J. R., 169, 172
Machin, G. I. T., 188
Mackintosh, Sir J., 41

market relationships, 107
Malthus, Revd. T., 102, 106, 183
Maurice, F. D., 164
Methodists, the, 16
Mills, J. S., 147, 164
Milton, J., 140, 159
moral(s), 75ff.
   and: free agency, 76–7, 120–1, 125; law, 80–1, 121; reason, 76–7, 124
   duty, 79
   obligation, 80
   person(s), 124–5
   reform, 17, 125
morality, 75ff.
   and commerce, 1–2, 23, 55ff., 94ff., 116ff., 144–5, 154–5, 161–3; external conduct, 75–6; free agency, 75–6, 89, 120–1, 125; individuality, 125; law, 78–9, 84–5; legal regulation, 106, 121, 125; patriotism, 85–6; political obligation, 77f., property, 41, 89–9, 117–21, 124–5; reason, 76–7, 84–5; religion, 122–5; statesmanship, 77, 84–5; the commercial spirit, 115ff.; the understanding, 77, 84–5
   Edinburgh Review on, 76, 106
   egalitarian nature of, 86–7
   Hobbes on, 78–80
   Kant on, 76
   Paley on, 75–7
   Rousseau on, 75, 84–5
   see also state, freedom, religion
Moses, 24–5, 27
Muirhead, J. H., 164, 187

Napoleon, B., 3, 71, 95–6
nation
   and: the National Church, 142ff.; the state, 118–19
   constitution of, 142ff.
national debt, the, 94–5
nationalty, the, 143ff.
Netherlands, the, 99
Neville, H., 159

Index

Newsome, D., 81, 159, 179, 187
Newton, Sir I., 86
Norman, E. R., 193

Oliver, W. H., 169, 170

Paine, T., 2, 22, 29, 171, 172, 184
Paley, W., 3, 7, 14, 75–7, 83, 84–5, 97, 106, 123
pantisocracy, 2, 4, 8–10, 19, 26–7, 36, 39, 54
  and the millenium, 9
  children under, 8, 27
  equality under, 8, 21, 26–7, 36, 39
  freedom under, 8, 26–7
  in relation to the Jewish constitution, 26–7
  its practical abandonment, 10
  Poole on, 9
  property under, 8–9, 27
  servants under, 8, 27
  Southey on, 7–10, 25
Papacy, the, 64–5, 147–8, 152
parliament, 127, 136–7, 140–2
  and the National Church, 127–30, 141–2
  omnipotence of, 141
  reform of, 6, 34–6, 40, 89–92, 136–7
  see also House of Commons; House of Lords
Patton, L., 33
Peel, Sir R., 105
person(s), 80, 101–2, 119, 132–3, 184
  and things, 80, 101–2, 119, 133, 135–6
  as: ends, 80, 84, 133; means, 80, 124, 133
Phillpotts, H., 141, 191
philosophy
  and: education, 122–7, 158–9, 162–3; the commercial spirit, 121–5, 162–3
  materialistic, 3, 122–3, 158–9, 163–4
  Platonic, 3, 122–3, 125, 158–9, 163–4
physiocrats, the, 102

Pitt, W., the Younger, 32, 57, 127
Plato(nic)(nism), 3, 86, 125, 158–9, 163–4
Pocock, J. G. A., 167, 173, 174, 175, 176, 177, 178, 180, 181, 187
Poland, 14
political economy, 102ff.
  and: morality, 122–4; the Bible, 103–4; the understanding, 103
  as an abstract science, 102–3
  differing views of, 102
  radical critics of, 107–10
  'reputed masters' of, 102ff.
political freedom, 13–15, 30–1, 41–2, 107
  obligation, 77ff.
  participation, 30–1, 36, 86–7
  power and property, 21, 24, 30–1, 36–7, 39, 41–2, 46ff., 92, 116–18
  rights, 33ff.
politics
  and: expediency, 84–90; morals, 77ff., property, 22–3, 46ff., 88ff.; prudence, 83–7; reason, 77f., 86–7; the understanding, 77ff., 84–7
  oppressive nature of, 8–9, 21–3
Poole, T., 27
Price, R., 6, 31
Priestley, J., 6, 21, 28–9, 31, 39
principles, 12–13, 18, 73ff.
  and: expediency, 84–90; maxims, 88–9; morality, 76–7; reason, 76–7, 88–9; reform, 12–13; statesmanship, 84–5, 87–8
  fixed, 12–13, 18
property, private, 1–2, 30ff., 46ff., 88ff., 118–19, 124–5, 133–7
  and: government, 133–42; political corruption, 30–1, 34, 46ff., 56–7, 93–4, 136; political power, 19, 21–7, 29–42, 46ff., 88ff., 133–7, 156–7; responsibility, 113ff., 124–5, 134–5; taxation, 93–4; the franchise, 46ff.,

88ff., 136–7; the origins of government, 22–3, 88–9
as a trust, 121
as propriety, 143–4
Cartwright on, 89–91
commercial, 1–2, 23, 56–7, 93ff., 134–6, 157–8
equality of, 8–9, 21–2, 24–7, 30–1, 37, 39, 40–1
fixed, 21, 57, 60, 118
'form of', 89, 97
freedom and, 22, 24, 27, 30–1, 36–7, 54–5, 89, 134
Harrington on, 30–1, 41, 50, 54
in: English constitution, 50–1, 56–7, 59–61, 89–92, 133–7; French Constitution of 1799, 46ff.
inequality of, 22–3, 24, 30–1, 37, 39, 60, 89ff.
Jews and, 24–7, 29ff.
landed, 1, 30, 50–3, 56–7, 59–60, 112–21, 124–5, 134–5, 157
'matter of', 89, 97
morality and, 30–1, 89, 104, 111–21, 124–5, 157–8, 161–3
moveable, 57, 94, 118
of the Church of England, 64–71, 127–31, 143–9
of the National Church, 64–71, 127–31, 143–9
oppression and, 21–4
political personality and, 24–5, 30–1, 40–1, 46ff., 88ff.
qualifications, 46ff., 88ff., 127
reason and, 89
rights to, 118
under Pantisocracy, 8–9, 21, 25–7, 39
under the Jewish Constitution, 24–7, 29ff.
understanding and, 89, 97
propriety, 143

Reeves, J., 15, 171
reform(ers), 12ff., 107ff.
 and: enlightenment, 12–13; the poor, 14

duties of, 13ff.
moral, 12–18, 40–2, 81, 108–9, 125
parliamentary, 33–5, 40–1, 89–92, 136–7
popular proponents, 13–17, 89, 107ff.
radical, 6–7, 36–7, 39, 69, 107ff.
religion (Christian), 19ff., 75ff., 121–5, 149ff.
and: education, 64, 121–5, 163; government, 64–6, 127ff.; intellectual activity, 122–3, 163; morality, 28–9, 75–6, 121–5; pantisocracy, 8, 21, 27; philosophy, 122–3, 163; popular reformation, 16–17; private property, 21–2; social and political change, 17, 39; the National Church, 143–9; the slave trade, 18, 22, 36; Trinitarianism, 19–21, 62–3; Unitarianism, 6–7, 20–1, 28, 39, 62–3, 75
Dissenting, 2, 4–8, 63, 146–8, 153–5
equality a requirement of, 6, 21, 39
established church and, 6, 19ff., 63ff., 149–54
Evangelical, 123–4
freedom a requirement of, 6, 21, 28
goals of, 19ff., 28
Jews and, 24–7
Protestant, 128, 148
radical, 2, 4–8, 19ff., 28–35, 39, 40–2
Revolution, French, 2, 6, 13–15, 61, 69, 71–2
Roman Catholics, 126–31, 142–3, 147–8; *see also* churches, emancipation, papacy
Roberts, D., 186
Robespierre, M., 16
Roe, N., 167, 168, 170, 174
Romantics, the German, 3–4
Rome, 58ff.
Rousseau, J-J., 75, 78, 80–1, 83–4

Index

Samuel, 26
Scott, J., 190
Shaffer, E. S., 62–3, 70, 176, 178
Sidney, A., 140, 190
Smith, A., 102, 104–5, 183
Smith, C., 195
Smith, S., 170
social contract, the, 79–80
Solway, R. A., 192
Southey, R., 6–10, 129, 169, 188, 193, 194
Spence, T., 169
Spencean socialists, 121, 187
Stafford, W., 167, 182
state, the, 77ff., 118–19, 126ff., 142ff.
  and: commerce, 23, 94–6, 98–9, 124, 135; morality, 77ff., 84–5, 97–8, 109, 118, 125; oppression, 8, 21–3; the nation, 142ff.; religious toleration, 153–4
  as an oppressive force, 8, 21–3
  commerce and, 23, 94–6, 98–9, 124, 135
  landed property in, 30–1, 60–1, 118–19, 124, 134–5
  Platonic conception of, 81–3, 125, 137
  the constitution of the, 133ff.
  the ends of the, 97–9, 118–19, 125
  the Jewish, 24–7, 29ff.
  the National Church in, 67–72, 127–31, 142ff.
Steuart, Sir J., 96, 102, 181, 182
Stuart, D., 43, 112

Sultana, D., 178

taxation, 93–4, 110–11
  and: national prosperity, 93–4, 110–11; political corruption, 23, 46–7, 110; the postwar crisis, 110–11
  compared with tithes, 111
  radical's views on, 30–1, 93–4, 110–11
Taylor, J., 151, 162
Test and Corporations Acts, the, 6, 127, 138
Thelwall, J., 5, 11, 15–18, 174, 175
Thompson, E. P., 44, 170, 175, 181, 182, 187
Thompson, N. W., 184
Thucydides, 122
tithes, 111
Tooke, H., 11, 16
Tories, High Church, 13, 68–9, 128–9, 137–8, 163–4
tradition, 161–3

understanding, the, 77ff., 89, 124
Unitarianism, 2, 4–8, 61–2

Voltaire, 162

Warburton, W., 67–8, 146, 177
Whately, R., 130, 142, 188
Whigs, the, 35–6, 100, 102, 164
White, R. J., 193
Willey, Basil, 73, 168, 176, 178
Winchelsea, Earl of, 119, 186
Wither, G., 140–1
Wordsworth, W., 44, 163

OHIO UNIVERSITY LIBRARY

Please return this book as soon as you have finished with it. In order to avoid a fine it must be returned by the latest date stamped below.

RETURN BY

FEB 2 2 1993

FEB 0 3 1995

SEP 1 1 2003

CF